THE ARTS OF ENCOUNTER

The Arts of Encounter

Christians, Muslims, and the Power of Images in Early Modern Spain

CATHERINE INFANTE

UNIVERSITY OF TORONTO PRESS
Toronto Buffalo London

© University of Toronto Press 2022
Toronto Buffalo London
utorontopress.com
Printed in the U.S.A.

ISBN 978-1-4875-0930-9 (cloth)
ISBN 978-1-4875-0932-3 (EPUB)
ISBN 978-1-4875-0931-6 (PDF)

Toronto Iberic

Library and Archives Canada Cataloguing in Publication

Title: The arts of encounter : Christians, Muslims, and the power
of images in early modern Spain / Catherine Infante.
Names: Infante, Catherine, author.
Series: Toronto Iberic.
Description: Series statement: Toronto Iberic |
Includes bibliographical references and index.
Identifiers: Canadiana (print) 20210287675 |
Canadiana (ebook) 20210287705 | ISBN 9781487509309 (cloth) |
ISBN 9781487509323 (EPUB) | ISBN 9781487509316 (PDF)
Subjects: LCSH: Spanish literature – Classical period,
1500–1700 – History and criticism. | LCSH: Christian art
and symbolism in literature. |
LCSH: Christianity and other religions – Islam. |
LCSH: Religion and culture – Spain. | LCSH: Spain – Religion.
Classification: LCC PQ6066 .I54 2022 | DDC 860.9/003 – dc23

We wish to acknowledge the land on which the University of Toronto Press
operates. This land is the traditional territory of the Wendat, the Anishnaabeg,
the Haudenosaunee, the Métis, and the Mississaugas of the Credit First Nation.

University of Toronto Press acknowledges the financial support of the
Government of Canada, the Canada Council for the Arts, and the Ontario Arts
Council, an agency of the Government of Ontario, for its publishing activities.

Canada Council
for the Arts

Conseil des Arts
du Canada

ONTARIO ARTS COUNCIL
CONSEIL DES ARTS DE L'ONTARIO
an Ontario government agency
un organisme du gouvernement de l'Ontario

Funded by the   Financé par le
Government   gouvernement
of Canada   du Canada

Contents

Illustrations

Acknowledgments

This book would not have been possible without the support of many individuals, and it is with great joy that I thank them here. I would like to express my deepest appreciation to Steve Hutchinson for his wise guidance, intellectual generosity, and for being a constant source of inspiration. I would also like to extend my heartfelt gratitude to Mercedes Alcalá Galán for being a sage mentor and exemplar role model for me, both professionally and personally. From Madison to Madrid, Steve and Mercedes have supported my work in many ways, for which I can never thank them enough. In Madison, I had the privilege of learning from Dustin Cowell, whose immense dedication to teaching Arabic allowed me to read texts that I might not have dared to tackle otherwise. Shukran jazeelan! I owe a special thanks to Paco Layna for his ongoing mentorship throughout the years. His enthusiasm and passion for Cervantes is contagious, and I credit him with my desire to pursue further graduate studies.

Throughout the course of writing this book, I have also benefited from exchanges with many other scholars. Since I first met Luis Bernabé Pons as a graduate student, he has generously suggested sources and shared his extensive knowledge of Moriscos. I appreciate the valuable comments he graciously provided me on a draft of Chapter 3. Javier Irigoyen-García read a draft of my book proposal and kindly shared sources and feedback on my work, for which I am profoundly grateful. I owe enormous thanks to Borja Franco Llopis for pointing me to sources and for conversations that helped me better understand the role of religious art in Christian-Muslim relations. I am grateful to Michael Armstrong-Roche for inviting me to present an early version of Chapter 2 at the Wesleyan Renaissance Seminar. His insightful feedback, along with the suggestions from other seminar participants, helped me tremendously. Other scholars have asked important questions, offered advice, or helped in other ways at different stages, including Laura Bass, Julia Domínguez, Esther Fernández, María Antonia Garcés, Enrique García Santo-Tomás, Michael Gordon, Paul Michael Johnson, Ana Laguna, Adrienne Martín, Mary Quinn, and Ana M. Rodríguez-Rodríguez. I would also like to acknowledge gratefully the suggestions offered by attendees at conferences where I presented earlier versions of some chapters in this book.

Funding from the National Endowment for the Humanities to attend the summer research institute "The Alhambra and Spain's Islamic Past" in Granada was crucial in allowing me to begin research on Chapter 3. Conversations at the Carmen de la Victoria overlooking the Alhambra with colleagues and guest lecturers enriched my research on the book. I am particularly grateful to the organizers of the institute, D. Fairchild Ruggles and Oscar E. Vázquez, along with colleagues M. Betsy Boone, Nabil Boudraa, María M. Carrión, Anna C. Cruz, Mahan L. Ellison, Ann C. Huppert, Taharee A. Jackson, Marco Katz Montiel, Thomas Kealy, Marilyn Kralik, Matilde Mateo, Karen Mathews, Christine Olson, Dannie Otto, Deborah Pope, María del Mar Rosa-Rodríguez, Dana Sajdi, Jeffrey Schrader, Jeffrey Scraba, Susan Slyomovics, Elizabeth Terry-Roisin, Tehseen Thaver, José R. Vázquez, and Ivonne Wallace Fuentes, who all helped me think in new ways about my project. A Dean's Research Fellowship during the 2017–18 academic year at Amherst College and generous financial support, including publication subvention funding from the Provost's Office, provided the resources and time necessary to write much of this book.

It has been a true privilege to write this book surrounded by supportive colleagues at Amherst College. I am particularly grateful to Sara J. Brenneis, Paul Schroeder-Rodríguez, and Ilan Stavans, who all have offered valuable advice and unwavering support since my arrival in the Spanish Department. I am likewise grateful to my colleagues in the "Global Pre-Modern" working group at Amherst College for stimulating discussions. In particular, Tariq Jaffer offered useful bibliographical suggestions and help with some Arabic translations. The wider Five College community has been a wonderful intellectual home for me. I am especially grateful to Nieves Romero-Díaz, Albert Lloret, and David Rodríguez-Solás for their warm welcome to the Pioneer Valley and for their collaboration and encouragement over the years. My thanks also go to the Interlibrary Loan department for fulfilling my many requests.

At the University of Toronto Press, I have had the good fortune of working with Suzanne Rancourt. I am immensely grateful for her encouragement and support of this project. I also extend my thanks to freelancer Barry Norris for his exceptional copy-editing, to Marta Steele for her work on the index, and all those involved in the publication process. I thank the two anonymous peer reviewers for their careful reading of each chapter and thoughtful suggestions, which undoubtedly helped make this book stronger. Chapter 1 expands on my article, "Los moriscos y la imagen religiosa: la cruz de Rafala en el *Persiles* rebatiendo a los apologistas de la expulsión," published in *eHumanista/Cervantes*. Portions of Chapter 6 previously appeared in my articles, "El renegado cervantino y el poder de las imágenes," published in *Hispanic Review*, and "Imágenes cautivas y la convivencia con las imágenes en el Mediterráneo de Cervantes," published in *eHumanista/Cervantes*. I thank the editors of these journals for their permission to incorporate some of these materials here.

I dedicate this book to my family. I sincerely thank my parents, Dave and Andrea, for their steadfast love, encouragement, and support. My husband's family in Spain has always loved and supported me, despite the distance. There are really no words to express the enormous debt of gratitude that I owe to my husband and best friend, José María, for so many (and probably too many) things. To him and our children, Lucas and Gloria, I am forever grateful.

Note on Translations and Transliterations

All translations into English are my own unless otherwise indicated. I incorporate the English translation within the body of the chapter and include the original language in the notes for reference. For longer quotations from Miguel de Cervantes's *Don Quixote*, I have used Edith Grossman's translation. For quotations from Cervantes's *La gran sultana*, I have used Barbara Fuchs and Aaron Ilika's English translation. When quoting early modern Spanish texts, I have only modernized the orthography to add accent marks where needed, and changed the capitalization of some words for consistency. For all transliterations of Arabic words, I have followed the guidelines of the *International Journal of Middle East Studies*. However, when quoting from published Aljamiado texts, I have not modified the editor's diacritical markings.

THE ARTS OF ENCOUNTER

Introduction

People are sexually aroused by pictures and sculptures;
they break pictures and sculptures; they mutilate them,
kiss them, cry before them, and go on journeys to them;
they are calmed by them, stirred by them, and incited to
revolt. They give thanks by means of them, expect to be
elevated by them, and are moved to the highest levels of
empathy and fear. They have always responded in these
ways; they still do.

David Freedberg, *The Power of Images*

In 1667 the Mercedarian friar Gabriel Gómez de Losada embarked on
a mission to rescue human captives in Algiers. Along with the 211 men,
women, and children that he liberated, he ransomed a coveted effigy of
Christ that had circulated among Muslims, Jews, and Christians in the
Mediterranean corsair capital.[1] The image was taken captive from a ship
in transit from Italy by Turkish corsairs, sold to a Jew in Algiers, intercepted by a Spanish merchant, and finally purchased and redeemed by
Gómez de Losada before his return to Madrid. According to his account,
some individuals wanted to possess the image for its special devotional
value, while others hoped to sell it and make a profit, to burn it, or to
protect it from harm. The captive image is, unexpectedly, desired and
valued by members of diverse cultural and religious communities, and
brings these groups into contact with one another. Given the extraordinary significance that religious images acquired for many Catholics
in early modern Spain, it comes as no surprise that this effigy of Christ
becomes the protagonist in the final part of Gómez de Losada's captivity
treatise. What is surprising, though, is how the captive image gains value
for all those involved in its circulation – albeit for different motives –
and how the trajectory of the image allows us to trace the encounters

between followers of various religious groups. The movements of this image tell a fascinating story of the interconnectedness between humans and religious images. It illustrates how the embedding of these images in written texts reveals a nuanced understanding of interfaith relationships in the early modern world.

The close proximity and constant contact between early modern Spain and the rest of the Mediterranean world offered a whole gamut of possibilities for writers to portray relations among members of these diverse cultures. The frequent and evocative encounters among Christians and Muslims, captives, slaves and corsairs, renegades, merchants, and redemptionist friars, among others, populate the pages of many early modern works by celebrated authors such as Miguel de Cervantes and Lope de Vega.[2] What is often overlooked, however, is the significant role that religious images play in many of the encounters described in these texts.[3] Like Gómez de Losada's captivity treatise, innumerable narratives in a variety of genres and languages offer accounts that underscore the importance of images in the development of many Christian-Muslim confrontations and exchanges, and attest to how sacred icons also coexisted with adherents of these two religions while sharing the same space. In some texts, the very reason different individuals are prompted to come in contact with one another is the image itself. In other cases, fictional or non-fictional characters associate themselves with specific religious icons to mould and shape their identities, especially under precarious circumstances. At other times, authors describe particular images that incite the religious conversion of their protagonists. On occasion, sacred representations are even purported to allow certain individuals passage across geographic and cultural frontiers. Verbal descriptions of religious images were undeniably incorporated into early modern literary and historical texts as authors sought to portray the intricacies of cross-confessional relationships.

The Arts of Encounter reframes our understanding of Christian-Muslim relations in early modern Spain by uncovering the significant role of religious images in interreligious encounters described in a range of literary genres, including narrative fiction, theatre, and poetry. I read these genres alongside a wide assortment of other early modern sources – namely, historical chronicles, Inquisition cases, religious treatises, miracle books, travel memoirs, captives' testimonies, letters, autobiographical accounts, paintings, and engravings. Drawing on this variety of texts in Spanish, Arabic, and Aljamiado (Spanish written in Arabic script), my book asks how the power of images omnipresent in everyday life influenced how early modern writers chose to portray relations between Christians and Muslims.

Many, if not all, of the writers examined in this book were aware that religious images were oftentimes a point of contention between Christians and Muslims in the Iberian Peninsula and throughout the Mediterranean. Although sacred icons of all sizes, types, and forms were pervasive in the daily life of Catholics in early modern Spain, Moriscos (Muslims forced to convert to Christianity in sixteenth-century Spain and their descendants) and their Muslim neighbours in North Africa often opposed religious images, evincing an aniconic tendency that, at times, resulted in public disdain. The power of images, as David Freedberg has masterfully explored, has the capacity to evoke a wide range of passionate and sensate responses, from desire and empathy to fear and rage – and in the case of early modern Spain, images elicited powerful responses among Christian and Muslim cultures. Yet many early modern texts reveal that, rather than simply cleaving to commonplace generalizations, writers showed much more complexity in representing Christian-Muslim encounters that centre upon religious images. Their fictional and non-fictional texts offered more possibilities than merely an acceptance or rejection of images. Whether or not the writers made claims to historical truthfulness, their writings do not necessarily paint a faithful reflection of reality, since their works may be influenced by their own ideological motivations. This could, of course, be the case with fictional works, but also with non-fictional genres that claim to tell the truth. By attending to the visual cues in the sources I examine, however, I argue that a more nuanced understanding of Christian-Muslim relations emerges. Reading narrative fiction, theatre, and poetry alongside an array of other non-fictional sources brings to light some of the anxieties about what it meant to belong to different ethnic or religious communities and how these communities interacted with one another within the fluid boundaries of the Mediterranean world, particularly in early modern Spain.

The Arts of Encounter

The encounters that transpired around religious images unfolded in virtually all places of public and private life, and were marked across a continuum by moments of forced tension and mutual respect. By "arts of encounter," I am referring to these diverse ways in which Christians and Muslims interacted with one another and the means by which these individuals negotiated meaning from the interactions that took shape around religious images. Given the varied ways in which early modern writers also represented these relations, one must account for the social and religious contexts in which they took place.

Fig. 1. Juan de Valdés Leal, *Cristo de Medinaceli arrastrado por las calles de Mequinez*, 1681.

Fundación Casa Ducal Medinaceli, Seville

In Catholic Spain, religious images were the object of veneration and worship. They were also used as effective tools of indoctrination, playing a prominent role in the defence of religious ideas.[4] In contrast, both the Muslim community that remained in the peninsula and followers of Islam in North Africa were inclined to reject religious images. These two opposing positions caused an inevitable barrier that was difficult to overcome, especially in the Spanish context, where encounters between these religious cultures were a daily occurrence. Art historian Felipe Pereda points out that "everything seems to indicate that the question of image worship was one of the insuperable barriers that separated Christians from Muslims and that this same barrier many times hindered their *convivencia* or at least the permeability of their cultural exchange" (Pereda 2007, 342).[5] Of course, stories that circulated in the peninsula describing accounts of damage done to Catholic icons on the *other* side of the Mediterranean only helped to reinforce this stereotype. Juan de Valdés Leal's painting, for example, portrays an alleged case of image destruction by Muslims in seventeenth-century Morocco (fig. 1).[6] As one of the chroniclers of the time explains, the image of Christ was stolen from the Spaniards in La Mamora and taken to Meknes, where King Muley Ismael ordered it to be dragged through the streets and then thrown into a cave with lions. The image of Christ was taken as one of the "spoils of their triumph" and profaned, not necessarily because of their rejection of figural imagery, but instead because of "a hate of the Christian religion" (San Juan 1686, 105).[7] As examples such as this reveal, the reception of religious images has very little to do with rejection of religious iconography by and of itself, and can be better understood in a context of tension between cultures, despite what the image represents.

Regardless of the truthfulness of accounts such as the one above, and despite a certain tendency in the peninsular Muslim communities and among their coreligionists in North Africa to reject images, it is essential to point out that this was neither universal nor extensible to all Muslims. Rather, the rejection of images was based more on cultural practice than on Islamic law. In fact, the Qur'an is even less explicit than the Old Testament in its opposition to figural images, since it contains no prohibition on the creation of images. As scholars such as Oleg Grabar have argued, many of the ideas and doctrines against the use of images were recorded after the revelation of the Qur'an, and were later collected in a variety of hadiths (sayings of the Prophet Muhammad) and fatwas (Islamic legal opinions) (Grabar 1987, 72–98).[8] It is important to take these ideas into account to uncover how the repudiation of images was more contingent upon the context in which it took place than on any hatred imposed by doctrine. Furthermore, as we will see in the sources I examine, images

were often used as an effective tool to strengthen a connection to or
rejection of one culture or another, beyond their intended meaning and
significance. A letter from the dey of Algiers protesting the damage done
to a small mosque in Cartagena in 1695 emphasizes these points. Since
the mosque's lamp and rugs had been destroyed and access to the masjid
had been restricted, the dey insisted that repairs be made to this holy
place for Muslims in Spain or else he would retaliate and harm Christian churches in Algiers, which, of course, included objects of devotion
(Vincent 2001, 197). Leaving aside the questions that arise about a Muslim community in late seventeenth-century Spain, it is clear that discussions about religious visual culture cannot be confined to one shore of
the Mediterranean and that images were accepted or rejected not only
because of beliefs about the use and creation of figural imagery.[9] In the
context of early modern Spain and the wider Mediterranean world, the
profanation of images needs to be understood within a larger framework
that also considers other possible motives aside from an aniconism based
solely on the rejection of anthropomorphic images.

This consideration is especially important in the case of the Moriscos. Due to their forced conversion in the sixteenth century, any understanding of the Moriscos' particular responses to religious images must
account for the specific religious and social context in which they lived.
Ecclesiastical authorities such as Hernando de Talavera, archbishop of
Granada, and Feliciano de Figueroa, bishop of Segorbe, urged these new
converts to keep images in their homes to promote Christian religiosity
and as a sign of their rejection of their Muslim identity (Franco Llopis and Moreno Díaz del Campo 2019, 111). Christian theologian and
son of Jewish converts Bernardo Pérez de Chinchón also preached to
Moriscos in Gandia (Valencia), teaching them the importance of religious images in Catholic practice. In his *Antialcorano* ([1532] 2000), a
collection of twenty-six sermons supposedly preached to Moriscos, he
recognizes the problem that images posed for Moriscos, but still suggests
that they "put images of the saints in their houses at the head of the bed
so that when they go to sleep and wake up they remember them," as Old
Christians did (373–4).[10] Nevertheless, a variety of sources, including
Inquisition records and writings by Moriscos themselves, indicate that
religious images were still problematic for many Moriscos.[11]

In December 1563, the twenty-fifth session of the Council of Trent
affirmed that images of Christ, the Virgin Mary, and the saints were to
be venerated in churches specifically "because the honor which is shown
them is referred to the prototypes which they represent, so that by means
of the images which we kiss and before which we uncover the head
and prostrate ourselves, we adore Christ and venerate the saints whose

likeness they bear" (Schroeder 1978, 216). Yet the notion of what Catholics' sacred images represented made them hard for some Moriscos to accept. In particular, there was opposition to the claim that the image was more than the materials from which it was constructed. The issue was not necessarily related to an aversion to figural images. Rather, the problem lay in the fact that these images were created to represent ideas such as the crucifixion and the divine nature of Christ, which many Moriscos renounced. For Ibrāhīm Ṭaybilī, born a Morisco and later exiled in Tunisia, the cross had no symbolic value, but rather was reduced to its material qualities: "a piece of wood" (1988, v.2253).[12] A selection of Inquisition cases likewise accused Moriscos of understanding images only in terms of their material nature and discrediting any similitude to their originals.[13] As we will see, the authors of the sources that I analyse throughout the book demonstrate their awareness of these issues and complicate these debates in their writings as they depict how they understood cross-confessional relationships in the early modern world.

Even though Moriscos in Spain and Muslims in North Africa tended to refuse figural imagery and to stress the importance of the word over images, this practice was not without exceptions.[14] Notably, Oleg Grabar reminds us that the Prophet Muhammad was said to have destroyed all the images at the Ka'ba in Mecca with the exception of a picture of the Virgin Mary and her son, which he spared (1987, 80). In our context of the early modern Mediterranean, the Moroccan ambassador al-Tamaghrūtī offers another illuminating case in his book *Al-Nafḥat al-Miskiyya fī al-Sifārat al-Turkiyya* [The perfumed breeze on the Turkish embassy] ([c. 1591] 2007), which describes his journey in and around the Mediterranean Sea. As he marvels at the Aya Sofya mosque in Istanbul, he notes how Muslims had removed almost all of the religious images left behind by the Christians, sparing only a few the physical affront:

> Inside the mosque, there are many types of images and crosses as well as images of the angels Gabriel, Michael, Azrael, Israfil, and others, and images of the prophets in the upper level like John, Zachariah, Mary, and her son Jesus in her upper arm, Jesus' manger, and other venalities of the infidels. When the Muslims entered, they took down all the images of the cross and some of the other images, and they left some other ones up. In this country, a lot of mosques have tried to imitate this grand mosque, but they were unable to do so.[15] (Al-Tamaghrūtī, 116)

In the case of Spain, household inventories document examples of images owned by Moriscos during the latter half of the sixteenth century. Archival records from the Provincial Historical Archive of Ciudad

Real indicate that a few Moriscos possessed small images of the Immaculate Conception, Saint Casilda, and a crucifix, among other objects of devotion (Franco Llopis and Moreno Díaz del Campo 2019, 115–18). Although these inventories lead to more questions about Moriscos' use of these specific images – especially since some of these figures shared an important connection to Islam – the records still reveal that not all Moriscos responded equally to figural imagery. Nevertheless, the writings of many sixteenth- and seventeenth-century authors often intentionally emphasized the differences and conflicts that religious images provoked, thus falling into what Nietzsche called the "habit of contrasts," instead of seeing only "differences of degree" (2006, 2:388).

At the other end of the spectrum of these encounters, there are some extraordinary cases of Christian and Muslim communities coming together and showing mutual respect for religious visual culture. One of the most striking examples is that of Lampedusa, a small island in the Mediterranean between Tunisia and Malta. The Spanish captain Alonso de Contreras, describing the Mediterranean coastlines in his *Derrotero universal* ([c. 1616] 1996), pauses to give an account of a common place of worship on Lampedusa that was respected by both Christians and Muslims. In a small shrine, on one side there was an image of the Virgin Mary and on the other a tomb of a Muslim holy man. Those who visited the shrine left alms, including items of food, so that any Christian or Muslim captives in need of sanctuary would find something to eat. According to Contreras, "Our Lady and the marabout are there in such a way that neither the Turks mistreat the image of Our Lady when they come to the island, nor the Christians do so to the marabout (192).[16] This shared space, where objects of devotion were treated with respect by those who entered the shrine, regardless of creed, serves as an exceptional example and counterpoint to many other encounters between individuals and images in early modern Spain and the Mediterranean.

Christian-Muslim Encounters in Mediterranean Perspective

The "arts of encounter" that I examine throughout this book focus on Christian and Muslim cultures, but because they took place within the porous boundaries of the Mediterranean Sea, they need to be contextualized alongside the wide range of communities and faiths that crisscrossed this space. Antonio de Sosa richly illustrates this diversity in his *Topografía e historia general de Argel* (1612), where he describes the "Christians, Moors, Turks, galley slaves, rowers, tradesmen, corsairs, merchants, and an infinity of other people" in the city of Algiers (Haedo [1612] 1927–9, 1:33).[17] Categories of religious identity were continually shifting, and thus the Christians and Muslims who appear in the texts I study here held a wide variety of beliefs and practices along this spectrum. This variety is magnified by divisions within certain religious communities, including differences between Catholics and Protestants, and Moriscos and North African Muslims, among many other distinctions that authors made in their writings. However, the connections and exchanges among these groups are just as important. Studying these Christian-Muslim encounters in Mediterranean perspective, then, helps us to see the "immense network of regular and casual connections" that Fernand Braudel emphasizes as well as the "connectivity" in what Peregrine Horden and Nicholas Purcell have called the "new thalassology" (Braudel 1972, 1:276; Horden and Purcell 2006, 733). This perspective helps to show that religious identities were not monolithic, and casts light on the complexities of these contacts as they developed across time and space.

That Christian and Muslim identities were not fixed will become clear in my analysis of the texts at hand in each chapter, but a few clarifications are in order about some terminology and connections among these communities. Since I examine texts both by and about Moriscos in early modern Spain and Muslims in the wider Mediterranean world, a few questions arise about the vocabulary used in sixteenth- and seventeenth-century Spain to refer to these cultural and religious communities. As specialists are already aware, the term "Morisco" carries with it a complicated history, partly because the word was not widely employed to speak about these Muslims forced to convert to Christianity and their descendants until the second half of the sixteenth century. And the forced converts did not tend to use this word to describe themselves. Instead, *cristiano nuevo de moro* or *Morisco* later in the sixteenth century were the terms used by the dominant majority of Old Christians to characterize the recent converts. In their own writings, these individuals usually referred to themselves as Muslims or as Christians (Harvey 2005, 2–6; López Baralt 1992, 28).[18] Furthermore, Morisco identity varied greatly depending on geographical territory. The manner in which many Muslims in al-Andalus began living under Christian authority was a gradual and varied process, and as a result created diversity among Moriscos. By 1501 some Muslims had already been living alongside Christians for four centuries, whereas in Granada Muslims had spent less than a decade under Christian rule (Bernabé Pons 2007, 52). Aside from these geographic considerations, other economic, cultural, and linguistic factors also influenced Morisco identity and religious beliefs. As we will see, identities were much more plural than these simple labels appear to imply.

In terms of Christian cultures, the authors of the texts that I study refer principally to Catholic practice, but varieties of Protestantism also make their way into the discussions about Christian-Muslim encounters around religious images. A variety of authors link Moriscos' reception of images to that of their Protestant neighbours, which developed along a parallel path. The mutual disdain for images in churches that many Moriscos and Protestants expressed gave these religious communities a strong point in common against their supposed adversary, the Catholic Church.[19] The exiled Morisco Aḥmad ibn Qāsim al-Ḥajarī, for example, documents his travels to the Netherlands and his affinity with Dutch Protestants in his *Kitāb nāṣir al-dīn alā l-qawm al-kāfirīn* [The supporter of religion against the infidels] ([c. 1637] 1997), remarking how he identifies with them on the subject of their mutual repudiation of Catholic religious images. He praises Martin Luther and John Calvin for opposing the teachings of the popes in Rome, who have "misled the people by worshiping idols" (194–5). Another Morisco exile, Aḥmad al-Ḥanafī, clearly distinguishes between Catholics and Protestants based on the value they attribute to religious visual culture, since "the Papist Christians"[20] make figural images of their saints to venerate, whereas "the Lutheran Christians"[21] reject and destroy religious effigies, affirming that making and worshipping images is unlawful (Cardaillac 2004, 121). These examples of Morisco and Protestant beliefs and actions towards Catholic images are significant to the texts I study in the following chapters, since early modern writers were attuned to these commonalities and the contentions that religious images incited.[22] Their diverse renderings of inter-religious relations, I argue, were highly motivated by the sacred visual culture that surrounded them.

The connection between Protestants and Moriscos was perceived to be so close that Moriscos could be accused of being simultaneously "Moor and Lutheran" (Cardaillac 2004, 134).[23] Julián, who continued to practise traditions important to his Muslim faith while incorporating Lutheran hymns into his lifestyle, was closely tied to the Protestant community because their rejection of images mirrored his own disdain for religious representations. His Inquisition case states that he did not attend mass because "the crosses were scarecrows and they should not be venerated ... and ... the images were all made up and weren't suitable to worship or venerate but instead only keep God in mind" (Cardaillac 2004, 134–5).[24] The Spanish humanist and Protestant Cipriano de Valera saw this mutual distain for Catholic objects of devotion as a key impediment to Moriscos' conversion to Catholicism (Franco Llopis 2010a, 95). Protestants thus served as an example for Moriscos who wished to reject Catholic images. In fact, some Moriscos were also inspired by Protestant texts, and based their anti-Catholic arguments on these writings. Aḥmad ibn Qāsim al-Ḥajarī, for example, uses Cipriano de Valera's Spanish translation of the Bible in his own work ([c. 1637] 1997, 53–4). He mentions how he came across one of Valera's books in Tunis that contained the Old Testament, the Psalms, and the Gospels, explaining how he took from it the story about King Nebuchadnezzar – a story in part against idols – to use in his own book (245–6).

Catholics in early modern Europe also viewed Protestants and Muslims as somewhat united due to their mutual distain of religious images. In 1625, Isabel Clara Eugenia commissioned Rubens to design a series of tapestries representing the Eucharist for the Monastery of the Descalzas Reales in Madrid. One of these tapestries portrays this close connection. In his painting, *La victoria de la Verdad sobre la Herejía*, used as a model for the tapestry, Rubens depicts an allegory of Truth pointing to the words *Hoc est corpus meum*, highlighting the bread transformed into the body of Christ, with the alleged enemies of this dogma painted together to the left (fig. 2). Among them are John Calvin holding a book in his hands and Martin Luther wearing a monk's habit and reaching out for a scroll,

Fig. 2. Peter Paul Rubens, *La victoria de la Verdad sobre la Herejía*, c. 1625.
Museo del Prado, Madrid

alongside a man donning a white turban and another grasping a knife. De Poorter believes these latter figures represent, respectively, Muslims and Jews as opponents to Eucharistic doctrine (1978, 379). By featuring these individuals adjacent to the iconoclast with a chisel in his hand, ready to profane the statue of the Virgin and Child, the painting hints at their shared rejection of religious images, in addition to the Eucharist. While the primary subject of this painting is evidently the victory of truth over heresy, and especially the triumph of the Eucharist in Counter-Reformation Spain, it also represents the connection between Protestants and Muslims and the tensions between word and image in the early modern world. Viewing these connections, and others I discuss, in Mediterranean perspective helps to nuance the complexities of the encounters that took place among Christian and Muslim cultures. The debates in early modern Spain were widely connected to parallel discussions about how images fit within the religious culture of the Mediterranean world.

Images in Context

Religious images in early modern Spain were pervasive and encompassed a wide variety of visual and material manifestations, so a brief clarification is necessary to define the ones we will be looking at in the following chapters. I use the word "image," and its equivalents, in the same sense that it was widely understood in early modern Spain and defined by lexicographer Sebastián de Covarrubias in his *Tesoro de la lengua castellana o española* ([1611] 2006). He principally defines *imagen* [image] by identifying the strong association of the word with Catholic practice: "Usually among the Catholic faithful we define images as the figures that represent our Lord Christ, his blessed Mother and Virgin Holy Mary, his apostles and the other saints and the mysteries of our faith, as much as they can be imitated and represented, to refresh our memory of them; and for the common people, who are illiterate, images serve as books" (1091).[25] According to Covarrubias's definition, images are to be appreciated as religious representations of figures such as Jesus, Mary, the apostles, and the saints, as well as other significant depictions of the Catholic faith. He later clarifies that any visual rendering of human beings in a secular context is instead a *retrato* [portrait]. In addition to the evident religious focus that Covarrubias affixes to this word, the second part of his definition highlights how images are intimately linked to tensions caused by differing opinions of their meaning and use, which continued to incite discord among his contemporaries. Namely, he addresses the problem of conflating a representation of a deity with its referent. In line with Covarrubias's definition of "image," I focus in this book on a variety of religious representations, especially images of the cross, Christ, and the Virgin Mary, since these are the figures most frequently described by writers that depict Christian-Muslim encounters. I consider these images in a wide variety of forms, from devotional icons and objects to sculptures, paintings, prints, relics, and ekphrasis, among other visual and material representations.

In the Arabic and Aljamiado sources that I examine, the vocabulary used to describe religious images is varied, since it often reflects certain attitudes towards sacred art. In texts written in Arabic by Muslims or crypto-Muslims, the word most frequently used to describe Catholic images is usually *ṣanam* (pl. *aṣnām*), meaning idol.[26] In other sixteenth- and seventeenth-century Arabic texts describing Christian-Muslim encounters that centre on religious symbols, the authors also use the word *ṣūra* (pl. *ṣuwar*) to refer to a pictorial representation, implying a more neutral term for image.[27] In Moriscos' Aljamiado texts, figural representations are regularly called *ídolos* [idols], or more often *ídolas*, denoting rejection of these objects of devotion. In some of these narratives, however, *ídolas* also refers to idols during *jāhiliyya* (the days before the advent of Islam), and not necessarily to Catholic images. As the various examples throughout each chapter reveal, the variety of vocabulary employed to describe the same objects shows some of the tensions represented by the writers I study.

I also consider a variety of fictional images that some Catholic writers associated with Muslims in the early modern Mediterranean. Due to the pervasivness of religious images in Baroque Spain, it seems as though some writers could not conceive of a religion whose followers did not have their own particular images to worship. A diverse array of authors of narrative, poetic, and dramatic texts in Spain embraces the idea that Muslims created their own versions of sacred icons that mirrored Catholic religious beliefs. These images included "idols" of the Prophet Muhammad, representations of the crescent moon, and the so-called *zancarrón*, a relic of the Prophet often described as his leg.[28] Allusions to these objects appear in works by canonical authors and lesser-known writers alike. Even Cervantes's Don Quixote admires Reinaldos de Montalbán above all other knights, in part because he has allegedly crossed to the other shore of the Mediterranean Sea to steal an "idol of Muhammad" (1978, I:1, 74).[29] And a quick search in the Real Academia Española's CORDE database reveals a varied list of works that mention the *zancarrón*, including Francisco López de Úbeda's *La pícara Justina* (1605), Luis de Góngora's *Comedia del doctor Carlino* (c. 1613), and Pedro Calderón de la Barca's *El príncipe constante* (c. 1629), as well as some poetry by Francisco de Quevedo and Sor Juana Inés de la Cruz, among other examples (Ceballos Viro 2009, 307n7).[30]

The past few decades have witnessed a boom in new research on Christian-Muslim encounters and exchanges in early modern Spain and their connections to the wider Mediterranean world.[31] Scholars have taken major strides in drawing attention to the nuances of how these interfaith relations were negotiated and how they contributed to rich cultural production. However, inquiry into the particular role that religious images played in cross-cultural encounters and exchanges has been limited principally to the discipline of art history. There has been no book-length study of the effects of religious images on Christian-Muslim relations throughout a range of literary genres, including narrative fiction, theatre, and poetry. Yet this approach is critical to understanding how interfaith and cross-cultural relationships were negotiated in the early modern world. Spanish art historians Felipe Pereda and Borja Franco Llopis have carried out the most illuminating research in this regard, particularly on Moriscos' reception of religious art and the place of images in their conversion and assimilation.[32] These scholars reveal that religious images were a key issue in debates about how to catechize Spain's cultural and religious minorities. Basing their meticulous research on Inquisition records and other historical documents, they demonstrate how Moriscos reacted in an iconoclastic manner to the introduction of these Catholic images, in an attempt to defend their identity.

The Arts of Encounter hopes to advance our understanding of interfaith relations by calling attention to the vital impact of religious images on Christian-Muslim encounters. Playwrights, poets, and writers of narrative fiction, among other genres, overwhelmingly reveal that the question of images went far beyond how these objects of devotion were actually accepted or rejected by diverse cultural and religious communities. Through their writings, these authors unmask some of their anxieties about what it meant to belong to one community of believers or another, how these images mediated among cultures, and even how certain individuals could use images to pass as members of other social groups.[33] To get to the crux of these questions, one needs to bring to the fore the religious visual culture described in the texts and put these images "on display," in an exercise that W.J.T. Mitchell calls "showing seeing" (2002b, 166). Since images of the cross, Christ, and the Virgin Mary, among other elements of Christian iconography, imbued nearly every space of the Spanish Empire, descriptions of this visual culture can be taken for granted unintentionally in writings that represent Christian-Muslim encounters. By tracing the significant presence of these objects of devotion and the responses they incited in cross-confessional negotiations, one can better capture the nuances of what Mitchell refers to as "vernacular visuality," or everyday seeing, and the complexities of how interfaith relations were perceived and conveyed in print (2002b, 178).

The context of early modern Spain and its connection to the broader Mediterranean world provides especially fertile ground for considering how cultural and religious identities were shaped through frequent encounters with images. After all, religious visual culture permeated almost every aspect of daily life in Catholic Spain, inciting writers to reflect in their writing – consciously or not – how the power of images influenced contemporary perceptions of cross-confessional interactions. As a result of the tight bond between the sister arts of poetry and painting, writers in early modern Spain appealed to the senses and infused their writing with a pictorial element, a "writing for the eyes," as Fredrick A. de Armas has appropriately labelled it (2004, 7). A flourishing body of scholarship by critics including Mercedes Alcalá Galán (2017, 2020), Laura Bass (2008), Emilie Bergmann (1979), Frederick A. de Armas (2006), Ana Laguna, Javier Portús Pérez (1999), and Antonio Sánchez Jiménez (2011), among many others, has made many important connections between the verbal and the visual in works by authors such as Cervantes and Lope de Vega. One of the consequences of this eminently pictorial writing, I argue, was that writers also understood Christian-Muslim relations in visual terms. Thus, it is critical to probe these writings particularly for their visual cues on religious visual culture, to appreciate more thouroughly how writers moulded the religious and cultural identities of their characters, and, more important, to interrogate what this reveals about broader understandings of how interreligious relations took shape.

Overview of the Book

The Arts of Encounter is divided into six chapters. The first three centre on literary and historical texts written both by and about Moriscos. These works reveal Moriscos' often precarious association with religious images in sixteenth- and seventeenth-century Spain and how this challenging coexistence with sacred icons was understood and manipulated by diverse writers of the time. The next three chapters cross imperial and cultural boundaries, and broaden the discussion of images as a site of contact between cultures in Spain and the Mediterranean world. Here, I pay special attention to the uses of Marian icons that both mediated and incited discord among Christian and Muslim characters. Finally, I consider the interplay of images that circulated around Mediterranean shores and cultures. Although the first chapters focus more on the particular situation of Moriscos in the Iberian Peninsula, their circumstances are intimately tied to the other fictional and non-fictional texts that I discuss in the remainder of the book. Because of how the "Morisco question" is intertwined with the broader Mediterranean context, I deliberately do not divide the book into two parts.[34] As Fernand Braudel reminds us, there is more that unites than divides these two shores, for "the whole sea shared a common destiny, a heavy one indeed, with identical problems and general trends if not identical consequences" (1: 14).

Chapter 1, "Moriscos between Cross and Crescent," sheds new light on Moriscos and their reaction to religious images in early modern Spain. It examines how early modern writers used the symbol of the cross in an attempt to represent interactions between Old Christians and Moriscos and to shape the religious identities of the characters in their texts. I take a close look at the use, value, and meaning that writers such as the apologists of the expulsion of the Moriscos ascribed to the symbol of the cross, contrasting it with the representation that Cervantes gives this Christian icon in his fiction. This chapter reveals that, although the apologists used the cross to justify their argument and pave the way for the expulsion of the Moriscos from Spain, Cervantes offered another alternative scenario for this cultural and religious minority.

Chapter 2, "Text against Image in Moriscos' Literary Culture," turns to Moriscos' own literary culture in sixteenth- and seventeenth-century Spain to demonstrate how their writings empowered them to resist the veneration of Catholic images. I analyse the religious images described in anonymous Morisco texts, including legends, epic-chivalric narratives, and prophetic texts, among various other genres. In these writings, Muslim characters transgress the established norm and actively reject the adoration of religious statues or idols, much as many in their Morisco audience opposed the Catholic cult of images. By examining this literature, I demonstrate how it emulates the challenging circumstances Moriscos faced in early modern Spain, and consider how it inspired them to reject the religious images of their own world. I also explore the importance of the Arabic script in these Moriscos narratives, both as a verbal means of resistance and as a visual image connected to Islam. Arabic letters and words are multifaceted, and can work in various ways throughout the manuscripts I examine in this chapter.

Chapter 3, "Granada and the Poetics of Sacred Space," advances our understanding of the role of religious images in Christian-Muslim encounters by focusing on the poetic descriptions of the Sacromonte hillside in Granada. In the spring of 1595, a cross was erected on the Sacromonte as a testimony to the discovery of lead tablets that highlighted theological affinities between Christianity and Islam. This cross was only the first of hundreds left by pilgrims, substantially changing the landscape of the Sacromonte. The early modern poetry describing the transformed landscape by Góngora, Fernández de Ribera, and Alonso de Bonilla, among others, uncovers how identities were formed in the crosses of the sacred hillside, particularly in the years leading up to the expulsion of the Moriscos.

Chapter 4, "Marian Images of Conversion," takes a fresh look at representations of the Virgin Mary, or Maryam in the Qur'an, an important figure in both Christianity and Islam. Although Mary figures prominently in Christian and Muslim cultures, images representing her could still pose problems for those who rejected figural representations. Early modern authors often attributed an aniconic predisposition to Moriscos in Spain and their Muslim neighbours in North Africa, highlighting their tendency to reject religious images. This chapter, then, examines how early modern writers attempted to reconcile this incongruity in their writings. With a shared cult of the Virgin Mary, yet differing opinions on religious images, sixteenth- and seventeenth-century authors used their writing as a tool to negotiate how they would represent Muslims' relation to Marian icons. What many of these texts reveal is that, while Moriscos and North African Muslims may have rejected images in practice, early modern writers tended to resort to the trope of conversion. Their writings suggest that the power of Marian icons often outweighed any aversion to figural representations, and that the miraculous power of images eventually would persuade the religious "other" to convert.

Chapter 5, "Images of Mary of the Battlefield," continues to examine the figure of the Virgin Mary, now as a frontier figure in the many early modern plays representing the so-called Reconquest of the Iberian Peninsula. As the previous chapter shows, many sixteenth- and seventeenth-century Spanish authors were aware of the important place that the Virgin Mary held in both Christianity and Islam. Yet some of these same authors who showcased Mary as a point of union between cultures represented her in a different light in these plays. A close analysis of some dramas of "Moors and Christians" by Lope de Vega, Calderón de la Barca, Rojas Zorrilla, and Fajardo y Acevedo – many of which stage the hiding and later reappearance of an image of the Virgin – reveals how playwrights negotiated their representation of Muslims' attitudes towards images of Mary on stage. Instead of resorting only to the trope of conversion, these playwrights suggest that the figure of Mary was intimately tied to conquest and local belonging, offering new possibilities for how to portray the Virgin Mary as both a contentious and an intermediary figure between Christianity and Islam.

Chapter 6, "Captive Images and Forged Identities," examines early modern captivity narratives – specifically, those that represent the capture and ransom of religious images and the broader role of images in North African captivity. Alongside human captives, sacred objects were also coveted and taken captive, sold, and redeemed by individuals on both sides of the Mediterranean. By contextualizing religious treatises, captives' testimonies, and autobiographical accounts that describe captive images alongside the works of other early modern authors such as Cervantes, I highlight the value that each writer places on these captive images as they cross geographical, religious, and cultural boundaries. Focusing on the travelling images in these texts, I argue that this approach can elucidate our understanding of interreligious and cross-cultural relations in the early modern Mediterranean world.

1

Moriscos between Cross and Crescent

On 22 September 1609, King Philip III issued the first royal decree for the expulsion of the Moriscos from Spain. This initial edict was directed towards the Moriscos in the kingdom of Valencia, who were ordered to leave their homes and embark at assigned ports for their passage to North Africa. Despite ecclesiastical attempts to acculturate them to Catholic practice, the edict portrayed Moriscos as "heretics, apostates, and traitors accused of lèse-majesté" ("Bando de expulsión" 1975, 252).[1] During the next two months, the process of banishing Valencia's Morisco population to Muslim lands was carried out relatively swiftly, with the exception that, in a few places, the royal order was met with armed resistance (Harvey 2005, 312–13). In the Valencian chronicler's eyewitness account, Gaspar Escolano documents the Morisco uprisings that took place in the surrounding mountain valleys in the weeks following the royal promulgation. Escolano notes on several occasions how Moriscos intentionally desecrated religious images during these rebellions. In one, between 22 and 24 October, Moriscos were accused of slashing images of saints, cutting the head off a crucifix, and repeatedly stabbing an image of the Virgin (Escolano 1879–80, 2:799a-b, 801a).

Accounts such as these of Moriscos' damage to crosses and other sacred images were taken advantage of by a group of principally religious writers to justify the expulsion of the Moriscos from Spain. These Catholic apologists of the expulsion, as they are known, included Jaime Bleda, Pedro Aznar Cardona, Damián Fonseca, and Marcos de Guadalajara y Xavier, among other minor players. Other writers, such as Antonio del Corral y Rojas, Gaspar Escolano, and the Valencian poet Gaspar de Aguilar, are among those who also participated in anti-Islamic propaganda in the years immediately following the expulsion. They produced a body of literature unlike any other corpus of texts inspired by historical events in sixteenth- and seventeenth-century Spain. Their writings exist for the sole purpose of projecting their ideological and propagandistic perspectives in an attempt to validate the decision to expel a cultural and religious minority.[2] As José María Perceval has demonstrated, these apologists of the expulsion characterize all Moriscos as one and the same. They intentionally exaggerate and attribute a series of unfavourable characteristics to these people, thereby making the decision to banish this community from Spain appear more just in their eyes (Perceval 1997). Yet, as this "official literature" tries to make sense of Spain's changing landscape, their writings also reveal the important role of religious images, especially the cross, in how Old and New Christians understood each other in the years leading up to the expulsion.

In this chapter, I trace the apologists' written descriptions of religious images to show how they tried to represent and shape the religious identity of Moriscos. The apologists focus particularly on images of the cross. This is no coincidence, since, aside from its being the most important religious symbol in Christianity, it was also one of the images that provoked the most tension for Morisco communities. One of the main issues was that, although Jesus/'Īsā is considered a prophet in Islam, in the Qur'an Jesus is not crucified and does not die on the cross. Thus, the symbol of the cross that represents Christ's death to Christians was blasphemous for Moriscos. Moreover, with images of the cross displayed nearly everywhere in Spain, Moriscos accused Christians of worshipping these images and not just what they represented, which they viewed as idolatry (Epalza Ferrer 1999, 230–2).[3]

In the last half of this chapter, I juxtapose the writings of the apologists with the Morisco episode in Cervantes's *Los trabajos de Persiles y Sigismunda* ([1617] 2004), which uncovers a unique perspective and complicates Moriscos' reception of the cross (3:11). This episode tells the story of a young Morisca woman in Valencia named Rafala who publicly displays a humble cross in her hands at the same time that the rest of her Morisco community is setting fire to the village and desecrating a stone cross before they set sail to North Africa.[4] Her treatment of this insignia clashes significantly with the way this cultural group was routinely characterized by numerous writers during this period. In the Cervantine episode, Rafala and her attitude towards this Christian symbol go against the grain of her Morisco relatives and neighbours, and as such she is represented as an exception. Thus, I contrast the story of Rafala with the writings of the Catholic apologists for the expulsion of the Moriscos who use the symbol of the cross and Moriscos' treatment of it to justify evicting this minority from Spain. Through the character of Rafala, Cervantes presents us with a different possible scenario of Moriscos' response to the symbol of the cross, challenging the one and only way the apologists were able to understand and represent the Moriscos.

The Cross in the Works of the Apologists of the Expulsion

One of the most renowned and influential defenders of the expulsion, Jaime Bleda, in his chronicle *Corónica de los moros de España* (1618), describes in great detail all of the reasons the Moriscos deserve to be expelled. For his part, Bleda ultimately contends that the Moriscos "very well deserved to be banished from the world" (896b).[5] In a chapter he titles "Due to the serious damage that the Moriscos did to the Blessed Sacrament, and to the most holy cross, our Catholic Monarch was forced to expel them," Bleda argues that one of the main reasons for the expulsion is specifically the repeated mistreatments of the cross (916b–921a):[6] "The treacherous Moriscos mocked and ridiculed the Blessed Sacrament, as has been said, every Sunday or holiday, while listening to mass they damaged all the crosses on the roads and on the way out of all their places: these crimes are what caused them to be expelled from Spain, without being allowed to stay here: *Expulsi sunt, nec potuerunt stare*" (917b).[7] Bleda continues to focus his argument in a way that exposes all of the offences done to the Holy Sacrament and the cross as principal and unavoidable motives for expulsion. In his view, these actions should not be tolerated under any circumstance, and the only solution is to expel the entire Morisco community from Spain.

Throughout his work, Bleda emphatically positions himself in favour of a drastic punishment: nothing less than expulsion. Yet, in an attempt to soften his discourse, he references a number of previous offences to the Blessed Sacrament and the cross that were reprimanded with heavier penalties, implying that expulsion would be a fair and appropriate ending for the Morisco community. He gives the example of the many Jews who had vilified these images and received a punishment much worse than exile. According to his account, it was not only the Jews who carried out these crimes who were punished; Jews who were related to these individuals suffered deaths, burnings, or were banished and stripped of their goods. In this manner, Bleda makes a comparison between Jewish and Islamic cultures, clearly justifying, in his view, the Moriscos' tragic ending (1618, 918a–b).

Although Bleda is the most unrelenting in his argument, other apologists add to this discourse, positioning themselves along the same lines as defenders of sacred images. They situate the Moriscos in a way that leaves them no option of being forgiven. In his *Memorable expulsión y justíssimo destierro de los moriscos de España* (1613), for example, Marcos de Guadalajara y Xavier recognizes Bleda's influence on his writings, especially Bleda's *Defensio Fidei* (1610), and includes the mistreatment of sacred images as one of the determining factors that leads to the expulsion of the Moriscos (156r). In order to foster their discursive strategies, these apologists evoke a more peaceful and compact Spain, free of Moriscos, where the cross can recover the admiration and respect the apologists believe it deserves: "We can now go around this kingdom without fear of these enemies; we rejoice to see the holy crosses free from so much damage that they used to do to them" (Bleda 1618, 1033a).[8]

The apologists of the expulsion also give the image of the cross its own autonomy and personality in a defence of Christianity and as an attack against what they believe to be a hostile threat to Spain. In their writings, the cross takes on other roles, such as being at the forefront of Christian troops. In this role, the cross not only serves as a visible support to the Christians and opposes the Moriscos; it also prevails over any image or symbol that metonymically represents its enemy. Bleda believes this Christian icon acts as a protagonist and fights in what he calls a "war against the crosses" (1618, 899b).[9] He bases his argument on a series of warlike passages in which the cross is victorious in its reproach against Muslims. He recounts the famous battle of Las Navas de Tolosa (1212) and the exploits of Count Fernán González (c. 910–70), both as historical references and as a sign of the unpromising future that awaits the Moriscos. Throughout his writings, he contends that no individual should dare to fight against such a powerful symbol as the cross and everything it represents (1618, 899b–900a).

While Jaime Bleda uses the representation of the cross as a tool against his opponents, the apologist Marcos de Guadalajara y Xavier goes one step further in his use of this Christian image. He manipulates the icon of the cross in a visual way, employing it not only as a tool to fight the Moriscos, but also as an instrument to contest any image representing the Prophet Muhammad that competes with the symbol of the cross. In other words, the tension exists not only between Morisco and Christian; the conflict is also a battle of religious signs, with the cross confronting any image that metonymically represents Islam. In his *Memorable expulsión y justíssimo destierro de los moriscos de España* (1613), Guadalajara y Xavier explains how Moriscos, conscious of the religious dichotomy present in the peninsula and interested in tipping the balance in their favour, harboured a desperate hope of receiving military aid from their Turkish neighbours.[10] In the author's view, the great majority of Moriscos "wished to leave triumphantly from the power of the Christians," and firmly believed that one day they would be rescued with the help of the Great Turk (1613, 103v).[11] Nevertheless, according to Guadalajara y

Xavier, other Moriscos were not as confident that the Turks ultimately would come to their rescue, and put their faith in other methods to discover their eventual fate (103v). Guadalajara y Xavier tells the story of a Morisca woman who placed various eggs in a sieve, all painted with a figure that she understood to be the Prophet Muhammad except for one, on which she drew the symbol of the cross (103v).[12] After she shook them forcefully in order to see which image would not be harmed, the only egg that remained fully intact was the one with the image of the cross. The Morisca understood this outcome as a clear sign of imminent victory for those who respect the cross, and warned her Morisco friends and relatives "to not undertake anything new, because it would only cause their downfall"[13] (103v).

This apologist continues with a similar account about a Morisco who goes to a candle maker and requests "two candles so equal, that neither one would weigh more than the other by even a single piece of hair" (Guadalajara y Xavier 1613, 103v).[14] On one he draws a figure of Muhammad and on the other an image representing Christ. He lights the two candles at the same time, then sees that the one with the representation of Muhammad is consumed more rapidly. The Morisco understands this as a visual indication of Christian triumph: "Our endeavour is going poorly, we are losing, the Christians will be victorious"[15] (103v). Considering the first-hand testimonies of many Moriscos in early modern Spain and their tendency to reject the creation of images, the apologists' stories likely were influenced more by their own imaginations than based in reality.[16] It is precisely these tales, however, recounted in Guadalajara y Xavier's works justifying the expulsion, that guide the way he chooses to represent and shape the identities of Morisco characters, portraying them all as one and the same.

Of Crescent Moons and Other Images

As we have seen in the writings of the apologists, the cross acquires a leading role that is not limited to confronting its opponents or any image that could metonymically represent these adversaries. In the eyes of the apologists, if the cross can be a determining factor in the expulsion of the Moriscos, the cross should also replace any other symbol that Christians could interpret as Muslim – specifically, the image of the crescent moon. In the opening dedication of his *Memorable expulsión* (1613), Guadalajara y Xavier establishes the expulsion of the Moriscos as a starting point, after which "their crescent moons" should be exchanged for crosses.[17] This intention to replace moons with crosses is also reflected in the ideas that Dr Lorenzo Galíndez de Carvajal expresses in his *Parecer*

(1526). In his assimilation plan for the Moriscos of Granada, he warns that "certain other symbols like the carved and painted moon"[18] should be removed and replaced with the cross and the Virgin Mary, since, in his eyes, the images that one possesses are a clear indication of one's religious identity: "people and things are recognized by the signs that they have and are deemed to be of the signs that they show" (quoted in Redondo 1983, 115).[19] Yet, Dr Lorenzo Galíndez de Carvajal's proposal was not uniform practice throughout the peninsula: in Valencia, Christian authorities mandated that Moriscos place "a crescent moon made of blue cloth the size of an orange" on their hats (quoted in Cardaillac 2004, 110).[20]

Some Inquisition cases do document that Moriscos carried symbols of the crescent moon, not necessarily as part of a religious tradition but rather for use as a talisman. In 1590, for example, Gerónimo Adulaas, a Morisco from Almoines, Valencia, was accused of carrying a crescent moon with Arabic letters written on it as an amulet (Labarta 2011–13, 233).[21] It is still hard to determine, however, to what extent and how Moriscos actually used this symbol, since surviving Morisco writings do not indicate that it had a significant religious meaning for this cultural minority in early modern Spain. Within a broader Mediterranean framework, Richard Ettinghausen (2014) notes that, although the *hilāl*, or crescent moon, was occasionally used in a pious context during the Ottoman period, such as on the reliquary that holds the cloak of the Prophet Muhammad in the Topkapi Palace, the lunar symbol was most often used in secular contexts, appearing on coinage, secular buildings, and the flags of Selīm I and Khayr al-Dīn Barbarossa. The apologists of the expulsion, however, attribute the crescent moon to be equivalent to the cross as a symbol for Moriscos. Fearing that the "Islamic" symbol will compete with their own Catholic figures, they strive to discredit any meaning it might have for Moriscos.

The apologist Pedro Aznar Cardona, in his *Expulsión justificada de los moriscos españoles* (1612), announces the total surrender of the Morisco community through a series of arbitrary parallels, using the symbol of the moon (1:192r–99r). Although this apologist condemns Moriscos for their mistreatment of the cross, he does the same to the image of the moon, which he takes as an equivalent religious symbol. He tries to diminish the symbolic value of the moon by insulting its prestige and legitimacy. Once Aznar Cardona has accomplished his goal of reducing the value of the crescent moon, he interprets a vision of a woman clothed in the sun and standing on the moon, basing his analysis on a passage in the Book of Revelation (fig. 3). He sees this image as an undisputable premonition of the supremacy of the Catholic Church over its Muslim

Fig. 3. Francisco Pacheco, *Inmaculada Concepción*, 1615–20.

Palacio Arzobispal, Seville
Photo Credit: Scala /Art Resource, New York

enemies: "What is very worthy of consideration in this miraculous vision
is that this shining woman had the moon below her feet, clearly showing
us that the day would come when (as the evangelist saw) the Christian
Church chosen by God will step on and keep below its feet the pomp
and majesty of the Muslim Turks, who are the delirious moon, according
to how they attribute it to themselves" (Aznar Cardona 1612, 1:196r-v).[22]

Aznar Cardona goes further to make a generalized interpretation of
this vision, which he sees as Christianity dominating Islam, by contextualizing the image within his contemporary surroundings and the situation
of the Moriscos. The apologist perceives this woman standing on the
moon as a prediction of the imminent victory that Christians will attain
in Spain after the expulsion of the Moriscos, along with the symbol of
the moon. Aznar Cardona's assertion that the image of the Virgin symbolizes a Christian triumph because of her power over the lunar crescent diverges from what theologians and painters would later write about
the iconography of the Immaculate Conception. Following the Spanish
Jesuit Luis de Alcázar's *Vestigatio arcani sensus in Apocalypsi* (1614), Francisco Pacheco outlines the acceptable religious iconography for the Virgin in Counter-Reformation Spain in his influential treatise, *Arte de la
pintura* (1649, 481–3).[23] He suggests that, by painting a crescent-shaped
moon below Mary's feet, the artist causes the light to reflect back on the
Virgin, glorifying the female protagonist. Yet Pacheco does not associate
the cosmological sign with a victory over Islam, as one of the apologists
of the expulsion contends.[24]

In Gonzalo de Céspedes y Meneses's novel, *Varia fortuna del soldado
Píndaro* ([1626] 1975), he includes a perverse inversion of an image of
the Virgin Mary with the moon under her feet. When the protagonist
returns to Seville near the end of the first book, we learn of an incident
between one of his old friends, Pero Vázquez, and a Morisco merchant.
Pero Vázquez discovers that the New Christian possesses a box containing a peculiar golden statue. Instead of a figure representing the woman
from the Apocalypse, it is "a little gold Muhammad, I mean gilded, with
the moon at his feet and a Qur'an in his hand and other diverse circumstances that made the case worse" (1:22, 210).[25] The gleaming image of
Muhammad is associated with the Morisco character in the episode, once
again representing this cultural minority alongside images in a way that
would make them appear idolatrous. Even Bleda extends the use of the
cross over the moon to the wider Mediterranean world while recounting
the miracle he titles "Of the cross that appeared over the moon."[26] In
this vision, the cross appears in the sky covering the crescent moon four
years before and in the same location as the Battle of Lepanto (1571).
According to Bleda, this cross dominating the symbol of the moon serves

as inspiration for the Christian captives and supposedly predicts the victory at Lepanto (Bleda 1600, 251–3).

All of these diverse uses of the cross appropriated and employed by the apologists for their own purposes acquire even more significance when they are referenced alongside the *Cofradía de la Cruz* [Brotherhood of the Cross].[27] This religious and military organization was formed on the recommendation of don Diego de Covarrubias to protect the holy crosses and with the premise of being "an association, or brotherhood of Old Christians, that takes care to protect them and place them in prominent places where their enemies will not be able to reach and harm them" (Bleda 1618, 960b).[28] Bleda became the ultimate driving force for this brotherhood, writing a memorial with regulations on how crosses were to be respected throughout Spain (961b). He tried to assure that the brotherhood would function properly in every way possible, despite a number of critics, including the Vatican, who opposed the association. Finally, with royal approval, the *Cofradía de la Cruz* took shape and grew beyond what Bleda had originally imagined (978b). In addition to this spiritual and dignified defence of the cross, the apologist's less theological intentions are also revealed. Using the *Cofradía de la Cruz* and the image of the cross, Bleda groups the whole community of Moriscos together as one and the same in order to justify a mass expulsion.[29] Within the context of this brotherhood, Bleda is unable to conceive of any event relating to the expulsion of the Moriscos without the involvement of the cross. To illustrate this point with an example, he explains how the final decree for expulsion, issued by the king himself, is based on the defence and protection of the cross and holy images, and the actual decision is justified "by way of the cross itself" (Bleda 1618, 981a).[30] Even for the apologist, the expulsion is not an action undertaken directly by the Christian forces. Rather, it is the cross itself that has the authority to expel the Moriscos (982a).

In an attempt to reinforce the idea of the cross as a tool to attack Christianity's enemies, Bleda recalls a miracle in which an image of the cross is intimately related to the expulsion of the Moriscos. In this miracle, mentioned various times in his works, a white and gleaming cross of Caravaca appears in the sky the night before the departure of the last Moriscos from the port of Los Alfaques (Bleda 1618, 1050b).[31] According to Bleda, this vision of the cross was the last image the Moriscos saw before leaving their homeland. In this way, the cross – the same cross that was once insulted and harmed and that had to defend and safeguard itself from the Moriscos – is responsible for completing the expulsion of the Moriscos (900a). Aznar Cardona takes advantage of the same miracle, giving it his own divine interpretation: "as if the heavens were telling us with such a miracle that the powerful staff of Christ our saviour, which is his victorious cross, with unsurpassed virtue left us free from the snares of the domestic infidels, and it remains free from their continuous blasphemies causing them to be tossed into those seas, clearing up the earth from their pestiferous illness so that free from the poor example of their infidelities and chilling scandals all of the faithful can worship it with greater fervour and purity" (Aznar Cardona 1612, 2:30r–v).[32] With these words, the apologist tries to frame the expulsion as a divine act in which the protagonist, the holy cross, arrives on the scene during the culminating moment of Christian triumph. With this backdrop, where divine and human misery are harshly juxtaposed, Aznar Cardona attempts to place all the pieces together to justify the expulsion of the entire Morisco community, from whom the apologist removes any trace of emotion or humanity.

Although the writings of the apologists are considered the "official literature" of the expulsion, at least seven oil paintings were commissioned by King Philip III that visually represent the official perspective of the Moriscos' exile from Spain.[33] The Valencian painter Pere Oromig, who might have observed the Valencian diaspora at first hand, depicts this momentous and tragic event in his *Embarque de los moriscos en el Grau de Valencia* (1612–13), including abundant details of some of the thousands of Moriscos who were forced to abandon their homes and their country as they left from this port (fig. 4).

Even though this painting was commissioned by the king and represents the official view of the expulsion, religious images such as the cross have virtually no prominence in it, contrary to their importance in the writings of the apologists. At the centre of the painting lies a stone cross in the middle of the plaza. Unlike the apologetic texts, the painting does not use the Christian icon as the focus of the action. Rather, the cross serves only as one more witness of this dramatic scene. Oromig includes no miraculous events using religious symbols, nor does he reproduce the stereotype of iconoclastic Moriscos, in this respect contrasting greatly with the works of the apologists, who take advantage of any opportunity to lay the blame on this minority.

In contrast to the Moriscos' iconoclasm, as seen in the texts discussed in this chapter, the apologists also present this community as idolatrous through their worship of what the apologists believe to be Islamic images. The practice of idolatry is the only alternative to image destruction that the apologists can imagine with regard to the Moriscos. In the eyes of Bleda, Aznar Cardona, and Guadalajara y Xavier, if the Moriscos reject Catholic images, they must have a parallel set of their own Muslim images and relics that they adore. This idea is especially surprising,

Fig. 4. Pere Oromig, *Embarque de los moriscos en el Grau de Valencia*, 1612–13.
Colección Fundación Bancaja, Valencia

considering that the apologists admit on various occasions that Moriscos do not worship any figural representations. Nevertheless, they still attribute certain images and sacred objects to the Moriscos, and assume that these items form part of their religious practices. Guadalajara y Xavier refers to this idea as he recalls an Inquisition case in which a Morisco is accused of possessing a canvas containing a representation of two human figures wearing Moorish attire. In the end, the Inquisition determines – at least according to Guadalajara y Xavier – that one of these figures is the Prophet Muhammad. In the words of the apologist:

> The canvas (which would be three hands long and two and a half wide) had a spacious room, a venerable old man dressed in a white and loose-fitting alb who had a blue cape over his shoulders and head, a Moor sitting at his feet, with whom it appears he communicated some serious matter, and a square pine-colored ear trumpet that had one opening placed on the wall and the other in the old man's ear. According to how it appears from how the case ended up and common knowledge and consideration from all around Andalusia, the old man was Muhammad.[34] (1614, 71v–72r)

After describing the content of the canvas, Guadalajara y Xavier deviates from the widespread belief and general acceptance of the Inquisition that one of the human figures is Muhammad. He contends, rather, that the Moriscos "don't venerate or honour an image of Muhammad's whole body, only his *zancarrón*, which is an adorned arm, according to every individual's possibility, with jewels, rings, and other riches" (1614, 72r).[35] Guadalajara y Xavier strengthens his anti-Morisco argument by cleaving to the notion of the *zancarrón*, or relic of the Prophet, and reproaching the Moriscos for worshipping one of Muhammad's extremities. This accusation forms part of a long list of idolatrous practices that the apologists use to justify the Moriscos' expulsion from Spain.

The *zancarrón* appears in a number of the apologists' writings, as well as in other literary texts of the period, each time with unique nuances.[36] Aznar Cardona and Damián Fonseca, for example, interpret the so-called Islamic object of worship in question as a representation of Muhammad's hand, instead of an adorned arm, as Guadalajara y Xavier understands it: "they took out a hand, which they call *ampsa*, to worship that resembles treacherous Muhammad's" (Fonseca 1612, 96).[37] Despite the distinctions between these texts, all of these apologists contend that this relic carries the same symbolic meaning for Moriscos as the cross does for their Christian counterparts. This interpretation is perhaps conditioned by the apologists' inability to comprehend any religion that would not make use of religious images, given the vast prevalence of such images in early modern Spanish culture. In this sense, the fictitious *zancarrón*, manipulated in the apologists' texts, could be understood as a distorted reflection of the Catholic cult of images, as José María Perceval has suggested (1997, 214). The inquisitorial case of the young Morisca Inés illustrates this idea clearly. This woman is accused for announcing publicly and without hesitation "that in their religion they took a donkey's leg and stood it upright and all the Moriscos got down on their knees in front of it, and one Morisco, whom Inés didn't name, said he dressed like a clergyman and said Mass in front of the *zancarrón*" (Dadson 2007, 254).[38] This telling example from the Inquisition reflects the crude inversion of Christian customs in a Morisco context. It is especially significant that the image of devotion in this case is not one of the Prophet's extremities, but rather part of an animal. The object of worship is transformed into a macabre item that heightens the act of idolatry in the eyes of the Christian authorities, while at the same time forming part of the discursive strategies employed to defend the exile of the Moriscos.

Valencian Moriscos and Religious Iconography

Turning now to the episode of the Valencian Moriscos in the *Persiles*, Cervantes offers another alternative besides iconoclasm or idolatry. This possibility contrasts dramatically with the apologists' discourse, but at the same time does not deny the reality of the period and the difficult coexistence of Moriscos with the religious images omnipresent in their daily surroundings. The Cervantine episode begins with the Morisca Rafala and her aging father greeting some pilgrims who are passing through the Valencian coastal village, populated mostly by Moriscos, on their way to Rome. The inhabitants offer a warm welcome to the outsiders, who gratefully accept it, although with a little apprehension. Their doubt is confirmed when Rafala warns the pilgrims of imminent danger. The Moriscos have concocted a scheme with a group of Barbary pirates, who intend to help the entire community abandon their town and set sail to North Africa, along with all the villagers and their goods. Taking into consideration Rafala's testimony and determined to protect their freedom, the pilgrims seek refuge within the walls of the church, where they are welcomed by the priest and the *xadraque* Xarife, Rafala's uncle. Before his new audience, Xarife angrily vents his anti-Morisco sentiments, embracing the viewpoints of the apologists of the expulsion.[39] Once the pilgrims shelter themselves under the protection of the church and after safeguarding the Holy Sacrament from the threat of the Moriscos, they arm themselves with guns and stones in preparation for the maritime attack that lies ahead. The narrator tells us that the Morisco community receives the arrival of the Turks with great rejoicing, which leads to the burning of the village, the destruction of a stone cross, and an attempt to damage the church, all in the name of Muhammad. At the end of the episode, once the danger is over and the Moriscos have set sail, Rafala and the scribe arrive at the scene. Holding her cross made of reeds, Rafala proclaims her physical and spiritual freedom: "A Christian, a Christian and free, and free by God's grace and mercy!" (Cervantes [1617] 2004, 3:11, 552).[40] The pilgrims' final view before continuing their journey is of Rafala worshipping the Christian images in the church and kissing the hands of the priest, all while her uncle Xarife carries on with his anti-Morisco harangue.

Considering this framework of circumstances, the church is presented as the unifying element in the sequence of events, becoming the central axis and conclave of the action in the passage. It is significant that all the characters finally converge at this venue and that some of the most dramatic scenes of the episode take place there. Most important, certain visual aspects acquire a special significance within the walls of the church. Given that the plot transpires with this ecclesiastical backdrop, it is no coincidence that the most obvious visual elements are the objects related to Catholic worship, which play a fundamental role in the development of the episode. While the pilgrims take refuge in the church alongside Rafala's uncle and the priest, the latter assures them of their safety, painting a picture of the church as strong and dominant: "we have a good tower, and the church has good and ironclad doors that, if it's not very intentional, can't be broken down or burned through" (Cervantes [1617] 2004, 3:11, 547).[41] Then comes the arrival of an angry crowd of Moriscos and their attempt to inflict whatever damage they can. The flames, the destruction of a stone cross, and the direct attack on the church are described subtly, to prepare the way for Rafala's appearance. Despite these details, it is significant that this description comes from the narrator, not from any of the crypto-Muslim Moriscos, who are continuously denied the opportunity to express themselves or to show any human qualities.[42] The Morisca Rafala and the scribe are the last characters to arrive at the religious sanctuary, and they appear, notably, from opposite directions and with contrasting dispositions. Moreover, the actions of the Morisca demonstrate visually the most revealing moment of the episode: the exhibition of a humble reed cross accompanied by a previously oppressed Christian declaration. Her statement is reinforced by her devout worship of the images inside the church.

Various scholars have pointed out that this episode, and the pilgrims' encounter with the Valencian Moriscos, was not far from the historical reality and that it presents the seriousness of the Morisco problem in the kingdom of Valencia. The fear of corsair raids on the Levantine coast of the peninsula was all too common, and Francisco Márquez Villanueva (1975, 288–90; 2010, 440n), Carlos Romero Muñoz (1997, 270–2), and Francisco Giner (140–5), among others, have related various historical examples of the events described in this episode of the *Persiles*. Steven Hutchinson (2012b) has underscored how the focus of the chapter is, in fact, on the exile of the crypto-Muslim Moriscos, who voluntarily abandon their homes in the Valencian village. Both he (2012b, 192–6) and Bernabé Pons (2013a, 168–9) opportunely situate the Morisco episode within this context, offering some revealing historical examples that shed light on the situation of these crypto-Muslims who willingly crossed over to North Africa.

In addition to these circumstances, the Valencian Moriscos who intentionally go into exile in this Cervantine episode also clearly portray the experiences of many of the crypto-Muslim Moriscos with the cross and the cult of images in early modern Spain. In his *Décadas de la historia de la insigne y coronada ciudad y reino de Valencia* (1610–11), the Valencian historian Gaspar Escolano documents various Morisco uprisings that took place in the region. In some of them, the Moriscos damaged crosses and sacred images inside and around churches: "[The Moriscos] did the same in the church and the parish house, where they killed a young man who served there; and stepping on and dragging the sacred vestments on the ground, they stabbed the images of the saints, and with a scimitar they cut off the head of Christ from a crucifix ... And it happened, to their surprise, that having set fire to the altar of the church, the whole altarpiece was burned except for the images" (Escolano 1879–80, 2:799a-b).[43] These affronts to the icon of the cross occurred not only on the Levantine coast, but elsewhere in the Iberian Peninsula, especially during uprisings and revolts (Franco Llopis 2011b, 121). In his *Historia del* [sic] *rebelión y castigo de los moriscos del reino de Granada* ([1600] 1991), the Granadan chronicler Luis de Mármol Carvajal describes one such action against Christian symbolism.[44] He depicts how Christians in a village in the Alpujarras of Granada suffer a Morisco attack that leads them to take refuge in the tower of the church, reacting in a similar manner to the Christian pilgrims in the *Persiles*. This time, however, the Moriscos of Granada do indeed manage to enter the sacred temple, unleashing their anger by damaging the crosses and sacred images and burning holy objects:

> [The Christian men], along with their wives and children, went into the church and protected themselves in the bell tower. Then the Moors from Bayárcal and other nearby places arrived, and while robbing the houses of

the Christians, they went to the church, and finding little defence, since
all of our people were up in the tower, they entered, and with ruthless
rage they destroyed the altars, breaking the altars and altarpieces, and
plundered whatever was inside, and they dragged all of the holy things
across the ground ... And for more scorn they shot with an arrow and
stabbed the crosses and images, and when they placed the pieces of all that
and of the altarpieces in the middle of the church, they set fire and burned
it.[45] (Mármol Carvajal [1600] 1991, 4:17, 106a)

As Felipe Pereda has observed, some of Francisco Heylán's early seventeenth-century engravings included in Antolínez de Burgos's *Historia
eclesiástica de Granada* ([c. 1611] 1996) portray Moriscos' aversion to figural images, just as many Christian writers imagined their response to
religious iconography (Pereda 2007, 352). One engraving, intercalated
in Antolínez de Burgos's account of what transpired between Christians
and Moriscos in Andarax during the War of the Alpujarras, depicts a
scene with much more cruelty than that described in the Morisco episode in Cervantes's *Persiles* (fig. 5). Here, Heylán juxtaposes the torture of humans with the sacrilegious destruction of religious images,
where both grief-stricken individuals and demolished objects of worship
become esteemed martyrs in the eyes of Christian authors like Antolínez
de Burgos. Heylán places a representation of a crucified Christ near the
top of the engraving, to serve as a model for all the men, women, children, and images that would be physically harmed and martyred because
of their irreconcilable differences. It does not seem to be a coincidence
that Antolínez de Burgos highlights 28 December, the Feast of the Holy
Innocents – which commemorates the life and death of the many infants
slaughtered by King Herod in an attempt to kill the Christ child – as the
date of this grievous event.[46] The manuscript that describes this engraving was completed, although not published, in 1611; meanwhile, the
expulsion of the Moriscos was already well under way. Together, the verbal and visual content of this episode would only help to present the
Moriscos in an unfavourable light as they were being exiled from Spain
(Antolínez de Burgos [c. 1611] 1996, 265–9).

The story that accompanies the first scene of the engraving in particular describes how the Moriscos in the Spanish village enter the church,
destroy all the crosses and sacred images, while also firing their weapons
at the Blessed Sacrament, leading to the burning of all the sacred objects,
including the temple itself (fig. 6). Although Antolínez de Burgos and
Francisco Heylán choose to represent the desecration of religious objects
alongside the martyrdom of countless villagers, it is precisely the defiled
images that serve as a model for the human protagonists. Describing a

Fig. 5. Francisco Heylán, *Mártires de Andarax*, c. 1611.

Archivo del Patronato de la Alhambra y Generalife, Granada

previous episode in Ugíjar, Antolínez de Burgos explains how a group of Christian men finds inspiration in a half-burned and destroyed image of the Virgin Mary while they themselves suffer the same torture as the Marian representation:

> With this proclamation, these courageous soldiers acquired a renewed spirit to die in defence of their faith; and, trusting little in their own strength, which was weak and deficient, they put their faith in the divine, turning to an image of the most holy Mother of the Angels, destroyed and half-burned by those infernal hands, they began to shout out: 'Repairer of our fall, solution to our miseries, hope for our glory, patroness and advocate for the afflicted, save us and protect us, Lady, in this extreme peril, so none of us miss the obligation we have.'[47] (Antolínez de Burgos [c. 1611] 1996, 262–3)

Considering how Moriscos destroyed Catholic objects of adoration in this scene and Heylán's engraving that illustrates it, the Morisco episode in Cervantes's *Persiles* appears much more moderate. Nevertheless, it still addresses the thorny issue of Moriscos' reaction to religious images in early modern Spain.

Christian authors who were in favour of the expulsion edict sometimes depicted Moriscos taking their contempt even further and experiencing malicious delight in seeing Christians themselves damaging their most

Fig. 6. Francisco Heylán, *Mártires de Andarax*, detail, c. 1611.
Archivo del Patronato de la Alhambra y Generalife, Granada

cherished symbols without knowing it. Guadalajara y Xavier tells of a Morisco shoemaker in the kingdom of Aragon who deviously placed a crucifix under a stone so that all the Christians who availed themselves of his services would have no choice but to stomp their feet upon the cross (1613, 59v). What the apologists try to show, thus, is that this icon does not always have to suffer visible and explicit abuse to be insulted.

Cervantine Moriscos and the Politics of the Cross

The apologists' focus on Moriscos' response to religious symbols only clarifies their intention to use these stories to justify the banishment of Moriscos from Spain. Yet, one cannot deny the complex coexistence of Moriscos with Catholicism in general, and with sacred images in particular.[48] The narrator of Cervantes's *Persiles* reflects this reality starkly in his description of the crypto-Muslim Moriscos who knock down a stone cross before exiling themselves to North Africa. However, the representation of Moriscos and their response to religious icons in the Cervantine episode deviates from the expulsion apologists' discourse in significant ways. Cervantes offers an alternate depiction of Moriscos' relationship to the Catholic cult of images that is embodied in the figure of the Morisca Rafala. Without denying her Morisca condition, she rejects certain stereotypes associated with her community by embracing a simple cross. This suggestive staging of Rafala with the cross in her hand hints at another possible scenario that contrasts with the narrowly conceived ideas of the apologists. In this episode, Cervantes offers the veneration of images as an alternative path that acknowledges some of the similarities between the Valencian Moriscos' behaviour in the *Persiles* and the accusations put forth by the expulsion apologists but that does not result in a soulless mass expulsion. By including Rafala and her uncle Xarife, the latter ironically cleaving to the anti-Morisco arguments of the apologists, Cervantes demonstrates that he is aware of the Morsicos' destruction and contempt of images in Valencia. Yet, without rejecting this reality, he instead chooses not to include any exorbitant accusations or miraculous events involving the cross and other sacred images, as the apologists do in their texts. And he certainly does not resort to attributing idolatrous practices to this minority, as many of his contemporaries do. This scenario makes Rafala's striking appearance possible, where the cross she holds serves as a symbol and fundamental key to present another potential outcome. In place of Rafala's humble reed cross, the apologists use a more robust, austere, and even overwhelming cross, but the cross itself is the same in the end, just used with a different purpose in each of their texts. Cervantes seems to suggest that Rafala and the younger generation of Moriscos, including Ana Félix, would be able to integrate themselves into Christian society more fully (Bernabé Pons 2016, 96).

The figure of Rafala with a humble cross in her hands reflects an attempt to institute the worship of images among Moriscos in Valencia and other regions of the peninsula, which some religious authorities tried to put into practice in the sixteenth century. Her public display of the cross parallels the focus on religious images in some evangelization campaigns in early modern Spain. In the kingdom of Valencia, Feliciano de Figueroa, bishop of Segorbe (1599–1609), writes in his *Constituciones de los nuevamente convertidos* that all the Morisco members of his diocese are required to have "a cross and images of saints in their homes with much decency and reverence all year long"[49] (Franco Llopis 2008a, 391; Saborit Badenes 1996, 435). Similar requirements appeared in other parts of the peninsula, as well.[50] In Granada, the Hieronymite Brother José de Sigüenza, while writing the biography of Hernando de Talavera, archbishop of Granada, explains how important crosses and other images were for him during the evangelization campaigns:

> When he went to visit these people he brought images on paper; from those old holy cards that at that time were thought to be good; he gave them to various people. He taught them how much reverence they deserved, and since having images was a point that was so prohibited in their Qur'an, he told them how deceived they were by thinking that and how they should consider worshipping them, showing them how they would not commit any type of idolatry, since their purpose is to uplift one's heart and awaken the memory of that which it represents, and to worship them for what they represent, which is God, his mother and the saints.[51] (Sigüenza 2000, 2:332)

In addition to this religious initiation through images, Hernando de Talavera mandates that the Moriscos in Granada carry a cross or display an image of worship in their homes.[52] Likewise, in his *Vida del capitán Contreras* ([c. 1630–41] 1982), Alonso de Contreras subtly reveals how Moriscos' homes were searched for an adequate display of religious iconography.[53] After Contreras is accused of being "King of the Moriscos" in Hornachos, a region known for its predominantly Morisco population, he gives an account of how he pretended to be sent by the bishop of Badajoz to check the residents' dwellings for images and crosses.[54] While he actually enters their homes for personal motives, he reveals that somebody must have passed through Hornachos selling religious prints, since every home had more than one cross displayed publicly: "And while first entering in other homes, they said that I was sent by the bishop of Badajoz to see if their homes had images and crosses, and since I was a hermit they believed me, and there was reason to believe that people came to Hornachos selling religious prints to get rich, and there was not a door that didn't have two or three crosses, so it looked like a battle ground" (Contreras 1982, 108).[55] Moriscos were often accused of not following the regulations issued by the ecclesiastical authorities and not displaying religious images such as the cross, as was the case of Pedro Tinel, who was accused of not having "an image or cross at home" (Franco Llopis 2010a, 94).[56]

Returning to the episode of Rafala and the Valencian Moriscos, the problems that could arise from either worshipping or scorning sacred icons are clearly seen through the actions of this Morisca character. The way in which the veneration of images occurs in the episode is sugges- tive, since, if we examine the attitude and behaviour of the Morisca pro- tagonist, we see that she appears to have a thorough understanding of how to worship and revere religious images. Not surprisingly, once the majority of the crypto-Muslim Moriscos exile themselves to North Africa, and Rafala is left on the Valencian coast, the first thing she does is go to the church, where she "prayed before the images and later hugged her uncle, first kissing the priest's hands" (Cervantes [1617] 2004, 2:11, 552). [57] There is no doubt that Cervantes intends the reader to perceive in the Morisca Rafala a strong Catholic devotion and a familiarity with worshipping religious images. It is no less significant that the Morisca also chooses such an opportune moment to do so: a village in flames, Moriscos with mixed feelings leaving their homes, the dawning sun, and Rafala's statement as she appears in the distance. A moment so subtly created makes the significance of Rafala and her worship of Catholic icons stand out even more. In order to highlight this Morisca's actions towards images, Cervantes has Rafala enter the church with the scribe, a character who is diametrically opposed to the Morisca and who fur- ther emphasizes her religious values: "The scribe didn't worship or kiss anybody's hands, because his soul was busy feeling sorry for the loss of his property" (3:11, 552–3).[58] Not even a slight concern over knowing whether his wife and children are safe hampers his thoughts, which are consumed by the loss of his burned and stolen belongings.[59]

The figurative dichotomy between the Valencian Morisca and the scribe is evident from the moment of their appearance together. Rafala comes from the coast, from the community of her own people who are on their way to North Africa, and she comes with a spiritual frame of mind superior to any physical or emotional loss. The scribe appears from the opposite direction, from inland, which suggests he was taking refuge from the actions related to the departure of the Moriscos. The only concern on the scribe's mind is the loss of his property. Hearing the ringing of bells but ignorant of what has happened in the Valencian town, the scribe appears on the scene only after the danger has passed. These opposite paths eventually meet to put both characters in a similar situation, both sheltered in the same church, apparently without physical assets and with the duty to build a new future. The temple doors are opened for both, regardless of their backgrounds; here, both Old and New Christians have a place, and the images act as their witnesses. All of this occurs as dawn breaks upon the Valencian town, a new day for the atypical characters, who will need to begin restructuring the foundations of a new life together, a future full of uncertainties but protected by the same walls. As María Soledad Carrasco Urgoiti reminds us (1997, 71), this future was not a choice for Moriscos like Rafala. Nevertheless, Rafala and her reverence towards religious images reveals an alternative scenario in which a simple cross in the delicate hands of the Morisca is capable of going against a more authoritarian cross used by the apologists, an imperative cross that helped pave the way for the expulsion of the Moriscos. Instead of grouping all Moriscos together, as the apologists do to justify the decision to exile the entire community, Cervantes presents us with two sides of the same situation, in this case the iconoclastic Moriscos alongside the devout Rafala, showing some diversity while representing Moriscos and their view of religious images. Through the Morisca Rafala, Cervantes contests the one and only way that the apologists of the expulsion understand and represent Moriscos. He thus upends assumptions about this community and their reception of religious iconography in early modern Spain.

The sources examined in this chapter reveal that many individuals in this period understood Moriscos' identity in terms of their response to religious images, particularly the cross. Images that are used and abused helped shape Morisco identity while also exposing what was at stake for this minority in the years leading up to their expulsion from Spain. In an attempt to justify the Moriscos' tragic fate, the apologists depicted all of them as either iconoclasts or idolaters – individuals who either destroyed images such as the cross or possessed representations of the crescent moon and *zancarrón*. Curiously, it is Cervantes's fiction that presents a more nuanced picture of Moriscos and their reception of the cross. The episode of Rafala shows he was aware of the debates and problems associated with Moriscos' reception of images, but it also illustrates the complexities of Morisco identity through the character of the young Morisca woman. By juxtaposing this female convert with a humble reed cross alongside the other members of her Morisco community that destroy the village's stone cross, Cervantes asks his readers to question the politics of the expulsion, and suggests that the thorny issue of image worship among Moriscos is not as uniform as the apologists make it out to be. But how did Moriscos themselves understand their own identity in relation to religious images, and how did they write about these issues from their own perspective? I address these questions in the next chapter.

2

Text against Image in Moriscos' Literary Culture

While the apologists of the expulsion were writing against Moriscos' disregard for religious images, the Moriscos themselves wrote against image worship in early modern Spain. Yet, as can be expected, both groups wrote for very different reasons. As we saw in the last chapter, the apologists used examples of image destruction in an attempt to justify their argument and pave the way for the expulsion of the Moriscos from Spain. However, throughout the sixteenth century and in the years surrounding their expulsion, some Moriscos wrote as a form of resistance against the practice of worshipping images. One Morisco who spoke out against Christian images and admired the actions of those Muslims who physically harmed sacred objects was Aḥmad ibn Qāsim al-Ḥajarī. In his *Kitāb nāṣir al-dīn* ([c. 1637] 1997, 141–4), al-Ḥajarī recounts the theological discussion he held with a French woman on the creation and worship of Christian images.[1] This dispute leads him to recall the words of the Prophet, collected in several hadiths, which rebuke the creation and worship of images, as well as of Muhammad's iconoclasm as he destroys 360 idols at the Ka'ba (145–6). Inspired by the actions of the Prophet, the Morisco likewise refers to a contemporary story of harm done to a Christian image by a Muslim captive as he praises his actions (146–7). In this narrative, the inhabitants of a particular village buy a statue – although to al-Ḥajarī they buy an idol – and order the Muslim captive Aḥmad to get it and transport it back to the town. After making sure he was not being observed, Aḥmad decides to tie the object to his donkey and drag it on the ground all the way back, in this way expressing his opinion on the worthlessness of the statue. Although the villagers are outraged by the way Aḥmad mistreats the holy effigy, significantly he does not receive any type of reprimand from the governor, since he only acted in accordance with the precepts of his religion.

Stories and legends like the one told by al-Ḥajarī played an important role in helping Moriscos preserve memories of great significance, and were particularly influential as a mode of resistance against Christian attempts to eradicate their culture and identity.[2] Many of these stories, which Moriscos read or listened to covertly, applauded the first Muslims' iconoclasm and criticism of idolatry. These texts would have been particularly relevant to Moriscos who sought to reject their modern-day "idols," or the Catholic images that they were required to venerate in early modern Spain.[3] Although hybridity is a characteristic feature of this literature, Luce López Baralt suggests that the essence of Aljamiado literature lies in its use as a tool of resistance for the Morisco community (2009, 28). It is especially revealing, then, that in nineteenth-century Aragon a concealed pile of rusted weapons was found hidden alongside an assortment of Morisco books, visibly linking Aljamiado texts to other, more traditional forms of resistance (Barletta 2005, x). Based on these considerations, we must ask how Morisco literature could sustain memories and function as a mode of resistance, particularly within the context of forced image worship.

Whereas Chapter 1 centred on Moriscos' attitude towards the Catholic cult of images in texts authored by Old Christians, this chapter focuses on the visual culture in Moriscos' own writings in Arabic, Aljamiado, and Spanish. Beginning in the years immediately following their forced conversions to Christianity at the start of the sixteenth century all the way through to the period after their expulsion, Moriscos wrote and copied letters, poems, legends, epic-chivalric narratives, and prophetic texts, among various other genres, that addressed their concerns and showcased their resistance to worshipping religious images.[4] Drawing on a variety of sources from this corpus of texts, I first consider how Moriscos wrote about the problem of "idols" and how they viewed the use of Arabic script as a means of resistance to religious images. I then examine anonymous Morisco literature in a variety of genres in which many of the Muslim characters transgress the established rules and actively repudiate the adoration of religious statues or idols, just as a great deal of their Morisco audience opposed the veneration of images. Although scholars have rigorously analysed Morisco literature from a range of perspectives, there are still no studies that delve into the important artistic elements they present – specifically, the various references to religious visual culture. A close examination of this aspect is both important and necessary, however, as it reflects the social quandary of the Moriscos in early modern Spain. By tracing the visual elements in these texts, we can begin to ask how Moriscos' literary culture compelled many crypto-Muslims enthusiastically to reject the very religious images they were forced to adore. The inclusion of written references to "idols" in a variety of their fictional texts raises the question of how these texts motivated diverse Morisco communities to uphold written texts against visual images.

The Problem of Idols through Morisco Eyes

Many Moriscos labelled Old Christians as *abīd al-aṣnām*, or idol worshippers, equating Catholic images with idols.[5] In fact, the criticism of idolatry or image worship was a frequent theme in Moriscos' writings, whether they referred to the disapproval of Christian icons in the churches surrounding them or the idols before or during the time of the Prophet Muhammad (Valero Cuadra 2000, 96). The exiled Morisco writer Ibrāhīm Ṭaybilī, for example, criticizes Christian dogmas that are incompatible with Islam in his polemical work. In his objections, Ṭaybilī underscores the idolatrous nature of the Catholic mass and denounces the veneration of religious images in the church, calling the statues idols and the cross a mere stick of wood (1988, vv. 2250–4). Another Morisco exile, Ibn Qāsim al-Ḥajarī, advances some of the same accusations towards the Catholic Church, "which is full of idols and crosses," as opposed to the "mosque that is devoid of idols and filth" ([c. 1637] 1997, 226, 123).

Even before Moriscos objected to the worship of "idols" after their forced conversion, some Muslims living in the Iberian Peninsula considered Christians to be idol worshippers, believing they adored the religious object instead of what it represented. In *Kitāb al-fiṣal* ([c. 1027–48] 1984), a work on Islamic theology, Ibn Ḥazm of Cordoba accuses his Christian contemporaries of idolatry for kneeling down and worshipping painted images in their churches, even though they themselves condemn idolatrous worship (3:112; Pereda 2007, 342n; Franco Llopis 2010a, 89). In addition to the issue of rendering cult to figural representations, Ibn Ḥazm is concerned with conflating the representation of a deity with the deity itself, making a similar distinction between the image and its referent to the one René Magritte would offer centuries later in his painting *La trahison des images* (1929). Scorning the value and place of images in a multiconfessional Iberia, Ibn Ḥazm contends that the paintings of human likeness worshipped by his Christian neighbours cannot be viewed as the very individuals they represent.

Shortly after the forced conversions of Muslims to Christianity began in Spanish kingdoms at the start of the sixteenth century, the problem of images became a greater concern for Muslims in the peninsula. To address this issue, Islamic legal scholar Aḥmad ibn Abī Jumʿah (d. 1511), more commonly known as the mufti of Oran, wrote a fatwa from Fez to crypto-Muslims living in Spain.[6] In it, he grants them permission to conserve their faith by dissimulating Islamic practices. According to the mufti's advice, they are allowed to comply with the precepts of the Catholic Church, as well as drink wine and eat pork, provided that the inward intention of their heart remains devoted to Islam. With regard to Christian visual culture, such as figures of Jesus and Mary, the mufti declares that these images are no more than mere *aṣnām*, "idols" made of wood and lifeless stone that serve no purpose (Harvey 1964, 172, 175).[7] The fatwa continues by directing how crypto-Muslims should respond to these Christian "idols." Even if they are forced to simulate outwardly their praise of the Christian statues, the Moriscos' inner intentions must remain committed to Islam: "If at the hour of prayer you are obligated to go and worship the idols of the Christians, you should have the intention to do the *takbīr al-iḥrām* and to carry out your prayer; and you should look at the idols when the Christians do so; but your intention should be directed towards God, although you may not be facing the direction of the *qibla*, the way in which those in war pray when they come up against their enemy" (Mufti of Oran 1975, 44–5).[8] As L.P. Harvey and María del Mar Rosa-Rodríguez have pointed out, Moriscos in Spain must have regarded the guidance in the fatwa as relatively significant, since it was copied and/or translated various times during the sixteenth and seventeenth centuries (Harvey 1964, 164, 158).[9] Even if Moriscos did not have direct knowledge of the mufti's guidance, they could know that Islamic practice would allow them to dissimulate their faith outwardly in times of religious oppression (Bernabé Pons 2013b, 526). This permission granted to Moriscos to be more flexible in their outward reception of religious images is especially significant, since it contrasts so markedly with the rigidity of the Christian world. As I outlined in the introduction to this book, Moriscos and Protestants were united in their beliefs and actions towards Catholic images. Yet, with the mufti of Oran's guidance, it was now possible for Moriscos to dissimulate their beliefs about religious images when confronted with precarious situations.

As a variety of letters from Moriscos to religious and political authorities in North Africa and the Ottoman Empire demonstrates, the issue of forced worship of Christian "idols" most certainly remained a great concern for this community in Spain. A few years after the conquest of Granada, one Morisco in particular articulated the sorrow caused by his forced conversion to Christianity in the form of an Arabic *qaṣīda* poem he sent to the Ottoman emperor, Bāyazīd II, in a plea for support. The poetic voice expresses lament that the Morisco children now go off daily with the priest, who instructs them in "unbelief, idolatry, and falsehood"

("Casida morisca" 1975, 38).[10] And the fact that the Islamic mosques of al-Andalus have been converted to churches, with Christian bells tolling from the minarets, causes distress among the Morisco community. Finally, the poem concludes with a supplication that the emperor intercede on behalf of the poet so that Moriscos can continue their Islamic practices or else relocate to North Africa with their belongings (33–41).[11]

Other Moriscos also requested help, citing similar concerns. Muhammad ibn Muhammad ibn Daud appealed to the Turks in Algiers for support. Although the letter was intercepted and never delivered to its intended recipient, the Morisco Alonso del Castillo translated it into Spanish, leaving a written testimony of ibn Daud's anguish, including his apprehension about forced image worship:[12] "They forced the people into their religion and make them worship figures [images] with them, pressuring them to do so, without anyone daring to talk about it. Oh how many upset people there are among those who don't believe! They call the people to come worship the figure [image] with the church bell, and they order the person to come promptly to their scornful religion" (Castillo 1852, 46).[13] From such Morisco pleas for help, the appeal of the mufti of Oran's fatwa is clear. His message explains to these concerned Moriscos how to preserve their faith through dissimulation and inner religiosity, despite being forced to worship Christian images.

Whether or not the Morisco exile Muhammad ibn 'Abd al-Rafi' al-Andalusī had first-hand knowledge of the mufti's fatwa, his behaviour towards Christian images indicates that he, too, acts according to such guidance. In his account al-Anwār al-Nabawīyya fī Ābā' Khayr al-Barīyya [The prophetic lights on the ancestors of the most excellent of all creatures] ([1635] 2009), written in Tunis after he fled Spain with his family in 1604, even before the expulsion, Ibn 'Abd al-Rafi' recalls how his father would secretly teach him about Islam in their home. Included in his Islamic teachings, Ibn 'Abd al-Rafi' received instruction on how he should respond to the many "idols" in Catholic churches. Just as the mufti of Oran explains, Islamic practices could be dissimulated, since the inner intention of the heart was most important. Likewise, Ibn 'Abd al-Rafi''s father insisted that his Morisco son look at the images, but, in his heart, recite verses from the Qur'an that negate all that these sacred effigies represent:

> My father, God almighty rest his soul, used to teach me what to say when I saw the idols. He said: "If you enter their churches and see their idols, say in your heart the words of God: 'O men, give ear to this parable: Those you worship other than God can never create as much as a fly, even if they get together to do so; and if the fly were to rob them of a thing, they would

not be able to snatch it away from it' [22:73]. Say: 'O you unbelievers, I do not worship what you worship' [109:1–2] and other holy verses, and the Almighty's words."[14] (Ibn ʿAbd al-Rafiʿ [1635] 2009, 195)

Along with instructing Ibn ʿAbd al-Rafiʿ on how to respond to the omnipresent Catholic visual culture, it is significant that his father also taught him the Arabic alphabet as an important part of his Islamic education. The young Morisco claims to remember vividly returning from school and his father's taking out an oak writing board on which he would write down the letters of the alphabet. As Ibn ʿAbd al-Rafiʿ sounded out each Spanish letter, his father would teach him the equivalent Arabic character. Knowing that his father was risking his life, he kept all this clandestine tutoring a secret from his mother and other relatives, even though they pressured him to reveal what his father was teaching (Ibn ʿAbd al-Rafiʿ [1635] 2009, 194–5). Along with opposing Catholic "idols," the act of writing with Arabic characters was in itself a form of resisting Christian culture and a mode of conserving Islam in Christian Spain. By using an alphabet that was considered dangerous and that was later proscribed in Spain, many Moriscos transgressed the linguistic boundaries set before them, in addition to opposing image worship through texts with Arabic letters or words. Since Arabic script gains relevance in the Morisco narratives that I explore at the end of this chapter, let us first look at how Moriscos considered the language of the Qur'an as both a verbal sign of resistance and a visual image connected to Islam.

Arabic Script as a Tool to Resist Idols

Ibn ʿAbd al-Rafiʿ and his father were among the countless Moriscos who covertly passed on knowledge of Arabic despite a growing distrust among Catholic authorities for Arabic script in seventeenth-century Spain. Regardless of the repressive laws that the Spanish Crown enacted against the use of Arabic, Moriscos disregarded the rulings and clandestinely preserved the Arabic characters. Moriscos' persistent use of the Arabic alphabet was principally due to the fact that it is the language of Allah and a visual reminder of the language used for the revelation of their sacred text, the Qur'an.[15] Writing in Arabic allowed Moriscos to connect themselves to the larger Islamic community in the Mediterranean and, more important, as Vincent Barletta argues, it "situated Morisco scribes and readers within a thousand-year-old tradition of God's relationship with Muslims" (2005, 137). Still, despite the importance of Arabic for Moriscos, it became increasingly difficult for them to read, write, or even possess texts with Arabic characters. Although the

Capitulations signed by the Catholic kings in November 1491 initially granted Moriscos permission to conserve their religious and cultural traditions, it was not long before the promises in the Capitulations were broken, and a series of prohibitions against Muslim customs, including the use of Arabic, was instituted. In 1501, Fray Francisco Ximénez de Cisneros, archbishop of Toledo, ordered the mass burning of Arabic books at Bibarrambla in Granada, salvaging only a few works of medicine, an event that Crypto-Muslims such as the Mora de Úbeda witnessed and painfully remembered. In his *Breve compendio* (c. 1532–3), the Mancebo de Arévalo recounts the great sadness of an elderly woman who told him about the massive book burning and how one sacred Muslim book in particular had been reduced to nothing more than children's papers (Narváez Córdova 2003, 54; López Baralt 1992, 194).

The book burning instigated by Cisneros was only one of a long series of decrees against the use of Arabic. In 1511 Arabic was still allowed, but in an attempt to distance them from their Islamic social and religious customs, Moriscos were required to turn in all books in Arabic to be checked by the authorities (Harvey 2005, 72). Decrees against continued to escalate until Arabic eventually became entirely proscribed. In 1566, a group of theologians, jurists, and other officials gathered and enacted a set of rulings against the use of Arabic, which Philip II published on 1 January 1567 (Domínguez Ortiz and Vincent 1978, 33; Caro Baroja 1957, 152–3). These rulings required Moriscos to stop speaking, reading, and writing in Arabic within three years and to turn in any books written in Arabic script to authorities for examination within thirty days. Luis del Mármol Carvajal records the reaction of Moriscos to the loss of their sacred language and customs in his *Historia del* [sic] *rebelión y castigo de los moriscos del reino de Granada* ([1600] 1991, 2:8, 69a), underscoring their despair and fear for their future.

Despite such prohibitions on the use of Arabic, the importance of this sacred language did not diminish among Moriscos. Some, like Ibn ʿAbd al-Rafiʿ and his father, continued to read and write it clandestinely. Copies of Arabic alphabets included in Inquisition cases demonstrate how Moriscos tried to pass along this forbidden knowledge from one generation to the next. Francisco Choplón confesses to the Inquisition that Mançor, a Valencian Morisco, had given him a copy of the Arabic alphabet and taught him to read it (Barceló and Labarta 2009, 281). In her study of books and written culture among Aragonese Moriscos, Jacqueline Fournel-Guérin notes that almost half of the Moriscos brought before the Inquisition between 1568 and 1620 were prosecuted for owning one or more Arabic books or loose pages with Arabic characters (1979, 243). In fact, possessing writings in Arabic was the most frequent crime for which Moriscos were found guilty by the Inquisition in Valencia (Surtz 2001, 424). Given the importance of Arabic texts to Moriscos, it comes as little surprise that they would go to great lengths to keep the sacred writings hidden. Yet, as many Inquisition cases demonstrate, authorities often found these forbidden books in their custody. This was the situation of the Morisca Beatriz Çahori, who fought with all her strength to keep her Arabic texts from being taken from her. When the Inquisitional officer was at her home, he claimed to have seen her hide something under her garments, and, after a long struggle, he finally discovered papers in Arabic concealed on Beatriz's body (Labarta 1980, 120).

Although Moriscos worked hard to hold on to this forbidden language, their knowledge of Arabic slowly began to decline. With the exception of Granada, Valencia, and a few small locales where there were still large communities of Arabic speakers, most Moriscos in the peninsula generally spoke different variations of Romance (Harvey 2005, 124; Bernabé Pons 2009, 69). Although many Moriscos were illiterate, and others gradually lost their ability to communicate in Arabic because of the repressive laws against their language, this did not weaken their interest in possessing and circulating texts in Arabic. In fact, the illiterate were precisely those Moriscos who were most apt to conserve these texts, even though they were forbidden and their owners could be punished for doing so (Labarta 1980, 115). An especially revealing case is that of the Morisco Amador Muarte, who carefully tried to conserve his copy of the Qu'ran, treating it as a holy image. He would hold the sacred text and kiss it "as a holy thing,"[16] even though he was illiterate and could not read the Arabic words (quoted in Fournel-Guérin 1979, 250). For Pedro Crespi, Arabic writings were not only sacred because of the language, but acquired special healing or even magical properties. This Morisco suffered a vision problem, but nonetheless treasured a talisman with Arabic characters that his wife had given him to help cure his eye disease. During his trial in 1583, Pedro testified that he did not know what the text said because of his vision impairment, but he claimed that, when he carried the Arabic text with him, his eyesight improved (Surtz 2001, 424). Morisco women, many of whom did not know how to read, were especially diligent in their attempts to hide and conserve writings with Arabic script (Surtz 2001; Perry 2005, 65–87). Juana Carpesa was just one of countless Morisco women who hid proscribed writings on their bodies to conserve the sacred literature, despite being unable to read it. In her trial for hiding Qur'anic texts under her skirt, Juana claimed that she had just found them, but that she was unable to read them (Surtz 2001, 427).

For all these Moriscos, the importance of Arabic or Aljamiado texts resided not only in the words written on the page, but also in the fact that the pages were populated with Arabic characters, the sacred language of the Qur'an. Drawing on these examples, we see how texts written in Arabic letters acted as a fetish of sorts, embodying inherent religious and magical powers.[17] As vital as the Arabic script might have been in these circumstances, it is important to consider that these examples materialize principally in Inquisition cases, and thus the fetishistic nature of these sacred objects might be overly emphasized. In fact, if the discourse of the fetish itself is one of "'secondary beliefs,' beliefs about the beliefs of other people, and thus inseparable from (in fact, constitutive of) systems of racial or collective prejudice," as W.J.T. Mitchell argues, then we must question the statements included in these Inquisition cases about the fetish powers of the Arabic text, despite their palpable importance for Moriscos (2005, 162). Reading these examples alongside Moriscos' own writings brings to light a more robust account of the uses and significance of Arabic characters for the Morisco community, which, of course, was as diverse as the geography it inhabited.

The Morisco known as the Mancebo de Arévalo explains the value that Arabic characters possessed in his *Tafsira* ([c. 1532–3] 2003), in which he devotes a chapter to the visual importance of *alif*, the first letter of the Arabic alphabet (fig. 7). Depending on the way in which it is composed, *alif* displays different attributes of Allah. When *alif* is written alone [ا], it is a visual symbol of the unity or oneness of Allah, but by adding different vowel markings to the letter, the meaning is visually superior. For instance, when *alif* has a *fatha* placed above it [اَ], the letter becomes more elongated, and the Mancebo interprets this as a visual representation of Allah residing above all things: "it denotes eminence, that Allah is exalted in everything; there is no equal or match to Him; Allah is exalted in name, Allah is exalted in all dominion, Allah is exalted in being and everything emphasizes His eminence; there is nothing that diminishes His name" ([c. 1532–3] 2003, 397).[18] The young Morisco concludes the chapter by commenting on each of Allah's divine attributes, which he visualizes in each of the different manifestations of the written image of the letter *alif*. María Teresa Narváez Córdova suggests that the association of the Arabic alphabet with Allah demonstrates the Mancebo de Arévalo's knowledge of Islamic mysticism. This discipline attributes a distinct value to each Arabic letter, allowing the Qur'an as well as other religious texts to be imbued with other meanings (Narváez Córdova 1995, 235). The Mancebo de Arévalo himself suggests that each letter painted individually possesses a unique meaning, but that all the letters placed

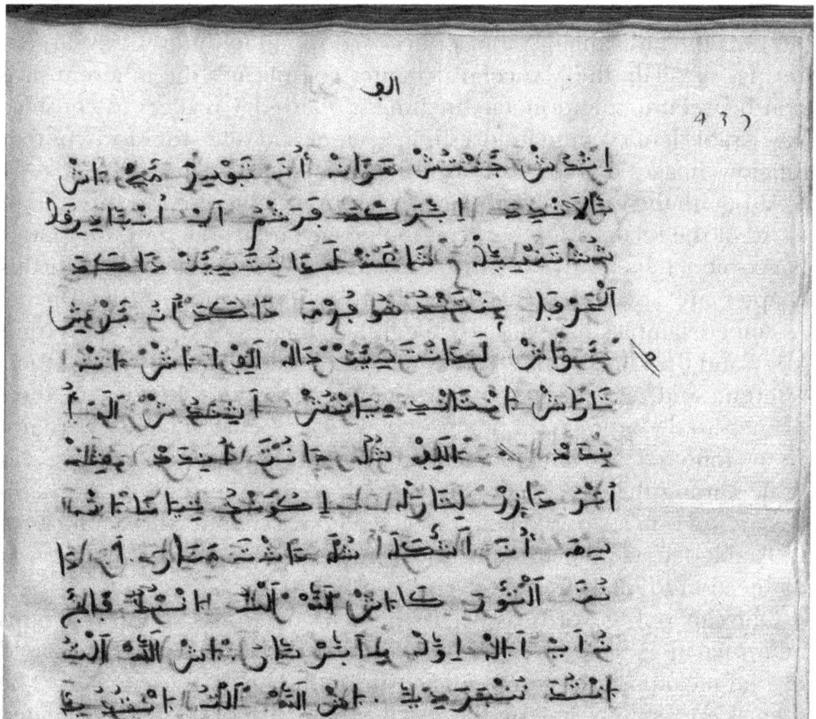

الع

٤٣٧

إشدمن جُلسس عوان أنت بقدر مهـ مامن
خلانيد الجرتع فرشم آب أشبايرقا
بمشتملاذ ، فاقسا طمعا نتيبا داكد
انزوبا بنتجنف هو بوهم داكدان تزوبش
نشوامن لمداشتدبت جال الفا مامش مانت
داراس مختلب مبانشر ابتجع من النبأ
بتـد الا علبن بل حا شت البيذح بعطا
أجر جارر بتارك لا كرمنح مما ماداشا
بمد أنت انكد شق عاشت مجارى ١ ما
نم انبوو كامن قلة ، الله بنجـة قالم
ما بـ اعا اذن ملاجر دان باش الله آنت
اشت بنجرى لا . اعل الله الد ا تنذبط
مارد ، مامش الله آند مامث ما الشمبطا لمجلا
كش شلة هوالشور دا بدحجر ك دا
مباشة لدش ننجروبا شد مامش ، مابت
انز البوومن لدا ده ل جا لاح البفطة
دمن لشمن مانت آنت بدازمن كا
شة لكشطارطدا ا انش لا أذش شوغلار
بانقا لاآنرى بير بامتا ال آنج الومـ

Fig. 7. Mancebo de Arévalo, *Tafçira*, fol. 437v, c. 1532–3.

together create an exceptional *tafsīr*, or interpretation ([c. 1532–3] 2003, 397). As the individual Arabic letters correspond to different visual renderings of Allah, the Mancebo's chapter complicates the inherent division between text and image, inciting modern-day readers to consider how Arabic letters could hold a similar power and value for Moriscos that religious images had for Catholics in early modern Spain.

Although the value of Catholic images, or lack thereof, is expressed in terms of the relationship between the image and its referent, the power of Arabic letters and words in the Aljamiado narratives studied in this chapter are also articulated through their connection to the Divine. As some examples have already suggested, images of Christ, the Virgin Mary, and the saints would not have the same value if it were not for their referent, and these representations demand devotion because of their likeness to the original. In practice, of course, these guidelines were not always followed, allowing for some images to acquire more meaning and value among their devotees.[19] Returning to the Mancebo de Arévalo's *Tasfira* and other Morisco texts discussed in this chapter, the significance of Arabic letters and words is also conveyed through their likeness or connection to Allah.

One can look at words, as W.J.T. Mitchell suggests, as both verbal signs and visual images: words can be read or listened to and interpreted based on the meaning they communicate through language; or they can be seen as images, focusing on the visual appearance of the text populated with letters of different sizes and shapes (2003, 51). In these Morisco narratives, words acquire a recognizable meaning through the stories and legends they convey, helping to preserve memories and acting as a mode of resistance against Catholic "idols." Equally important, however, is the visual aspect of the Arabic alphabet that its authors or scribes employ. Arabic is the language of Allah, the language chosen to reveal the sacred text of the Qur'an. The Qur'an itself alludes to the significance of writing and to the special nature of Arabic, linking the Divine with the practice of written expression (Schimmel 1970, 1).[20] Arabic letters and words, therefore, are not just verbal signs of a language used to communicate meaning; they carry a visual relevance of their own. While Arabic script evidently does not represent the Divine in the same way that a Catholic image does, it still has a sacred connection to Islam and can depict Allah.

As we have seen, the Mancebo de Arévalo used the Arabic alphabet to write his *Tafsira*, but he also manipulated the letters in an exercise to visualize the different attributes of Allah, regarding the letters as images of the Divine ([c. 1532–3] 2003, 397–8). As noted earlier, the function of Arabic letters as images was especially important to illiterate Moriscos, who sought and possessed texts with the sacred letters. In other instances, Moriscos responded to letters and words written in Arabic script in a fashion similar to those who venerated Catholic images – or, at least, that is what some Inquisitional cases would lead us to believe. The Aragonese Morisco Juan de Portugal, for example, was accused of organizing gatherings of crypto-Muslims at which he would display his copy of the Qur'an as all those present "kissed and adored the book of the Qur'an as a holy thing" (quoted in Fournel-Guérin 1979, 257).[21] The religious texts and other narratives that Moriscos fought to conceal and preserve thus in many ways stood as substitutes for the Catholic sacred images that many Moriscos renounced.

In his study of religious visual culture, David Morgan suggests that, when different religions or religious groups demonstrate iconoclastic behaviour towards another's images, they often replace that which they seek to destroy with another mode of imagery. He argues that those "who express disdain for visual imagery in religious practice and seek to proscribe its use as 'idolatrous' typically put in its place alternative forms of material culture that provide a different form of iconicity" (2005, 117). In sixteenth- and seventeenth-century Spain, some Moriscos who resisted or sought to damage Catholic images substituted Arabic letters and texts that possessed a comparable meaning for this religious visual culture. For example, as we have already seen, Ibn 'Abd al-Rafi''s father taught him to negate Catholic "idols" by substituting Qur'anic text that he could recite in his heart. And some of the Aljamiado narratives that I discuss shortly show how Muslim characters resist idols, giving primacy to textual manifestations in their stead. Without the value of Arabic characters as images, these texts would fail to maintain their relevance for many Morisco communities. In this way, the Aljamiado texts discussed in this chapter, composed with the visually significant Arabic script, displayed a similar value for Moriscos that religious representations had for Catholics in early modern Spain. While Catholic images were esteemed as depictions of Jesus, Mary, or the saints, Arabic letters were regarded as textual images that encompassed the sanctity of Islam. With these written images, Moriscos could oppose competing figural representations, and these texts may have functioned as a replacement for the Catholic images that surrounded Moriscos in their everyday life.

Text and image, however, did not always stand in for each other. At times, the written word and the visual image coincided to form a new hybrid imagetext, to use W.J.T. Mitchell's term. In a letter to the General Inquisitor, the Morisco Jesuit priest Ignacio de las Casas discusses his observations and concerns about Morisco assimilation in the years leading up to their expulsion, taking note of a curious representation on a church altar in Valencia in which text and image, Muslim and Christian, occur simultaneously: "there is a painted image in which the priest is raising the host and from one side to the other of the host there are some intertwined designs painted, and they are nicely done and formed Arabic letters and say from one side – there is no God – and from the other – but God – which is the phrase that Muslims and heretics have used and use today to deny the divinity of Jesus Christ our Lord and all of the sacraments, and all of the Moriscos from that city know this very well" (Las Casas 2006, 547).[22] Although Ignacio de las Casas does not indicate who might have placed the Arabic words on the church altar or when this might have occurred, he suggests that many Moriscos were fully aware of the meaning of the text and that, in reading these words, they scoffed at Old Christian beliefs. Thus, this Christian painting with Arabic words on the church altar is both Christian and Muslim, possessing value for followers of both religions. It is also a visual example of the Morisco literature that I discuss below – a visible representation of text against image.

Within the context of Moriscos' literary culture, Arabic script acquires a renewed importance when juxtaposed with the ubiquitous Catholic visual culture of early modern Spain. As many of the narratives I examine below show, Arabic texts, words, and individual letters are inherently linked to Islam and connect the beholder of the text to Allah. As we will see, Arabic texts are used in battle, for conversion, and, above all, to oppose idolatry, among other uses. By honing in on the written descriptions of visual culture in Morisco literature, added layers of meaning surface, revealing a more nuanced understanding of their circumstances in the Iberian Peninsula. This focus on the subtext of visual references offers a new approach to Aljamiado texts, and sheds light on the value of these texts against images to express Moriscos' cultural practices and beliefs.

Legends of Idolatry and Iconoclasm

Moriscos wrote in a variety of genres, but the vast majority of Aljamiado literature was anonymous and religious in nature.[23] Among this corpus of texts, many of the legends that Moriscos penned could be categorized as didactic literature because of how the characters model certain aspects of Islamic culture and religion. One important characteristic of this genre is the use of dialogue to transmit religious and cultural knowledge, which allows the authors to present the moral of legends in simpler and more direct language, making them more accessible to their Morisco audience (Valero Cuadra 2000, 79–80, 86–9). In the legends I discuss here, the didactic aspects of the texts, including the use of dialogue, come to the fore as the characters model resistance to "idols" and, in some cases, condone iconoclastic acts.

One of the most popular of these Aljamiado legends was *La leyenda de la doncella Carcayona* ([c. 1578–87] 2000), a Morisco version of the Handless Maiden tale, which has a number of variations in European languages, as well as in Arabic.[24] Carcayona's story offers inspiration, and teaches Muslims to defend their cultural and religious identity in the face of adversity. The numerous and distinct versions of the Aljamiado narrative that were conserved attest to its likely popularity among Morisco communities in early modern Spain (Valero Cuadra 2000, 65). Even after their expulsion, Moriscos brought the Aljamiado legend with them to North Africa, where it was written in Spanish with Latin characters, most likely by a Morisco in Tunis (Valero Cuadra 2000, 27–8; Galmés de Fuentes 1957, 274).[25]

The Aljamiado versions of this narrative tell the story of Princess Carcayona and her father, King Najrab, who worships a gilded idol embellished in jewels and precious stones. As the king's daughter is worshipping her own bejewelled idol, a golden dove adorned with coloured pearls lands on her statue and declares the oneness and omnipotence of Allah. The dove continues to instruct the maiden about Islam, explaining the rewards for believers in Paradise, as well as the consequences in Hell that await those who are unfaithful to Allah. Above all, the dove advises Carcayona to stop worshipping her idol, since it will not hear her prayers. The maiden accepts the dove's advice, leaving her idol and converting to Islam. When she tells her father of this news and advises him to reject idol worship as well, he rebuffs her advances and has his idol brought out to be publicly adored. Carcayona destroys the idol, inciting King Najrab to threaten his daughter by telling her that, if she does not reconsider her conversion to Islam, he will be forced to cut off her hands as a punishment. The maiden remains faithful to Allah, disobeying her father as she proclaims her emphatic rejection of idol worship: "[Oh, father!], do what you will, but I will not turn from my ways nor will I give up my obedience for disobedience, nor the Creator for the [created, nor *al-janna*] for *jahannam*, nor will I give up [Allah] for the idols" (*La leyenda de la doncella Carcayona* [c. 1578–87] 2000, 279).[26] As a result, the king cuts off Carcayona's hands and has her exiled indefinitely from his kingdom. After withstanding a number of trials and tribulations, Carcayona's hands are miraculously restored because of her faithfulness to Allah. The tale then concludes with the princess's decision to found a city on the fertile banks of the Euphrates River, dedicating it to the service of Allah.

Various scholars have highlighted the didactic qualities of this Aljamiado legend, which teaches the excellence of Islam.[27] It illustrates the
rewards of those who are obedient to Allah above all else, despite any
difficulties or cruel injustices. Carcayona rejects and destroys her father's
idols but remains faithful to Allah, even after her father punishes and
exiles her. When she is exiled a second time, this time by her husband,
the young maiden remains committed to the Muslim faith and seeks
refuge through her prayers to Allah, eventually being rewarded for her
faithfulness. Thus, the story of Carcayona would have appealed to its
Morisco audience, who confronted increasing adversities in sixteenth-
century Spain. Moriscos who read or heard about the maiden's circumstances must have felt comforted or even confident and motivated to
follow their Muslim faith. Mary Elizabeth Perry interprets Carcayona's
story as a metaphor for Morisco individuals who were victims of cruel
injustices. In the legend, Carcayona is persecuted because of her Muslim
faith, just as many Moriscos who continued to practise Islam in early
modern Spain were oppressed. Yet, as Perry notes, Carcayona's steadfast
faith in Allah was not only a source of suffering but also a foundation for
inspiration and perseverance, just as many Moriscos found support in
their religious beliefs (2005, 19–37).[28]

Reading this Aljamiado narrative within the context of the religious
visual culture of early modern Spain illuminates how this text could
model resistance for Moriscos who questioned how to respond to the
pervasive Baroque imagery in their quotidian surroundings. In the
Aljamiado version of Carcayona's story, the idol plays a major role in
all of the characters' actions and behaviour throughout the tale. King
Najrab is defined by his close association to the idol, and his decisions
revolve around the importance he places on this object of worship. The
maiden's rejection of idolatry, on the other hand, is a considerable part
of what characterizes her as a faithful follower of Islam. Throughout the
story, there is a clear binary framework between those who worship idols
and the minority, including Carcayona, who are able to resist and revoke
them. Given these circumstances, it is important to consider the story
of Carcayona specifically in light of Moriscos' rejection of the religious
visual culture that surrounded them. The maiden's actions could serve
as inspiration to withstand their contemporary idols, such as images of
Jesus, Mary, and the saints.

In the same way that Carcayona found her father's praise of statues
immoral, many Moriscos in sixteenth-century Spain found the Catholic
images that they had to worship idolatrous. Those who heard Carcayona's
story likely would have seen a connection between the maiden's resistance of idol worship and their own rejection of Christian images that

they saw as false gods. While it is true that none of the references to idols makes explicit any connection to Christianity, by reading this Aljamiado story within the cultural context of the Moriscos it becomes apparent how the criticism of idol worship could be a metaphor for Catholic material devotion. As the examples at the beginning of this chapter demonstrated, Moriscos referred to Old Christians as "idol worshippers," and important figures such as the mufti of Oran specifically labelled Catholic objects of devotion as "idols." Furthermore, as Pino Valero Cuadra notes, the connection between Carcayona's story and the Moriscos' own situation could be made even clearer given that the maiden's father, Najrab, is described as "King of the Romans" (*La leyenda de la doncella Carcayona* [c. 1578–87] 2000, 241).[29] Here, "Romans" is derived from the Arabic term *rūm*, one of the various names used to describe Christians, suggesting that Najrab can be viewed as a Christian king who professes idolatry (Valero Cuadra 2000, 97).[30] Moriscos certainly would have been able to make this connection, since they employed the word *rūm* to portray their Christian neighbours.[31] Even near the end of the seventeenth century, the Moroccan minister Muhammad ibn ʿAbd al-Wahhāb al-Ghassānī referred to Spain as "*bilād al-rūm*," or the land of the *rūm*, when he travelled there to negotiate the release of Muslim captives and books in Arabic (2005, 48).

The worthlessness of the idols in Carcayona's world surely would have reminded Moriscos of how little they valued Christian images. After the dove visits the maiden, as she is adoring her bejewelled idol, and tells her that the gleaming statue has no value, Carcayona relays the same message to her father: "Oh, father! First I ask for forgiveness from [Allah], my Lord and your Lord. Give up the service to idols, those that neither hear nor see, they harm and are not beneficial" (*La leyenda de la doncella Carcayona* [c. 1578–87] 2000, 272).[32] The maiden's allegation offers a similar word of warning about idols as the one that the mufti of Oran had given to Moriscos: images or idols are mere objects, with no use or power (Harvey 1964, 175).

It is significant that Carcayona is emboldened to speak out against her father, an authority figure. She is willing to risk the consequences as she declares the emptiness of her father's object of worship and refuses to accept the idol as part of her own devotional rituals. Could the maiden's actions reassure the Moriscos that read or listened to this story that they, too, could be audacious and announce their disapproval of "idols" to Spanish authorities? Certainly, the various Inquisition cases that attest to Moriscos' verbally defying Catholic images in the face of those in power could lead one to believe that this occurred more than once.[33]

Other Morisco narratives also suggest that contention with authority around the precarious issue of idol worship, albeit with different outcomes, was of great concern to Moriscos. The tale of 'Umar ibn Zayde involves a prolonged dispute between 'Umar and his father concerning the value of the idols Allāt and al-'Uzzā, which his father worships (Corriente 1990, 69–80).[34] 'Umar uses similar arguments to those of Carcayona as he explains to his father that the idols will not help him or benefit him in any way, whereas Allah will hear their prayers. Their conversation turns violent when neither one of the two is able to accept the other's viewpoint, both standing firm in their beliefs. Ultimately, 'Umar is willing to die for his principles as his father threatens to harm him for not accepting the idols. Just like Carcayona, 'Umar perseveres, and Allah protects him for speaking out against these objects of worship. The passage in which Carcayona criticizes her father's veneration of religious statues also communicates the same views as those found in the sixteenth-century Aljamiado story *Alhadiç del-alárabe i la donzella* (Valero Cuadra 2000, 154; Bouzineb 1987, 125–6). Here, too, a young girl calls into question her father's devotion to idols while affirming her own faith in Allah: "Oh, father! You live in error and lies, since the idol Alāta w-Al'uzzā does not have any power or wisdom or benefit, nor does it harm or protect" (Hegyi 1981, 190).[35] These three Aljamiado stories, among others, are important for our understanding of how marginalized characters model resistance to authority figures, especially since in each case these dominant individuals try to impose their faith in religious objects on the minority.

To demonstrate the worthlessness of her father's idols, Carcayona breaks her father's idol and donates the precious metals and pearls to the poor in service to Allah (*La leyenda de la doncella Carcayona* [c. 1578–87] 2000, 273–4). The maiden's treatment of King Najrab's object of adoration evoke the responses of some Moriscos to the visual culture that surrounded them in early modern Spain. As we saw in Chapter 1, Moriscos were punished by the Inquisition not only for harming or destroying Catholic icons, but also for verbally expressing their contempt for religious images. Doña Constança Lopez was just one of these Moriscos tried in Granada for her actions against sacred figures. Because she stored a broken piece of the altar stone and wood from a church altarpiece in her home to use as firewood, Doña Constança was sent away to Castile and punished with an unpardonable sentence of life in prison (García Fuentes 1981, 114–15). In the Aljamiado story of the handless maiden, Carcayona's father severely reprimands her for a similar reason. While the king's idol is not a Christian icon by definition, it is the cause of conflict between him and his daughter, and Carcayona's rejection and destruction of it is the reason for her punishment and eventual exile from his kingdom.

The story's ending, nevertheless, provides hope and encouragement for its Morisco audience. It teaches the rewards for remaining faithful to Allah above all else, especially in withstanding any pressure to adore images or idols in his place. The dove, a messenger of Allah, addresses Carcayona and reminds her that she will be rewarded for persevering in her Muslim faith and enduring persecution for resisting her father's idols. The dove promises her a place in Paradise on Judgment Day, and later Allah restores her hands to compensate her for her devoted actions. The story of Carcayona models resistance for Moriscos, reminding them that, if they adhere to the precepts of Islam and renounce religious visual representations, they too will be compensated.

Legends of Textual Supremacy

As its title suggests, the sixteenth-century Aljamiado narrative *Reconta-miento de la conversión de Omar* recounts the religious conversion to Islam of 'Umar ibn al-Khaṭṭāb, the second caliph and a significant figure during the early days of Islam. The account is included in ms. 4953, a miscellaneous collection of religious texts and legends located at the National Library of Spain in Madrid.[36] In addition to relating 'Umar's change of heart and proclamation of the Muslim faith, this text is also a story of the triumph of the Qur'an over idols, exposing the importance of the written word for Moriscos in the face of the religious images omnipresent in their daily surroundings in early modern Spain.

The legend begins with a forewarning from the Qur'an condemning all those who worship idols in Allah's stead and establishing the primacy of the word over figural representation. Outraged by this message, 'Umar and his tribe, who worship idols, set out on a mission to kill the Prophet Muhammad. During his journey, 'Umar encounters a friend who advises him to go and visit his sister and brother-in-law, who had recently converted to Islam, before carrying on with his campaign. As he arrives at his sister's home, he hears them reading the Qur'an out loud behind closed doors. Despite his initial rejection of Islam, the act of listening to the sacred text is, significantly, what incites his eventual conversion, prompting him to compare the textual description of Allah with the visual representation of his idols, and finally to conclude that the former is superior to the latter. As a recent convert, 'Umar then encounters Muhammad, and the two go to the Kaʻba at Mecca to destroy the idols. According to this account, no physical force is used to tear down the idols. Rather, the words they articulate against the idols cause

them to collapse on the ground. As the idols break to pieces, Allah sends
a verse from the Qur'an to praise Muhammad, testifying once again to
the power of the Qur'an over the idols – of text over image.

Despite the miscellaneous nature of the manuscript, Hawkins argues
that there is, nonetheless, "an integrated theme," and reads ms. 4953 as
a type of Morisco-Aljamiado treatise that presents "a coherent Morisco
philosophy of suffering" (1988, 200). The meaning of the manuscript,
he posits, should be found in the compilation of texts as a whole and in
the parallels that it presents with Moriscos' social situation in Spain. As a
cohesive whole, it offers a paradigm for Moriscos to withstand their own
uncertain circumstances (213). Looking particularly at *Recontamiento de
la conversión de Omar*, Hawkins believes that Moriscos could have found
hope from this story in that, if they endured suffering, like 'Umar's sister who was punished for not eating the meat that was brought to her,
eventually the unbeliever would have a change of heart and "the intol-
erant Christians trying to suppress Islam could yet be brought into the
community" (206). Although many aspects of the manuscript do centre
on the question of suffering, to focus exclusively on this element would
be to marginalize other important uses of the manuscript.[37] This story,
I contend, should also be read in terms of the conflict between image/
idol and text/Qur'an, especially since Moriscos' writings do not aim to
convert Christians or bring them "into the community," as Hawkins suggests. As we have seen throughout this chapter, Morisco culture attributes opposing values to the power of the word versus the power of
the image. In this story, in particular, the power of the words from the
Qur'an converts 'Umar and negates the value of visual representations.
The idols are eventually destroyed because of the mighty words 'Umar
speaks against them. And, as the legend ends, the text of the Qur'an
appears over the broken idols, testifying to the power of the word over
the powerlessness of the image.

Broadening the thematic understanding of the manuscript beyond
Hawkins's proposal by piecing together the other narratives that reinforce the power, and sometimes even magical properties, of the written
word, another aspect of the text's coherence emerges. The materiality
of Arabic letters and words is not only present in the story of 'Umar's
conversion, but is also embedded throughout the other stories, unveil-
ing how both the manuscript as a whole and the individual texts within
point to the sacred nature of Arabic script. In the tenth section of this
manuscript, for example, Qur'anic verses offer protection to Muhammad's followers in challenging times. This section recounts the legend
of Tamīm al-Dārī,[38] one of the Prophet Muhammad's companions. In
the tale, a group of jinn suddenly appear before Tamīm while he is

performing ablutions and take him to a large and ghastly cave. Despite his relentless prayers and readings from the Qur'an, Tamīm continues to undergo numerous trials as the other jinn mock and insult him. Eventually one of the evil jinn accuses Tamīm of waging war on him by reading the words of the Qur'an, ultimately causing this jinni to melt like wax (Hegyi 1981, 164). Words acquire even more power later in the manuscript, where they are included as the key ingredient of a miraculous potion. The Arabic words are written out and placed inside a glass to be consumed, which the Morisco text promises will cure various ailments and convert unbelievers to Islam (207–8).[39] The Arabic characters possess the ability to work in various ways throughout the manuscript, from converting unbelievers and casting away evil spirits to curing maladies and, most significantly for my argument in this chapter, opposing visual representation.

Epic Battles against Idols

Apart from legends like those about Carcayona and ʿUmar ibn al-Khaṭṭāb, Moriscos also cultivated epic-chivalric narratives. This genre of texts, which recounted heroic exploits, was one that most captivated Morisco audiences (Montaner Frutos 2010, 54). These works can also be framed within the popularity of legendary *maghāzī* or pseudo-*maghāzī* literature, narratives that told of the epic military expeditions that took place during the time of the Prophet Muhammad (Galmés de Fuentes 1975a, 24–6). The *Libro de las batallas* is one of these epic-chivalric narratives, copied down in the sixteenth century and included in ms. 5337 housed at the National Library of Spain in Madrid. This Morisco-Aljamiado compilation of stories recounts the triumphant expeditions during the first days of Islam with ʿAlī ibn Abī Ṭālib, the Prophet Muhammad's cousin and son-in-law, playing the leading role as the hero in the majority of the accounts. Although the different narratives include some magical and fictitious elements, the core of each story focuses on historical events during the time of Muhammad. Many of the characters, geographical locations, and battles fought during the early days of Islam can be identified (Galmés de Fuentes 1975a, 82–3).

In the epic battles included in the *Libro de las batallas*, the Prophet Muhammad, ʿAli, and other Muslim characters are triumphant against the *kuffār*, or unbelievers, and because of their victories some of the defeated convert to Islam. The stories in the *Libro de las batallas* were popular among Moriscos and, like other Aljamiado literature, were copied and circulated frequently (Galmés de Fuentes 1975a, 92–3). As Luis Bernabé Pons highlights, it is not hard to see why these tales of chivalry might have been meaningful to Moriscos in sixteenth-century Spain: they underscore the triumph of Islam in challenging circumstances, thus offering Moriscos hope that Islam will continue to be victorious despite the trying conditions they faced in Spain (Bernabé Pons 2010, 41).

Similar to other pseudo-*maghāzī* literature that narrates fictionalized accounts of the early Muslim military expeditions, in these Aljamiado narratives many of the battles revolve around idols or conquered enemies portrayed as idol worshippers.[40] In the stories in the *Libro de las batallas*, the Muslim characters warn the unbelievers to stop adoring idols, and in some instances destroy the images that compete with Allah. These narratives would have given Moriscos faith that, despite of their trials and their obligation to respect and worship Catholic images, they, too, like the first Muslims, would be triumphant.

The *Batalla del rrey al-Muhalhal ibnu āl-Fayadi* recounts the expedition of Khalid ibn al-Walid, Arab commander during the early Islamic conquests, and his encounter with the idolatrous King Muhalhal and his army (Galmés de Fuentes 1975b, 213–44). Throughout the story, the narrator clearly juxtaposes the two groups and their interests: Khalid and the Muslims, on the one hand, fight to defend the name of Allah and the Prophet, and, on the other, the unbelievers engage in battle seeking strength in their idols. Khalid's mission begins when Muhammad asks him to deliver a letter on his behalf to King Muhalhal requesting that he convert to Islam and consequently replace his idols with Allah. In the course of his journey, Khalid meets and contests a number of men from the king's army, and when finally reaching the king finds him standing before his cherished idol. The Muslim commander orders Muhalhal to remove the statue from his sight before speaking with him and conveying Muhammad's message. The king sets aside his object of worship and reads the letter containing Muhammad's threat either to embrace Islam or engage in battle. He is so infuriated that he takes Khalid captive and wraps him in the skin of his horse. 'Ali comes to the rescue, releases Khalid, and the two join in battle with Muhalhal and his army, who pray to their idols for fortitude. Ultimately, 'Ali and Khalid kill all those who refuse the message of Islam, including the king and many of his best knights.

On the surface, this story chronicles King Muhalhal's defeat by the Muslims and showcases the extraordinary abilities of Khalid and 'Ali in battle. Yet, on a more meaningful level for the Moriscos, this narrative serves as a reminder of Muslim glory in the face of their enemies during the early days of Islam. Even when Khalid and 'Ali are outnumbered, they are victorious, since they worship Allah and do not seek their strength in gold and silver idols like the knights of King Muhalhal. Many Moriscos felt a close connection to the Islamic world, and therefore these stories about the triumphs of Islam certainly would have encouraged them during challenging times and bolstered their sense of community (García Arenal 1975, 73). The Morisco Francisco de Espinosa, in particular, took pleasure in participating in a group reading about Muhammad's achievements, likely in stories similar to the Aljamiado narrative of King Muhalhal's defeat. In his Inquisition case, this Morisco from El Provincio (Cuenca) was accused of being "present when certain people read things in a book about Muhammad and his evil sect, especially about how Muhammad had won and ruled over many lands and other things, and by listening to the abovementioned be read Francisco de Espinosa enjoyed himself" ("Acusación y sentencia del proceso inquisitorial contra Francisco de Espinosa" 1975, 100).[41] Due to the nature of Inquisition cases, the extent to which Francisco de Espinosa actually gathered with other Moriscos to listen to narratives of Muhammad's exploits could, of course, be questioned. Even so, those who read or listened to the stories in the *Libro de las batallas* or similar narratives would have felt inspired by the values that Muhammad and his followers upheld. The clear rejection of images and the lack of value attributed to pre-Islamic idols would have been a great encouragement for Moriscos who faced the question of how to reject Catholic images or idols.

Although the stories of Muslim victories at the dawn of Islam have no explicit connection to the situation of Moriscos in early modern Spain centuries later, in other writings Moriscos did draw a parallel between the two contexts, thus exposing the potential value of the Aljamiado narratives contained in the *Libro de las batallas*. In one of Ibn Qāsim al-Ḥajarī's arguments against the creation and veneration of images, the Morisco exile references Muhammad's destruction of 360 idols in the Ka'ba as an exceptional model for his coreligionists.[42] By following Muhammad's obliteration of idols with an anecdote of how Aḥmad, a Muslim captive and contemporary of Ibn Qāsim, did the same to a Christian "idol," Ibn Qāsim bridges the temporal gap between the days of Muhammad and the plight of Moriscos in early modern Spain ([c. 1637] 1997, 146). Moriscos, thus, would have been inspired by the Aljamiado narrative of the Battle of King Muhalhal or similar stories to reject modern-day idols or, at the very least, find respite in knowing that the first Muslims prevailed in defiance of the prevalence of the idolatrous visual culture in their society.

Moriscos likewise would have linked the defeat of the idol-worshipping King Muhalhal to that of their contemporary rulers who depended on Catholic images for strength in battle. In 1541, less than one month after Carlos V's failed expedition to Algiers, Moriscos in Granada sent a letter to Sultan Suleiman al-Qānūnī in Constantinople explaining how

Carlos V had planned his attack to help prevent North Africans from lending their support to Moriscos in Spain (Temini 1989, 27). The letter reveals that Moriscos believed the Muslim victory in Algiers occurred because they sought strength in Allah, whereas the Christians only knelt before their material objects: "with their priests they seek help from their idols, and as for us, we turn to the Prophet Muhammad. They were determined [in their plan of attack] on Algiers, but Allah is excellent and destroyed them, and he protects his religion because he is the best defender" (quoted in Temimi 1989, 37).[43] Like the narrator of the *Batalla del rrey al-Muhalhal,* who ascribes the king's defeat to his idol worship, the Moriscos in the letter to the sultan credit the Muslim victory in Algiers to the Catholic ruler's idolatry.

While the Battle of King Muhalhal offers a warning to those who place their trust in idols, another Aljamiado narrative praises those who destroy idolatrous objects. In the *Batalla de al-Āšyab ibnu Ḥanqar,* the narrator chronicles the encounter and battle between the Muslim hero ʿAli and al-Āšyab Ibn Ḥanqar, king of Taima (Galmés de Fuentes 1975b, 245–56). The battle is instigated because Ibn Ḥanqar has a gilded idol that he worships in place of Allah. The Prophet Muhammad sends a letter to the king asking him to stop his idolatrous practices and to pronounce the *shahāda,* the profession of Islamic faith. When Ibn Ḥanqar reads the letter criticizing his idol worship, he furiously throws his crown to the ground, refusing Muhammad's recommendations, and, as a result, accepts battle against the Muslim army. When it appears that the Muslims will be defeated, Muhammad sends forth his best knights to face the king of Taima's men. One by one, they die in battle, but once ʿAli arrives on the scene, the apparent defeat is transformed into a victory. The problem of idol worship, however, remains in Taima. To resolve the issue, one of Ibn Ḥanqar's elderly subjects suggests to the king that, if ʿAli is capable of breaking the idol, they should all convert to Islam. When Muhammad receives the message, he sends ʿAli to fight against the king's cherished statue, shattering the idol with his sword. Ibn Ḥanqar and all his men then abandon their idol worship to become Muslims (Galmés de Fuentes 1975b, 245–56).

Like the other narratives in the *Libro de las batallas,* this story is a reminder of the triumphs of Islam in the face of its enemies. By juxtaposing service to Allah with idol worship, the story of Ibn Ḥanqar also communicates a didactic message against the use and adoration of idols in place of Allah. Throughout the story, the characters and their values are defined by the visual culture, or lack thereof, that surrounds them. Thus, when ʿAli destroys the king's idol, he affirms the omnipotence and oneness of Allah for Moriscos.

Prophetic Narratives of Victory and Defeat

The moral lessons of the narratives in the *Libro de las batallas* share some striking similarities with Morisco *jofores* (from the Arabic *jafr*), or prophecies. These *jofores* present eschatological views of the world, usually prognosticating what will happen to particular Muslim groups in the End Times. In composing these prophecies, Moriscos drew on both Islamic and Christian traditions of divinations about the future, adapting them to their own particular context (Green-Mercado 2019, 7–10). As Green-Mercado shows, prophetic narratives circulated among Morisco communities in the Iberian Peninsula during the late fifteenth and early sixteenth centuries, putting Moriscos in contact with other individuals in the broader Mediterranean world and revealing some of their strategies of resistance (3–17).

Like the *Libro de las batallas*, whose message is a reminder that the Muslim religion was and will be victorious despite the obstacles its followers face, many Morisco *jofores* also predict a future in which Muslims will be victorious, thus encouraging disheartened Morisco communities. Just as reading and listening to the *Libro de las batallas* or similar narratives about Muhammad's exploits was a collective act among Moriscos, as demonstrated in the case of Francisco de Espinosa mentioned earlier, these prophecies also usually involve a shared experience. In studying Moriscos' End-Times discourse, López Baralt indicates that, although some prophecies focus on one individual, Moriscos often used the prophecies to serve a collective purpose: in essence, as tools to build political awareness (López Baralt 2009, 184).[44]

El guaçía del Gran Turco llamado Mohammed el Otsman is one of these Morisco prophecies that offers hope to crypto-Muslims, especially those who passionately resist Catholic images. The text is presented as a testimony of the Grand Turk, conqueror of Constantinople, in which he offers a series of recommendations to his son and promises him the successful future conquest of Christian territories, such as Rome and all of Spain. The Grand Turk longs for his son to be victorious in many feats against the Christians, including the destruction of the gold and silver idols in Catholic churches, which go against the teachings of the Prophet Muhammad (Cardaillac 2004, 417).[45] Similar Aljamiado prophecies seek to encourage Moriscos and relieve their painful reality by foretelling the eventual defeat of the Christians along with their idols. One Morisco prophecy included in ms. 774 in the National Library of France in Paris, for example, predicts what will happen in the Iberian Peninsula and how Islam will prevail. The *jofor* prophesizes how some Christians in Spain will profess Islam when they see their king captive, and in the end "the idol worshippers and pork eaters [the Christians] will be defeated; there will be no *dīn* [religion] left except Islam" (Sánchez Álvarez 1982, 242).[46] Not all of the Morisco *jofores*, however, were optimistic about the future of Islam in the peninsula. In another prophecy in the same manuscript, the Prophet Muhammad has a dream in which the archangel Gabriel shows him a vision of a conquered Andalusia, one where "the idol worshippers and pork eaters [the Christians]"[47] will rule over the land and all Muslims (252).

Reading these prophecies alongside the narratives in the *Libro de las batallas* reveals the parallel between the first Muslims and the Moriscos in early modern Spain. By juxtaposing the faithful followers of Allah with those who worship "idols" – whether they be the unbelievers during Muhammad's time who adored their own ornate statutes or the Christians who venerate religious images in their churches – these narratives were a guide to how Moriscos could interpret the pervasive religious visual culture in their own society.

By tracing the references to visual culture in Moriscos' own writings, this chapter has shed light on how Morisco communities engaged in debates about religious images and how many of them collectively resisted these "idols" through writing and listening to stories. Moriscos wrote about the problem of "idols" that they encountered on an increasing basis in their daily lives, and sought ways to counteract this religious visual culture, even if that meant their outward displays of response to these images did not correspond with their inner beliefs. Whether they wrote in Arabic or Aljamiado, they viewed Arabic script as an important tool to remind them of the supremacy of text over image. Significantly, they used this script to compose and copy the Aljamiado literature reviewed in this chapter. Texts of various genres, including legends, epic-chivalric narratives, and prophetic texts, model resistance to idols and suggest that those who oppose religious visual culture will emerge victorious just like the first Muslims.

Despite the wide variety of texts discussed in this chapter, the nature of these sources does not allow us to hear the voices of certain Moriscos in early modern Spain who might have had different views about the place of images. Completely assimilated Moriscos would have many reasons not to write about their Muslim past or ancestors, especially not in Arabic or Aljamiado.[48] And the exiled Moriscos who wrote from North Africa also would not have benefited from highlighting those who had assimilated fully into Christian society back in Spain (Harvey 2005, 250–2; Márquez Villanueva 1998, 166–71; Remensynder 2011, 559). Thus, many of the extant texts on which we must rely to understand Moriscos' reception of religious images and which, significantly, were written by

Moriscos themselves inevitably tend to focus more on the tensions that arose from the forced worship of images in early modern Spain.

Yet, the Morisco sources examined in this chapter are crucial because they present a nuanced perspective of Moriscos' reception of religious images that scholars thus far have analysed only from Christian sources. A close examination of texts written by Moriscos themselves suggests that many did use literature to resist some of the visual culture of the period. References to "idols" in a variety of their fictional texts, coupled with other Morisco writings about how they should or did deal with religious images, reveal how Morisco communities upheld text against image. Finally, focusing on references to religious images and idols in Morisco literature opens new ways to read this literature, since mentions of visual and material culture in Aljamiado narratives reveal subtle aspects of Moriscos' own lived experience in the Iberian Peninsula. In the following chapter, I broaden this perspective by looking at how debates about images were manifested in the very landscape of early modern Spain.

3

Granada and the Poetics of Sacred Space

On 12 April 1595, the first cross was erected on the Sacromonte hillside in Granada as a result of the extraordinary discovery of lead tablets with surprisingly revealing inscriptions.[1] It all started on 21 February of that year, when treasure hunters who were surveying a cave on Mount Valparaíso, later known as the Sacromonte, unearthed a lead plate written in what they believed to be Arabic script. The inscription claimed that a certain Mesitón had been martyred and buried there during the reign of Nero in the first century. Five days after the lead plate was deciphered, another one was found, this time stating that Hiscio, a disciple of the Apostle St James, had also suffered martyrdom on the hillside of the Sacromonte. Soon after, the excavation yielded a third lead tablet containing exceptional details about a Christian convert named Tesifón, another disciple of St James, who allegedly had inscribed a book on lead tablets like the others already discovered on Mount Valparaíso.

With the local community now filled with anticipation and religious fervour, a series of books, ashes, and other relics began to appear in Granada in the weeks and months that followed (Hagerty 1980, 30–3). The texts provided information on Christian doctrine, emphasizing the theological affinities between Christianity and Islam. Since Granada's Islamic heritage was still very present in Spain's collective memory, these texts seemed to offer a Christian past for the last stronghold of Iberian Islam (Bernabé Pons 2014a). Yet, with the learned Moriscos Alonso del Castillo and Miguel de Luna as the likely authors of these forgeries, the discoveries in the caves of the Sacromonte could also be read as "a desperate last-resort attempt" for Moriscos to anchor their place in Spain before King Philip III issued the definitive expulsion decree (Harvey 2005, 267).[2] In their syncretistic presentation, the lead tablets appealed to both Muslim and Christian audiences, igniting fervent religiosity as well as intense debates about their authenticity.

These discoveries, as A. Katie Harris has demonstrated, significantly affected the sacred landscape of Granada, transforming the hillside that was once important for the Morisco community into a key site for Catholic *granadino* identity (Harris 2002).[3] The hundreds of crosses that eventually studded the hills overlooking the Albaicín neighbourhood greatly contributed to this topographical conversion. After the first cross was left in the spring of 1595, men, women, and children from all walks of life set out on foot to place crosses on the rugged terrain. Members of different professional guilds, from blacksmiths to scribes, also left their mark on the Sacromonte. Even prisoners from the local jail sent a cross, and beggars made a penance stop to leave a Christian symbol there. The solemn processions were accompanied by the sounds of festive music and by people, dressed in their best clothes and jewels, rejoicing, suggesting that these events also contributed to the social atmosphere and a sense of belonging for the local community (Centurión y Córdoba 1632, 79v–89v).[4] One contemporary witness estimated that, in only eight days, the Sacromonte had already been covered with four hundred crosses (López Madera 1601, 6r). Francisco Bermúdez de Pedraza gives a more modest assessment, claiming that, in less than a month, faithful citizens had erected two hundred crosses, a "sight so beautiful that it caused spiritual joy in the virtuous and incited devotion in the most distracted hearts" (1608, 171r).[5] Among the few crosses still visible on the Sacromonte today lies an imposing one built of stone that faces the abbey, embedded there by the stonemasons and soldiers of the Alhambra in 1595 (fig. 8). Verses are inscribed on two sides of the pedestal that subtly link the individuals who brought the cross to the newly baptized Sacromonte: "To the divine and strong courage of some soldiers, who were such that they defeated and subjected death to the world, and to their spoils won with such force and so much light, other pious soldiers raised this cross. To the memory and example of those famous stones whose precious columns were a living temple of God in the mountain where they saw so much glory and so much good, the stonemasons also offered this cross of stone."[6] By erecting a cross, the soldiers from the Alhambra inscribed their professional guild into the local history and associated themselves with the metaphorical soldiers of God, the martyrs whose remains were allegedly discovered on the Sacromonte.

The affair of the lead books has been rigorously studied by a variety of scholars and approached from different perspectives, focusing mainly on their falsity, authorship, and their role in creating a new Christian identity in Granada. Yet the crosses that spread across the Sacromonte still need to be understood within the broader context of Moriscos' reception of the Christian symbol, especially since, in all other matters

Fig. 8. Cross brought to the Sacromonte by the stonemasons and soldiers of the
Alhambra, 1595.

Photo: author

related to the lead books, the "seal of Solomon" (*khātam Sulaymān*) is much more conspicuous than the cross. This symbol of a six-pointed star appeared on many of the *plomos* and has now come to be associated with the Sacromonte and its surroundings. In Morisco cultural practice, King Solomon was highly regarded for his wisdom, and his influence enveloped both natural and occult spheres (Harris 2007, 32). As a consequence of his power, some Moriscos carried the Solomonic seal as a talisman, invoking it for curative and preventative effects. The pervasiveness of this leitmotiv also pervaded Christian spaces, and was painted on the walls of some of their homes in Granada. Even as late as 1626 the Inquisition detained a certain don Pedro Arce for placing an order with a jeweller for eight silver crosses engraved with the star of Solomon (García Arenal and Rodríguez Mediano 2010, 276–7). This fusing of religious practices with supernatural beliefs thus led the Morisco Jesuit priest Ignacio de las Casas to censure the widespread use of this symbol throughout Granada (Magnier 2006, lvi).[7] So, the fact that hundreds of crosses dominated the landscape presents a different view of the discoveries unearthed there in the years leading up to the Moriscos' expulsion from the peninsula.

The Place of Poetry

Poetry was an important means used to record these extraordinary events, but it is usually only mentioned in passing in the more specific studies on the Sacromonte.[8] Starting with Luis de Góngora's sonnet "Al monte santo de Granada" (1598), several poets described the local interest in the recently discovered lead tablets and the changing Christian landscape. In addition to Góngora, some Granadan poets, such as Pedro Rodríguez de Ardila, and writers from other parts of the peninsula, including Rodrigo Fernández de Ribera, Agustín Collado del Hierro, and Alonso de Bonilla, dedicated verses to the recreation of the Sacromonte, highlighting the crosses that shaped this new panoramic view and gave this enclave a peculiar identity. This space also aroused interest in Francisco de Quevedo, who approaches this topic in his *Discurso de las láminas del monte santo de Granada*, of which no copy is extant (Magnier 2006, xvii). Even don Pedro de Granada Venegas, a Morisco and heir to the Nasrid Sultans, was said to have written "some songs on the Sacromonte of this city" (Bermúdez de Pedraza 1608, 131r).[9] This Morisco was a patron of poetry and organized literary *tertulias* in his home with other poets, including Juan Latino, Gregorio Silvestre, Hernando de Acuña, and Gaspar de Baeza (Terry 2015, 77–90). However, the *Poética Silva*, which records much of this literary activity in Granada, unfortunately does not include Pedro de Granada Venegas's verses about the sacred hill (Osuna 2003, 32).[10] By reading the poetry on the Sacromonte alongside contemporary theories of landscape, I ask how these poetic descriptions, especially those of the crosses, could be used to veil the memory of a recent Islamic past. The poets frame our vision to see a religious orography and thus a Christian past and present on the Sacromonte.

Cultural geographer Denis E. Cosgrove has drawn attention to the critical role of vision in determining the human relationship to the world. He understands landscape as "a way of seeing – a way in which some Europeans have represented to themselves and to others the world about them and their relationships with it, and through which they have commented on social relations" (1998, 1). Thus, landscape is not just about the moulding of land, as he argues; it is also intimately tied to society and its cultural practices. In a similar vein, W.J.T. Mitchell gives prominence to the sense of sight, and suggests that we consider "the way landscape *circulates* as a medium of exchange, a site of visual appropriation, a focus for the formation of identity" (2002a, 2; emphasis in original). Furthermore, Mitchell clarifies that landscape "naturalizes a cultural and social construction, representing an artificial world as if it were simply given and inevitable, and it also makes that representation operational by interpellating its beholder in some more or less determinate relation to its givenness as sight and site" (2). In other words, we must consider landscape not only in terms of what it represents, but also as a continuous process in which spectators position themselves (or, more passively, are positioned) within different social and cultural frames of reference. And it is through this process that "social and subjective identities are formed" (1). Drawing on these theories of landscape, the poetry on the sacred orography of the Sacromonte invites us to ask how the poets shape the landscape with their verses and especially how they position the viewer in a way that substantially influences how the landscape is perceived and identities are fashioned.

Góngora's sonnet in honour of the Sacromonte is one of the first poems to describe the Granadan landscape after the discoveries of the lead tablets. Only a few years after the hillside was transformed by the Baroque spectacle of crosses, he composed "Este monte de cruces coronado" (1598), which was later included in Pedro Espinosa's *Flores de poetas ilustres de España*, published in 1605 in Valladolid (178v). Góngora paints a picture with his verses of the sacred hill "crowned with crosses," contrasting it to Mount Etna (1982, v. 1).[11] Unlike the volcano that was home to the Titans in classical mythological, however, the Sacromonte boasts of the remains of the ancient Christians who suffered martyrdom there. By juxtaposing the sacrilegious ways of the Titans who tried to rise up against the Olympian gods with Granada's humble martyrs, the poet highlights the level of holiness of these human beings and the magnitude of the discoveries on the Sacromonte. Despite contemporary debates on the veracity of the finds, Góngora's poetic voice appears to align itself in favour of the lead tablets, as the sonnet concludes by inciting the reader/spectator to venerate this space "with tender eyes, with reverent feet" (v. 14).[12]

The first stanza appeals to the senses not only because of the visual spectacle that is presented crudely before us, but also for the way in which it is presented, since the viewer is situated vis-à-vis the landscape. The use of the demonstrative adjective "this" creates a direct encounter with the natural enclave, since nothing stands between the spectator and the Sacromonte (Góngora 1982, v. 1).[13] This gesture calls the attention of onlookers to stop and contemplate what is before them (Orozco Díaz 1983, 500). Furthermore, the shape of the hillside seems to unfold before the eyes of its beholders, so that the spectacle can be lucidly contemplated. By describing the mount that "exhales light," Góngora directs our gaze to the glow emanating from this sacred space, temporarily eclipsing other aspects of the material world (1982, v. 3).[14] As Emilio Orozco Díaz reminds us in his study of the spatial visualization of Baroque poetry, several poems of the Golden Age are not intended to be recited, but to be engraved or written in stone, marble, or bronze, as Góngora had clearly intended in his sonnet entitled "Inscripción para el sepulcro de Dominico Greco" (Orozco Díaz 1983, 500–1). Likewise, his poem on the Sacromonte tries to move the viewer facing the landscape to devotion, as if the sonnet were an epitaph carved on one of the crosses. Indeed, some of the crosses did include inscriptions in verse, such as the one brought by the stonemasons and soldiers of the Alhambra mentioned above (Orozco Díaz 2002, 156–7).

Before such a sea of crosses symbolizing the discoveries of the remains on the mount, the pious behaviour demanded by the poet is the same as one might expect from a devotee who is inside a church or sacred place of worship. Such an attitude undoubtedly would predispose the viewer to understanding the hillside as an element of mediation between the earthly and the celestial worlds, placing it alongside the martyrs on an intermediate plane in which the enclave itself would also act as a mediator. Góngora presents us with a space radiating in holiness, a "trophy" that stands in honour of Christian martyrs (v. 5).[15] In this sense, the poet creates a parallel between the Sacromonte and Mount Etna, the same Mount Etna that Góngora would later incorporate into his *Fable of Polyphemus and Galatea* (1613), to highlight the magnitude – in this case, spiritual – of the remains that lie below. The bones and ashes of the martyrs present a sanctified version of the mythological giants that were condemned to be buried for daring to wage war on the gods of Olympus, although in this case the martyrs employ "holy strength" – that is, the same as that of heaven – thus acting as mediators between heaven and earth (Góngora 1982, v. 11).[16] The intermediary role that emanates from the landscape is understood by its consideration as a sacred space, so that, as an artificial element – in this case, a place of worship, yet represented as a natural environment – it appears inevitable to the spectator. The landscape initially could be taken for granted, as something that has always been present, since the process of transformation is hidden from view. Yet it is in this process, as Mitchell posits, that "social and subjective identities" are shaped. In Góngora's sonnet, this visual and spatial evidence is taken in by the viewer, reinforcing the perception of a sacred place in which the natural gives way to a religious and cultural environment.

After pilgrims contemplate both the physical and spiritual meanings of the Sacromonte, Góngora controls their vision by telling the beholders how to direct their gaze. The landscape is not left to open interpretation; instead, the poet exhorts spectators to approach the site with reverence and devotion, blinding wayfarers to other possible readings, particularly any that might suggest a connected history and space with Morisco inhabitants. In their study of landscape and vision, Harris and Ruggles propose that drawing attention to the ways in which we are made to look "illuminates cultural discourses that are essentially spatial, yet normalized to the point of invisibility" (2007, 18). In effect, Góngora's sonnet functions as a type of topographic map, detailing the physical land as well as what lies beneath the sacred site. And with the poet as our guide, we come to understand how to decipher this panorama. Unlike other regions of early modern Europe that showed a preference for representations of cityscapes that were as precise as possible, Spain tended to prefer what Kagan calls communicentric views that present a more idealized rendering of the landscape and often link it to local religious practices and beliefs. Like Góngora's sonnet, these communicentric views hint at the ways in which a particular community's inhabitants visualized and understood where they lived (1998, 77, 88–104). The various maps produced in the years after the lead tablet affair do just that. They present a graphic representation of Granada that focuses on the new Christian identity of the city, overlooking any physical signs of its Islamic heritage that still lingered at the end of the sixteenth century (Harris 2007, 119–26). It is relevant that Góngora not only situates the spectator in front of this sacred terrain; he also draws us into the transformation as eyewitnesses of the Baroque spectacle on the Granadan hillside.

Over a decade after Góngora dedicated his sonnet to the Sacromonte, Alonso de Bonilla composed verses about the sacred hill with the similar purpose of venerating it as a site of pilgrimage, but from a different approach.[17] His sonnet "A las cruces del monte santo," included in his *Peregrinos pensamientos de misterios divinos* ([1614] 2004), focuses precisely on the transformation of the landscape as a natural process, rather than an already fixed identity.[18] Bonilla highlights the expanse of land on Mount Valparaíso that, over time and caused by the discoveries of the martyrs' remains, has become a sacred enclave of worship. The first two quatrains of the sonnet begin by illustrating a flower's life cycle, which the poet later equates with the proliferation of crosses and altars that have sculpted the silhouette of this place:

> Usually the tender and gifted plant
> of some flower of desired smell
> pays a generous and pleasant tribute,
> if it is transplanted and placed in good soil.
> But after its beauty withers
> the cruel ignominy of ungrateful time,
> results in a seed instead of an ornament,
> and on what was, it rises up.[19]
>
> (Bonilla [1614] 2004, vv. 1–8)

In what follows, the seeds are compared to the crosses, and the martyrs to the flowers, thus embellishing the landscape, since, with their act of faith, they endow the natural space with an aura of unmistakable holiness. Bonilla situates the beholder of this scenery within a normal process of change – that is, the spectator perceives a gradual conversion of the landscape in its essence, which entails an eminently visual component. This transformation materializes with the crosses that populate the landscape and, like its natural environment, follows a cycle of change that affects the viewer's perception of the panorama, a process in which the reader also participates, acting as a witness.

A few years later, in 1617, the Sevillian writer Rodrigo Fernández de Ribera published a poem entitled *Canción al Monte Santo de Granada,* which he dedicated to Archbishop Pedro Vaca de Castro y Quiñones, a staunch defender of the authenticity of the lead books and founder of the Abbey of the Sacromonte.[20] Although Fernández de Ribera has been recognized primarily for his satirical works *Anteojos de mejor vista* (1623) and *El mesón del mundo* (1631), the rest of his literary production should not be dismissed, as his verses on the Morisco experience and the discovery of the lead books in the Sacromonte provide a unique perspective.

He was likely an eyewitness to the embarkation of the Moriscos at Seville during their expulsion from the peninsula, and the verses he writes on it in his early seventeenth-century unpublished poem *La asinaria* highlight the alleged acts of charity carried out by the Sevillians in favour of the Morisco children who were forced to stay behind, despite largely criticizing Morisco cultural practices and beliefs.[21]

Fernández de Ribera's *Canción al Monte Santo de Granada* (1617) is of special interest because of its description of the Granadan landscape of the Sacromonte. Like Bonilla's sonnet, this poem also dedicates a large part of its argument to the natural environment, which the poet elevates to a supernatural level worthy of being qualified as the greatest of wonders. This grandeur that emerges from the slopes is mainly prompted by the events that recently took place, now underscored by the new physiognomy of the terrain and part of its recreation. After the "mortal invierno" (mortal winter) in which the martyrs suffered death, the Sacromonte is now living a "Mayo eterno" (eternal May), crowned with hyacinths and violets (3r). As explicitly shown in the following verses in an apostrophe to Archbishop Pedro de Castro, Fernández de Ribera endows the newly sanctified Sacromonte with an unquestionable natural character: "Oh farmer of this concealed cultivated land,/which bears divine fruit,/and sprouts lead sheets for books" (7r).[22] Here we see how the poet stages the discovery of the lead tablets as if they were fruits of the trees, and the archbishop himself plays the role of a farmer who cultivates the land, suggesting that he keeps guardianship of the recently unearthed tablets and relics. Granada's fertile land is nourished by the Darro and Genil rivers that irrigate the region. The fecundity of this earth that yields fruit is a metaphor for the sacred fruit that the land has born in unearthing the lead tablets, a terrain where crosses multiply, carried there by devote pilgrims from throughout the peninsula (3v-4r). Finally, Fernández de Ribera alludes to these flowing rivers not only for enriching the landscape, but also for their role as exceptional messengers of the miraculous findings on the Sacromonte, springing from the Darro to the Genil, leading into the Guadalquivir, and flowing into the sea (4r). Here, Fernández de Ribera seems to draw on Bermúdez de Pedraza's *Antigüedad y excelencias de Granada* (1608), where he extols the rivers and their watershed, springing miraculous water that both Christians and Muslims have sought (11v-14v).[23]

The song also makes visible a relation of power between the viewer and the landscape. In the first stanza, the poetic voice addresses the sacred mount, praising its magnitude: "Divine mount, you will be able to lustily turn your sublime neck and serene brow to the high heavens" (3r).[24] As these verses reveal, the first attribute that characterizes the hillside is its elevation, placing beholders on an inferior level and thus inviting them to prostrate themselves reverently in front of the Sacromonte. The poet later characterizes the hillside as a "pyramid," and evokes Mount Olympus in his description of the revered gradient, among other metaphors that signify its stature (5r; 4v).[25] Although the poem transitions in the last verses to Pedro de Castro, the poetic voice continues to situate the viewer symbolically in a position of reverent submission. The archbishop occupies a "holy altar" and is compared to the biblical prophets Moses, Aaron, and Elijah (7r). Spectators, therefore, remain with their gaze fixed upward like one of the many pilgrims who made their way to the Sacromonte or a devotee who is persuaded by Archbishop Castro's support of the lead tablets.

Aside from extolling the Sacromonte studded in crosses and wrapped in holiness, Fernández de Ribera's poetic voice directs our gaze to Archbishop Castro, a "second venerable Elijah" on his own Mount Carmel (7r).[26] These verses suggest that, when Pedro de Castro reaches his last days, the converted landscape will endure as his legacy and, more important, the slopes will be a site of spiritual redemption. Góngora had already contemplated the role of the Sacromonte as a mediator in his sonnet, although in this case it is not the martyrs who reach to the heavens, but the very landscape that mediates between earthly and celestial beings. The poem closes by alluding to the redemptive nature of the sacred enclave, which is capable of inciting tears and repentance in even the most irreligious human beings: "The strangest people/most barbaric and remote/live tears pour, because you cause/their devout compunction" (7v–8r).[27] These last verses are especially striking if we consider them with Francisco Heylán's engraving of Pedro de Castro baptizing recent converts in Granada (fig. 9).[28] In this visual representation, Heylán presents the archbishop's role in the baptism of new Christians alongside the newly converted Sacromonte landscape covered in crosses. The inscription below the image with a reference to Psalm 77 ties the memory of miraculous biblical redeptions to the content of the engraving. Thus, Fernández de Ribera's poem coupled with Heylán's engraving present the Sacromonte as a site of atonement, connecting Pedro de Castro's role in both the newly "baptized" mount with its crosses and the baptism of new converts on the sacred hillside.

In a poem of nearly 250 verses on the Sacromonte, a space that in reality had much to do with the Moriscos, the silence about their presence is stark. Yet, these last verses of Fernández de Ribera's poem faintly hint at Archbishop Castro's belief that the new cult could help ensure the Christianization of Granada coupled with the conversion of Moriscos and heretics. In 1609, with the expulsion of the Moriscos already

Fig. 9. Francisco Heylán, *Bautismo de los moriscos*, detail, c. 1611.

Museo Casa de los Tiros, Granada

under way, Castro meets with the *junta* and shares his opinion that the Sacromonte exemplifies the coming to fruition of the prophecy of Obadiah 20–21, a passage that Castro interprets as the conversion of many peoples to Christianity and a condemnation of Islamic practices and beliefs (Harris 2007, 43; Urquízar Herrera 2017, 171). One year later, in a letter the archbishop wrote from Granada to King Philip III, he expresses his concerns about the expulsion of the Moriscos, especially since he believes they merit some exceptions – namely, young children and Morisca women married to Old Christian men, as well as Moriscos who conduct themselves as Christians, since they could help promote more conversions within their communities ("Carta de don Pedro Vaca de Castro" 2003, 281–1). Although Fernández de Ribera published his poem after the expulsion of the Morsicos was officially completed, the final verses subtly unveil Castro's posture towards the "Morisco problem" and represent the Sacromonte as a site of atonement.

Fernández de Ribera's song is one of the few poems about the Sacromonte that allude to the Moriscos or to Spain's Muslim past. Góngora, Alonso de Bonilla, and others make no mention of the cultural and material vestiges of the Moriscos' significant influence on the peninsula. In the Sevillian poet's *Canción al Monte Santo de Granada,* aside from touching on Archbishop Castro's hope for Moriscos' conversion, Fernández de Ribera glosses the "Saracen hands" in a way that represents Muslims only as an "interruption" of Spain's Christian identity (1617, 4r).[29] Like other narratives of Christian images allegedly hidden from Muslim conquerors that only reappeared centuries later during the Christian conquest of the peninsula, the lead books and martyrs' remains persisted throughout the Islamic period, implying, in the poet's opinion, that Spain was and continues to be a Christian land, thus erasing hundreds of years of Islamic legacy from the collective memory.[30] Fernández de Ribera's verses on the Sacromonte, alongside those of Góngora, Alonso de Bonilla, and other poets, are not just mere descriptions of the landscape and the spectacle of the crosses that adorn the slopes. Taking Mitchell into consideration, this landscape is part of an active process in which ideological identities are fashioned. By focusing the spectator's view on the terrain, the poets shape the landscape in a way that predisposes the audience to interpret the panorama in a certain way. Through their verses and sculpting of the land, whether intentional or not, the poets obscure the memory of a recent Islamic past.

Miguel de Luna and the Cross of Caravaca

For much of the population of late sixteenth-century Granada, the crosses visibly signified a Christian meaning for the Sacromonte, while for some Moriscos the true meaning of the landscape was hidden inside the *plomos.* The lead tablets, as Luis Bernabé has argued, "are deftly designed so that each reader, Christian or Muslim, could recognize themselves in them according to their own beliefs" (Bernabé Pons 2008, 79).[31] The authors of these tablets likely knew that the Christian audience would read them with a Christian interpretation, and that they lacked sufficient knowledge of Islam to decipher their significance for Moriscos. Using "Spirit of God" (*Rūḥ Allah*), instead of "Son of God," for example, to characterize the Prophet Jesus would still be acceptable to the Christian recipients of the *plomos* without having to make a statement about his divinity (Bernabé Pons 2008, 74). Scholars of the lead tablets generally believe that at the centre of the forgeries were Moriscos, including the doctor and translator Miguel de Luna, the same Morisco who had also crafted a falsified history of the

Muslim conquest of the peninsula in his *Historia verdadera del Rey don Rodrigo* ([1592] 2001).[32] He played an important role translating the parchment found in the Torre Turpiana and later with the lead tablets on the Sacromonte (García Arenal and Rodríguez Mediano 2008; 2010, 165–96).

Around the same time as his involvement in these activities, Miguel de Luna was embroiled in another forgery – that of fabricating new details related to the legend of the Cross of Caravaca, which is the focus of the remainder of this chapter. Reading Luna's role on fomenting the legend of the cross alongside the poetry about the Sacromonte that focuses our gaze on the multiplicity of crosses provides another angle from which to examine Moriscos' reception of religious art, especially when compared with the texts examined in the first two chapters.

In 1615, Juan de Robles Corbalán published his history of the miraculous apparition of the Cross of Caravaca; the work was quickly translated from Castilian to both Latin and German only a few years later. Although written records referring to the Cross of Caravaca existed as early as Fernando Colón's *Descripción y cosmografía de España* ([1517] 1988, 2:327), Corbalán's publication revealed Miguel de Luna's involvement and interest in the miracle, including an attempt by various individuals to fabricate new elements of the legend and forge a new history for the cross.[33] The different versions of the legend recount how Zeyt Abuzeyt, the Muslim king of Valencia and Caravaca, had taken the Christian monk Ginés Pérez Chirinos captive. Recognizing that Chirinos and the other captives were deteriorating in health, he agreed to let them say mass and helped to gather the supplies to permit them to do so. When they were about to begin, Chirinos realized that they had forgotten the cross, at which point two angels flew through the window with the Cross of Caravaca. Astonished by the miracle, the Muslim king converted to Christianity along with his wife Queen Heyla (Robles Corbalán 1615, 23v–28r; García Arenal and Rodríguez Mediano 2010, 218–22). According to Corbalán's account, the same cross later went on to perform a number of other miracles around the world, including in the Indies, Japan, and China (1615, 30v–36r). As García Arenal and Rodríguez Mediano recount, Corbalán later went on to craft his own version of the legend, which also consisted of the deciphering of strange inscriptions and paintings on the walls of the room where the cross originally had appeared. According to this account, after searching far and wide for someone to translate the inscriptions, Luna was the only one with the skills and knowledge to take on the challenge, especially because of his role as translator of the lead books (Robles Corbalán 1615, 46r–56r; García Arenal and Rodríguez Mediano 2008; 2010, 218–22).

The inscriptions and paintings materialized on the walls and around the window in the room where the Cross of Caravaca was first flown in by angels, and they depict the events related to King Abuzeyt's conversion. The murals portray the Muslim king on horseback, in conversation with his *alfaquís* and a priest, and during his baptism. Corbalán attempts to bolster his account by leaning on Luna's expert translations and interpretations. By using visual "evidence" and by including reproductions of them in his written text, he claims a certain authority for his rendering of the legend:

> For the investigation and assessment of ancient things, a very well received thing among learned men is the authority of letters, paintings, characters, and figures, which our ancestors used to leave the news of great and memorable things sculpted on stones, altarpieces, and walls for us. Because they were not inclined so much to writing, as they are now, they left them with this belief alone: [these representations] are so strong in showing the truths of past things and occurrences that cannot be ascertained by writing, and there is no one who puts this in question.[34] (Robles Corbalán 1615, 46v)

The inscriptions and murals thus become sites for anchoring memory – what Pierre Nora calls *lieux de mémoire* in his seminal work on memory and history. Nora posits that memory "takes root in the concrete, in spaces, gestures, images, and objects," but in Corbalán's account it is a fabricated memory, a recreation of the past in an attempt to create a new memory that could benefit those implicated in the manipulation of the legend (Nora 1989, 9).[35]

Miguel de Luna's interest in the Cross of Caravaca is filtered through the lens of Corbalán's *Historia*, so we must approach his translations therein with caution. Corbalán claims that he had exchanged letters with Luna on this project in September 1603 and March 1604, affirming that the characters inscribed around the window and on parts of the paintings were "Arabic, similar to those that we call Gothic here" (Robles Corbalán 1615, 47v).[36] Regardless of the veracity of his account, some peculiar interpretations arise. In the painting depicting the Muslim king on horseback, the letters on his embroidered clothes are intended to serve as a memory of his conversion to Christianity. The needlework on the horse's saddle cover continues the story of his religious transformation: "With this horse I praised the law of God, and defeated his enemies in battle many times. In that it shows us having taken up arms in favour of the Christian religion. And the stories of Castile, and Aragon tell us, that he was accompanying King don Fernando the Saint, when he won

Seville, and King don Jaime when he took Valencia" (Robles Corbalán 1615, 51r).[37] García Arenal and Rodríguez Mediano read Luna's interpretations of the murals depicting King Abuzeyt, focusing on his voluntary conversion, as compatible with his larger plan to present a less Islamic past for the peninsula (2008, 132; 2010, 221). Complementary to this reading, we can also consider the characterization of the king as a recent convert to evoke the Apostle Paul. Similar to Saul of Tarsus, who persecuted Christians before converting to Christianity, King Abuzeyt in Corbalán's account previously had responded with rage and killed those Christians who had approached him to preach the Gospel (even though Corbalán suggests elsewhere that the king secretly maintained friendships with other Christians) (Robles Corbalán 1615, 20v–21r; 19r). And after the king converts and is baptized, he changes his name to don Vicente Belvís and now fights on the Christian side (66r).[38] Despite the fact that Paul was a controversial figure in Christian-Muslim polemical literature, including in some Morisco Aljamiado manuscripts, Luna dismisses the Muslim view of Paul and instead presents a biblical model of conversion.[39]

In the years before Corbalán published his history on the Cross of Caravaca, the apologists of the expulsion of the Moriscos had already included references to this cross, but for a different purpose. Jaime Bleda recounts the story of the apparition of this Christian symbol in nearly all of his principal works in an attempt to propagate its miraculous powers, including its alleged approval of the Morisco expulsion. In his *Libro de la Cofradía de la Minerva* (1600a) and *Quatrocientos milagros y muchas alabanças de la Santa Cruz* (1600b), Bleda includes the Cross of Caravaca as one of his many miracles of the cross.[40] He alludes to King Abuzeyt's conversion from Islam only in passing, however, and for him the real miracle of the cross is how it helped set free Abuzeyt's Christian captives, especially since he evokes their fragile emotional and physical state (1600a, 325–8; 1600b, 239–44). In later works, such as his *Defensio fidei in causa neophytorum siue Morischorum* (1610) and *Corónica de los moros de España* (1618), Bleda tries to prove that the Cross of Caravaca endorsed and helped carry out the expulsion of the Moriscos (1610, 596; 1618, 1050b). During the last embarkations at Los Alfaques, on Iberia's eastern coast, Bleda claims that the expelled Moriscos had been waiting for last-minute help from the "Turks," but instead were greeted by "the holy cross that is their scourge, which just expelled them from there" (1618, 1050b).[41] Pedro Aznar Cardona, likewise, buttresses his anti-Morisco arguments with the Cross of Caravaca, interpreting its apparition during the Moriscos' forced departure from the peninsula to signify its approval of their expulsion (1612, 2:29v–32r). Even in Corbalán's *Historia*, he includes miracles of the Cross of Caravaca that appear to align themselves slightly more with the rhetoric of the apologists than with the message of the *plomos* that his Morisco collaborator likely had helped propagate.[42] One miracle in particular concerned King Abuzeyt's cousin, Aben Maho- mat, and his son with the same name. After his father's tragic death, the younger Mahomat was baptized as don Fernando and had joined King Fernando III in his fight against Muslim troops, when a shining Caravaca cross appeared in the sky as if to guarantee the Muslims' defeat (Robles Corbalán 1615, 91v–93v).

Why would Miguel de Luna help to promote a legend about the Cross of Caravaca, the same cross that apologists of the expulsion later would use to justify the Moriscos' expulsion from Spain? This apparent contra- diction needs to be understood within the larger framework of projects in which Luna was involved. As García Arenal and Rodríguez Mediano suggest, the Morisco doctor and translator endeavored to de-Islamize the Islamic legacy of the peninsula in an attempt to show that individuals of Muslim heritage could be "good" Christians. In the Caravaca affair, which effectively links the conversion of a Muslim king to a popular religious cult, Luna helps to advance the idea that illustrious Muslims had already converted to Christianity voluntarily centuries before the Moriscos' forced conversions. And since the Christian legend is alleg- edly revealed through Arabic script, he suggests that the language of the Qur'an is acceptable for Spain's sacred history (2008, 132–3; 2010, 221–2).

It is important that we also consider how Miguel de Luna might be presenting a certain view of the Cross of Caravaca depending on his audience, especially if we reflect on his activities with other Moriscos in Toledo. One of the witnesses of the trial of the Morisco shopkeeper and merchant Jerónimo de Rojas in Toledo between 1601 and 1603 provides revealing details about Luna's involvement with the Morisco community there.[43] The witness claims that Luna would meet clandes- tinely with other Moriscos who eagerly listened to him as an authority on Islamic religion and culture, with one Morisco even asserting that "there is no better Moor in Spain" (García Arenal 2010, 260).[44] The trial also indicates that Luna spoke about the lead books as Islamic texts, claim- ing that the Christians had been deceived (258). In terms of visual cul- ture, according to the Inquisition trial, Luna's friend Jerónimo de Rojas also spoke out against the Catholic cult of images, complaining "that what they have invented to worship images of wood and stone is evil and treachery" (257).[45] All of these details provide a sharp contrast to Luna's promotion of the Cross of Caravaca discussed earlier. Thus, it seems likely that he could have been promoting a certain view of the Cross of

Caravaca when speaking to a Christian audience while saying something different about religious images when meeting with crypo-Muslim communities. At the very least, this example should prompt us to pay attention to the fluid boundaries of images and to consider the ways that the Cross of Caravaca could be used within different contexts.

Reading Miguel de Luna's promotion of the Cross of Caravaca alongside his likely involvement with the *plomos*, which resulted in the proliferation of crosses on the Sacromonte, exposes parallel uses for the Christian symbol: that which dominated the landscape's physical terrain, and that which was fixed in the spiritual imagination. While early modern poets shaped the sacred space with their verses, focusing on the transformed orography of the hillside, Corbalán's *Historia* helped carve a wider space for the Caravaca cross. Even though there is not a direct correlation between these two events, albeit Luna likely had connections to both, they reveal broader questions about how writers – Old Christians and Moriscos – envisioned and manipulated Christian iconography in shared religious and cultural spaces.

In the first two chapters, we saw how a variety of authors treated Moriscos' often precarious association with religious images, especially the cross. In their fictional and historical writings, Cervantes, the apologists of the expulsion, and the Moriscos themselves approached the question of images largely around issues of iconoclasm or conversion. As we saw, apologists of the expulsion aligned themselves along the same lines as the Inquisition cases that accused Moriscos of abusing religious images, thus exploiting the symbol of the cross in their attempt to justify the Moriscos' forced departure from Spain. Cervantes, meanwhile, was more attuned to visual cues, suggesting multiple possibilities for how Moriscos might respond to religious art and how these images put characters of different backgrounds in contact with one another. We also saw how Aljamiado writing could be a powerful tool to respond both verbally and visually to "idols," including Christian icons, as well as to establish the primacy of text over image in Moriscos' literary culture.

The cases I have explored in this chapter present another alternative. Neither the poetic texts nor Miguel de Luna's translations filtered through Corbalán's history explicitly expose the anxieties surrounding Moriscos' reception of religious images, yet the authors adapt their use of the cross within the same shared space of the Sacromonte. They move away from the context of iconoclasm and image destruction, and instead sculpt a landscape that superficially veils the memory of the recent Islamic past. The texts studied here are important because they present a more complex vision of how writers manipulated religious images across perceived cultural and religious boundaries, showing how poetry and history converge and illuminate each other within this context. Ultimately, verbal descriptions of the cross are embedded in these texts, uncovering how religious and cultural identities were fashioned within the material and spiritual landscapes of early modern Spain.

These texts describing the landscape of the Sacromonte direct our attention principally to the iconography visible on the terrain – above the ground – of the holy mount. The poets sculpt the land with their verses and guide the viewer's line of vision towards the multiplicity of crosses on the Sacromonte, thus rendering Granada's Islamic heritage out of sight. Below the surface of this sacred orography, however, it is not the cross, but rather the Virgin Mary – or Maryam, as she is known in the Qur'an – who takes on a leading role in the lead tablets. Mary is the focus of the majority of the twenty-two tablets, and she is also one of the key figures tasked with relaying the new Christian doctrine that has been revealed to her by the angel Gabriel. This Mary of the Sacromonte, however, was unique. Among other exceptional qualities, she praises Arabic, a language that Moriscos had been banned from using since Philip II's 1567 decree, above all other languages. The Virgin Mary in the lead tablets is conveniently situated between Christianity and Islam in a such a way that she could be acceptable to all (Martínez Medina 2006, 447–54; Remensnyder 2011, 547–51).[46]

In one of the lead tablets, the Virgin Mary responds to a series of eight questions about the truth of the Gospel. When Peter asks her about the "excellence of the Arabs," she highlights how God has chosen them and that Arabic is superior to all other languages (Harvey 2005, 389). The authors of this lead tablet credit Mary for gathering the twelve disciples in her home and illuminating their hearts, attributing a central role to her in the revelation of these newly discovered scriptures. One can easily begin to see how Mary was fashioned in a way that would be appealing to the Morisco community on the brink of expulsion, while she could still be suitable to their Old Christian neighbours. Even after the expulsion, some Moriscos in North Africa continued to recall the importance of Mary in these lead tablets. Ibn Qāsim al-Ḥajarī had been responsible for translating the lead books after their discovery in Granada; years later, in Tunis, he transcribed a manuscript of one of the books – curiously, one focused on Mary – which he includes as an appendix to his autobiography (Matar and Christodouleas 2005, 200). Likewise, in a Morisco prayer written down in the years after the expulsion, its author reveals how at least some exiled Moriscos had brought their devotion to the Mary of the Sacromonte with them to North Africa. They looked to the Mary of the lead tablets for strength and encouragement in their trials, this time from the other side of the Strait of Gibraltar (Barkaï 1983, 257–8).

Thus, focusing on the abundance of crosses on the Sacromonte shows only part of the complexities of how cultural and religious identities were shaped through frequent encounters with religious images in early modern Spain. Below the sacred terrain of the Sacromonte, the figure of Mary straddled Christian and Muslim cultures. This notion was far reaching, and many early modern Spanish authors – both Old and New Christians – were congnizant of Mary's revered place in both faith traditions beyond just the context of Granada's hillside. In the next two chapters, I take up this question and examine how a wide variety of authors used their writing as a tool to negotiate the Virgin Mary's place between Christianity and Islam.

4

Marian Images of Conversion

Mary, God has chosen you and made you pure: He has truly chosen you above all women.

Qur'an (3:42)

And the Virgin Mary was so good that even though I do not say anything about her except what your Qur'an says, it is enough for you to believe how holy she was. [Y fue tan buena la Virgen María, que aunque yo no diga della sino lo que dize vuestro alcorán, es harto para que creays quán sanctíssima fue.]

Bernardo Pérez de Chinchón, *Antialcorano* (347)

In Miguel de Cervantes's *La gran sultana*, the captive Christian protagonist, Catalina de Oviedo, enters the scene with a rosary in her hand and invokes the Virgin Mary for comfort in her affliction. Instead of objecting to her strong religious devotion, the Grand Turk encourages Catalina to continue praising Mary and seeking her protection: "Pray, Catalina, pray, for without divine aid human things do not last; and call on your Lela Marién, for it doesn't frighten me, on the contrary, it seems good to me, for she is sainted among us as well ... You can praise her as you like, for we do the same, and we honor her above all for her virginity" (Cervantes [1615] 2010, 140–1).[1] Catalina is unmoved by the sultan's comments, and is quick to acknowledge that Mary is honoured in many nations. Like Cervantes, many early modern Spanish authors were well aware of the important place Mary holds in both Christianity and Islam.[2] The Qur'an dedicates its nineteenth sura (chapter) to her, and other *āyāt* (verses) praise her above all women. Indeed, she is the only woman to be honoured with a sura named after her, a privilege that not even Hagar, mother of Ishmael, is conceded in the Qur'an (Pelikan 1996, 68–9; Smith and Haddad 1989, 162). Even a book such as Bernardo

Pérez de Chinchón's *Antialcorano* ([1532] 2000), a text clearly intended to refute Islamic doctrine and practice in Spain, recognizes Mary as a key figure and common ground between Muslims and Christians, as the second epigraph to this chapter suggests.

Muslims living in the Iberian Peninsula were also keenly aware of Mary's revered place in Christianity and Islam. Even at times when they might have considered their Christian neighbours as foes, Mary's elevated status was undeniable. Roughly a century before the Catholic kings' conquest of Granada, Ibn al-Jayyab, one of the court poets of the Nasrid sultanate, composed a poem comparing three of the most important women in Islam: the Prophet Muhammad's wife 'A'isha, his daughter Fatima, and the Virgin Mary. Of these feminine figures, he places Mary at the top, even though she is "lady of the house of idols," a reference to the Madonna that his Christian neighbours venerated in images:

> Love three women, pure in conduct.
> 'A'isha was bestowed with great glory and stature
> and God the Merciful freed her from the people of deceit.
> And ahead of her is Fatima, the one of high lineage.
> And, in first place, the purest among them is lady of the house of idols
>   [Mary].[3]
>
> (Quoted in Rubiera Mata 1972, 141)

After the forced conversions of Muslims in sixteenth-century Spain, many Moriscos also recognized Mary as a figure important in both Christian and Muslim cultures, most significantly in the apocryphal lead books of the Sacromonte discussed in the previous chapter. Other Morisco texts, such as the Mancebo de Arévalo's *Tafsira*, also concede an important place to Mary/Maryam. In a chapter devoted to the greatness of Maryam, the Mancebo praises her for her spirituality and for the protection that God has granted her (2003, 265–6).[4] Likewise, Aljamiado Morisco legends about the birth of Jesus, or 'Isā ibn Maryam, as he is known in Islam, highlight Mary's elevated position among Morisco communities in early modern Spain.[5] Even in a late sixteenth-century Aljamiado Morisco manuscript containing an Islamic hadith on the life of Jesus, Christian and Muslim beliefs about Mary are quite literally fused together. This particular version of the hadith conserved at the CSIC in Madrid curiously contains two lines of the Latin Ave Maria prayer written in Arabic script that are coupled with the remaining hadith in Arabic characters exalting the Virgin Mary (*Narraciones y leyendas* n.d., 58v).[6]

Although Mary figures prominently in Christian and Muslim cultures, images representing her could still pose problems for those who rejected figural representations. As we saw in the past few chapters, early modern authors often attributed an aniconic predisposition to Moriscos in Spain and their Muslim neighbours in North Africa, highlighting their tendency to reject religious images. And, in some of their own writings, Moriscos confirmed this inclination by denouncing the creation and veneration of "idols," even though it was not a generalized practice nor extensible to all Muslims, as some of the cases studied thus far have shown. This chapter, then, examines how early modern writers attempted to reconcile this incongruity in their literary texts. With a shared cult of the Virgin Mary, yet differing opinions on religious images, sixteenth- and seventeenth-century authors used their writing as a tool to negotiate how to represent Muslims' relation to Marian icons. What many of these texts reveal is that, although Moriscos and North African Muslims might have rejected images in practice, early modern writers tended to resort to the trope of conversion in their literary texts. Their writings suggest that the power attributed to Marian icons often outweighed any aversion to figural representations and eventually would persuade the religious "other" to convert.

Among those men and women who converted due to the Virgin Mary's influence were a series of North African princes and high-ranking individuals from other Islamic lands who made their way to Europe for a variety of reasons. Some of the most fascinating cases are those of Muley al-Shaykh (later known as don Felipe de África), Muhammad al-Attaz (later named Balthasar de Loyola), and Muley Alal Merin (baptized as Gaspar de Benimerín).[7] Spanish Golden Age authors helped popularize these conversion narratives by representing some of them on the early modern stage.[8] Lope de Vega enacts one of these well-known conversions, with Muley al-Shaykh (Muley Xeque in Lope's play) starring as the protagonist.[9] In 1593, the Moroccan prince converted to Christianity, and was baptized in the Escorial with Philip II and the Infanta Isabel Clara Eugenia serving as his godparents. Although a number of early modern historians and contemporaries of Lope de Vega, such as Luis Cabrera de Córdoba, Antonio de Escovar, Antonio de León Pinelo, Jerónimo Quintana, and Jerónimo de Sepúlveda, among others, describe Muley al-Shaykh's life and baptism, Lope is the first to describe the young man's interest in Marian icons, whether authentic or conceived by the playwright.[10] He dedicates the entire second act of the play to his instruction in Marian iconology and his reaction to the image of the Virgin of la Cabeza, which Muley Xeque initially hoped to mock until his miraculous conversion occurred. Only decades after Lope wrote his play, others elaborated on details revolving around the image of the Virgin of la Cabeza's influence over Muley Xeque, such as Manuel de Salcedo Olid in his *Panegírico historial de Nuestra Señora de la Cabeza* (1677) or the Italian theologian Matteo Gianolio di Cherasco's late eighteenth-century biography of Muley Xeque. For this reason, Lope's play offers a fascinating starting point from which to examine how early modern authors attempted to portray Muslims' precarious relation to Marian icons in the Iberian Peninsula.

Marian Icons between Christianity and Islam

Despite the complexities of figural images in Christian-Muslim encounters, a variety of miracle stories placed the power of Marian icons in a central place for the conversion of their Muslim protagonists, offering visual testimony of the images' influence. In late medieval Iberia, as Remensnyder has shown, Mary was already celebrated as the "Mother of Conversion," known for prompting Muslims and Jews to convert to Christianity. Early modern writers later inherited the common motifs from the medieval miracle stories as they recorded new accounts of Mary's ability to impel men and women to convert (Remensnyder 2014a, 175–205). Yet, miracles of conversion incited by an image of Mary added an extra layer of meaning, since they also implied the convert's new tolerance of Marian icons. The combination of verbal and visual elements, "the whole ensemble of *relations*" as W.J.T. Mitchell terms it, worked in tandem to offer proof not only of Mary's controlling sway, but also, significantly, of the efficacy of images to convert (1994, 94; emphasis in original).

In Alfonso X's *Cantigas de Santa María*, for example, *cantiga* 46 tells of a Muslim man who travelled to the Holy Land and pillaged Christian sites, taking a statue of the Virgin Mary for himself. He wrapped the image in gold cloth and positioned it in a place of honour in his home, gazing at it often and struggling to accept the doctrine of the Incarnation (fig. 10). Even though the issue is not centred on the problem of figural images, but rather on accepting Mary as the Mother of God, the *cantiga* reveals the influence of Marian icons.[11] When the miraculous powers of the devotional image take effect and the statue's two breasts turn to flesh, from which streams of milk flow, the Muslim protagonist and many of his followers convert (Alfonso X 1986, 1:171–3).[12] Other miracles attributed the conversion of Muslim individuals – even those who categorically rejected Christian iconography – to figural images of the Virgin Mary. In the sixteenth century, Fray Gabriel de Talavera recounts the miracle of a Muslim slave on his way to the Virgin of Guadalupe in Caceres with his masters. Due to this servant's stubborn and rebellious demeanour, no one had been able to convince him to enter a church and contemplate

the cross, lest they risk his fury. Yet the image of the Virgin of Guadalupe performed a miracle, prompting the Muslim slave to look at the
Marian icon, at which point he experienced an immediate change of
heart and was baptized along with some of his followers (301v–302r).
What these miracles show is that medieval and early modern Christian
authors did not always view figural imagery as an obstacle to conversion
via Marian icons. They reveal the triumph these authors saw in Christian
iconography – especially of the Virgin – to influence Muslims to convert
to Christianity.

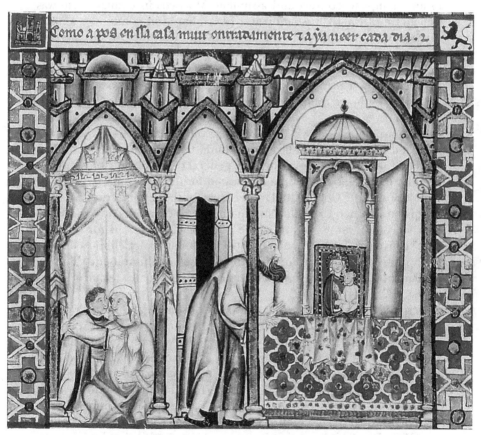

Fig. 10. Detail of *Cantiga* 46, in Alfonso X's *Cantigas de Santa María.*
Real Biblioteca de El Escorial, MS T-I-1, fol. 68v
Photo credit: Patrimonio Nacional, Biblioteca del Real Monasterio de San
Lorenzo de El Escorial, T-I-1

The use of Marian icons to convert Muslims and bring them into the Christian fold did not go unnoticed by those holding positions of power in the first years after the Capitulations of Granada. Queen Isabel I commissioned a number of religious images to be sent to the mosques-turned-churches, most of which were located in the Albaicín, where a majority Morisco population resided. As Pereda has demonstrated, the iconography of the images sent to these recently converted churches was likely influenced by the fact that they were principally intended for Moriscos, as only images of the Virgin and some saints were sent, but no large crucifixes (2007, 293–308). Hernando de Talavera, the queen's confessor and archbishop of Granada, also resorted to images in an attempt to convert and assimilate Moriscos in Granada. He was well aware of what Christianity and Islam shared in common – among the books in his library was a Latin translation of the Qur'an, offering him keen insight on these points. Consequently, it was no accident that images of Mary were chosen in particular for the evangelization of Moriscos and for their places of worship, even if the Moriscos themselves did not always embrace them with open arms (2007, 254–373).

In other regions of the peninsula, however, there were few cases of the use of Marian icons for Moriscos' conversion similar to those Queen Isabel I and Hernando de Talavera had undertaken in Granada. In Valencia, San Francisco de Borja, superior general of the Society of Jesus and founder of Colegio de Gandía, advocated for using an image of the Virgin Mary with the Christ Child in her arms for the Jesuits' evangelization campaigns. Franco Llopis has shown on various occasions how San Francisco de Borja was cognizant of the value of Marian icons for the "sincere" conversion of Moriscos, and how this Jesuit leader employed them for a more pacific assimilation of the Morisco community in Valencia, similar to what Talavera had accomplished in Granada (Franco Llopis 2008a, 389; 2014, 106, 112).[13]

Despite Mary's place as a link between Christianity and Islam, a variety of written and visual sources suggest that Moriscos had mixed reactions to figural images representing the Virgin.[14] An anonymous painting displayed in the Parish Church of Ugíjar (Granada) depicts one such reaction to figural representations of Mary, this time of the Virgin del Martirio, patron saint of the Alpujarras (fig. 11).[15] The painted canvas illustrates how Moriscos desecrated the figure of Mary alongside the martyrdom of Christian men and women during the War of the Alpujarras (1568–70). By juxtaposing human and icon in this visual representation, the artist elides the fate of earthly and divine beings, highlighting a martyrdom in which the tortured men and women gain strength in their suffering from the disfigured Marian image.[16] Isabel de Melgar, wife and

mother to two of those martyred at the hands of Moriscos in Ugíjar, gave
an account of these events to Justino Antolínez de Burgos in 1600, once
again underscoring Moriscos' treatment of Marian icons: "In the same
way [her son] cried when he told this witness that in the church of Ugíjar, they had put a rope around the neck of an image of Our Lady and
she had been dragged and thrown into the fire and, with contempt, they
had sat on top of her most holy face" (*Informaciones* 2014, 104).[17] Regardless of the veracity of Isabel de Melgar's testimonial account, it is revealing that, in all the details of the sacrilege of the Virgin del Martirio, this
witness offers no indication that Moriscos act as a result of their aversion
to figural images. Instead, her account is more closely guided by the
context of confrontation between Old Christians and Moriscos in Ugíjar.
Likewise, Justino Antolínez de Burgos records how Moriscos burned the

Fig. 11. Anonymous, *Profanación y rescate de una imagen de Nuestra Señora del
Martirio*, seventeenth century.

Parroquia de Nuestra Señora del Martirio, Ugíjar, Granada

altar, broke religious images, and turned the sacred ornaments into turbans and *marlotas*, not because of any objections they might have had to figural images, but rather because of "their contempt and hatred of our sacred religion" (262).[18] Although the use of these narratives should be questioned, given the context in which they were produced, the visual and textual accounts of Moriscos' response to the Virgin del Martirio, among other images of the Virgin Mary, indicate that Marian icons were, at times, objects of contention among members of the Morisco community.

Other accounts provide a very different picture of Moriscos' association with Marian icons, including some that suggest a certain attachment to images of the Virgin Mary even after their expulsion from Spain. In a curious *relación de sucesos* published in Málaga in 1612, Gaspar Serato describes how a Morisca named Mencía cultivated a strong devotion to an image of the Virgin of la Caridad, despite having to conceal her affection for Marian icons from her husband and family. She initially had hoped to enter a convent to avoid marriage, but her father arranged for her to marry a Morisco from Hornachos, who acted violently against her to prevent her from worshipping Mary. Even after suffering her husband's physical abuse, she clandestinely purchased a print of the Virgin of la Caridad while in Seville to take with her after her expulsion to North Africa. Once in Morocco, she took out the printed image to worship covertly, until her husband discovered her kneeling in front of it and tried to destroy the image by throwing it in a fire. As a result of her devotion to Marian icons and her Christian faith, Mencía was eventually martyred on African soil (Serato 1612, 1r–3r).[19] Furthermore, in at least one case, a descendant of Moriscos in Tunis values a statue of Mary well into the eighteenth century, nearly a hundred years after the expulsion of the Moriscos from the peninsula. Cherite Castelli, a descendant of expelled Moriscos, cherished a small Marian figure that he kept at his storefront to protect his merchandise, although more for its talismanic properties than for any pious motives (Carlos Varona 2011, 329; Ximénez 1934, 190). Irrespective of the possible motives behind these two accounts, at the very least they offer an alternative scenario to the cases of iconoclasm discussed above. More important, they also suggest that some Moriscos might have taken their interest in Marian icons with them to North Africa following their expulsion.

Staging Conversion

Although Moriscos were negotiating their own precarious association with Marian icons in the years before their expulsion, Lope de Vega stages the conversion of a Moroccan prince whose own conversion is provoked by an image of Mary in the play *Tragedia del rey don Sebastián y bautismo del príncipe de Marruecos* (c. 1593–1603).[20] As the title suggests, his *comedia* represents two historical events: the disastrous results of the Battle of Alcazarquivir (al-Qaṣr al-Kabīr) in 1578, including the death of the Portuguese king, Sebastian, and the conversion and baptism of Muley Xeque in 1593 after witnessing the pilgrimage of the Virgin of la Cabeza in the Andalusian town of Andújar. Despite the diverse content represented in the three acts of Lope's *comedia*, many scholars have sought to find unity in the play. Oliver Asín affirms that it is precisely Muley Xeque who, as the protagonist, adds cohesion to the play (2008, 171), while Pedraza Jiménez suggests Lope's work was commissioned by Muley al-Shaykh himself and that he might have asked the playwright to follow his personal life closely, even if the overall structure of the play would suffer (1997, 137–8).[21]

The play begins *in medias res* as the characters anxiously contemplate the Saadian dynastic dispute in Morocco, which eventually leads to the battle of Alcazarquivir at the end of the first act. One of the contenders to the throne is Muhammad al-Mutawakkil (Muley Mahamet in Lope's play), nephew of the sultan in power and father of Muley al-Shaykh. Al-Mutawakkil requests military assistance from the Portuguese king and in exchange presents him with the Moroccan port in Asilah. As Fernand Braudel reminds us, "It may not have been the greatest disaster in Portuguese history, but the importance of the battle of Alcazarquivir should not be underestimated, for it was heavy with consequences" (1972, 2:1179). One of these consequences was that al-Mutawakkil, King Sebastian, and reigning sultan ʿAbd al-Malik all died in the battle, resulting in Ahmad al-Mansur's being named the new ruler and some members of the Saʿdian dynasty being forced into exile.[22] Among those displaced were Muley al-Shaykh and his uncle, Muley Nasr, who first went to Portugal and then to southern Spain. Although the first act of Lope's play ends with the devastating outcome of the battle and the death of a Christian king, the religious transformation and baptism of a Moroccan prince in the last two acts helps compensate for the initial tragedy, as Mariscal (1990, 161) and Romanos (1999, 190) have suggested. By concluding the drama in this way, Lope reaffirms the triumph of Christianity over Islam despite the Portuguese loss in North Africa.

Early modern literary and artistic renderings of the pilgrimage to the Virgin of la Cabeza attest to the popularity of this April event and especially the reputation of the Madonna herself. Bernardo Asturiano's seventeenth-century painting on the subject notably links the past with the present, portraying the apparition of the Virgin of la Cabeza to Juan

Alonso de Rivas in the thirteenth century alongside contemporary celebrations carried out in the name of the Virgin (fig. 12).[23] Miguel de
Cervantes also highlights the popularity of this particular image of the
Virgin in his *Trabajos de Persiles y Sigismunda* when the protagonists come
across an aged woman on her way to visit a number of holy sites, including the festival of Nuestra Señora de la Cabeza in Andújar ([1617] 2004,
3:6, 487). In this ekphrastic passage, the female traveller in question
describes the miraculous image and the countless people who journey to
this sacred place for the festival, basing her description on a painting in
the Royal Palace in Madrid.[24] Despite the varied motivations for attending the festivities, for Lope the outcome is always the same. In his play, we
see Christian and Muslim characters encounter one another as a result
of the aura of the Marian image. Any differences that might be present
initially are nearly erased by the religious conversion and baptism staged
at the denouement of the play. Moreover, any reluctance to accept the

Fig. 12. Bernardo Asturiano, *Romería de Nuestra Señora de la Cabeza*, seventeenth
century.

Museo de Nuestra Señora de la Cabeza, Andújar, Jaen
Photo: Wenceslao Infante Burón

validity and worth of the Marian icon is resolved before the end of the *comedia*, when the effigy's miraculous and inherent power to provoke the conversion of a noble Muslim prince is validated.

Although Muley Xeque's conversion on stage does not take place until the end of the second act, Lope slowly begins to mould and transform his protagonist in the preceding verses, preparing the audience for the Moroccan prince's encounter with Marian icons and eventual conversion to Christianity. On his way to the festivities celebrating the Virgin of la Cabeza in act 2, Muley Xeque comes across a group of three women who serve as an analogy to the principal Marian image (Mariscal 1990, 160). Muley Xeque's initial interest in these three earthly women is later substituted for his desire to learn more about the divine woman – namely, the figural representation of the Virgin Mary celebrated in Andújar. Driven by their senses, the women exoticize the Moroccan prince, as they look at, listen to, and touch him. He defines himself as a hybrid subject, speaking both Arabic and Spanish, with one foot in Africa and the other in Spain. The women mark their differences with Muley Xeque, accentuating his supposedly unbridled sexuality and desire to take more than one woman as his wife. As Edward Said argues, "the Orient seems to suggest not only fecundity but sexual promise (and threat), untiring sensuality, unlimited desire, deep generative energies" (1978, 188). Thus, with an Orientalist gaze, the women paint Muley Xeque as an exotic outsider in need of conversion. The Moroccan prince, however, disguises himself in "Christian" clothes in order to fit into the Andalusian environment surrounding the pilgrimage to the Virgin. It is only after he has modified his outer appearance that his inner intentions also begin to transform. Likewise, his conversations with the three Spanish ladies are soon substituted with discussions about Marian representations, and his desire to mock the festivities and religious image dissipates as he learns more about the different images of the Virgin. Although the anonymous women ultimately reject him as a "Moor," the Virgin of la Cabeza accepts him into the Christian fold as he converts in the presence of her image.

If the three women hint at Muley Xeque's need for conversion, then it is the friar from the monastery of Nuestra Señora de la Victoria who provides the theological backing for him to do so, underscoring the power and prominence of religious images for the prince.[25] While waiting for the procession and image of the Virgin to pass by, the friar instructs Muley Xeque on the most important Marian icons in Spain, among them the Virgin of Montserrat, Atocha, and Guadalupe. Although the friar might not be aware of Muley Xeque's initial intention to mock the festivities and the image of the Virgin, he does recognize that figural images had been a point of tension for Muslims living in the Iberian Peninsula

(Vega [c. 1593–1603] 2012, vv. 1666–8, vv. 1949–68). It is worth noting, then, that Muley Xeque's instruction in Marian iconography is focused solely on images of the Virgin with the Christ Child in her arms, an image that Muslims and new converts from Islam would be more willing to accept (see figs. 13, 14, and 15).[26] In Islamic doctrine, Mary – mother of Jesus – is praised for her exemplary maternal role and female virtue. The Qur'an, in particular, asserts that Mary and her son are "a sign for all people" (21:91), extolling mother and child together (Schleifer 1997, 45–54, 46). Furthermore, according to prophetic traditions, when the Prophet Muhammad destroyed the idols at the Ka'ba in Mecca, it was only an image of Mary with her son in her arms that he chose to spare (Grabar 1987, 80).[27] In the context of early modern Spain, Franco Llopis has suggested that images of the Virgin Mary embracing her son might have been the most widely accepted by Moriscos, especially since they also valued Mary as a model of feminine virtue. San Francisco de Borja, for example, favoured an image of Mary with her child in his evangelization campaigns, including in the principally Morisco region of Gandía.[28] Unlike other advocations of the Virgin, such as the *Mater Dolorosa* associated with the Passion of Christ, an image of the Virgin Mary holding her son was much less polemical for members of the Morisco community (Franco Llopis 2014, 111–13). For this reason, the exclusive focus of the friar in Lope's play on images of the Virgin Mary with the Christ Child in his instruction of Marian iconography could function as a strategy to have Muley Xeque finally accept the Virgin of la Cabeza and hasten his conversion to Christianity.

These Marian icons that the friar describes to the Moroccan prince are also associated with miracles and legends of Muslim individuals who convert to Christianity after hearing about the Virgin Mary or after gazing at images representing her. In this way, the account of Muley Xeque's conversion by way of a Marian icon inscribes both the prince and the image of the Virgin of la Cabeza in this tradition, highlighting the power of sacred representations to convert individuals with diverse beliefs. The Virgin of Montserrat, for example, surfaces in early modern miracle stories and literary narratives of Muslims' conversion to Christianity (fig. 13). In his *Libro de la historia y milagros, hechos a invocación de Nuestra Señora de Montserrate* (1536), Pedro de Burgos gives various accounts of Muslims who convert to Christianity after coming in contact with the image of the Virgin of Montserrat or after seeing the miracles she has performed.[29] In one instance, a Muslim slave aboard a ship off the coast of Algiers suddenly began praying the Ave Maria as he saw the Virgin of Montserrat appear above the boat, guiding them through a storm. Astonished at the help she provided to the Christian sailors on the rough sea, Ali converts to Christianity, changes his name to Pedro in honour of one of the rescued seafarers, and gives thanks to the Virgin of Montserrat (Burgos 1605, 188r–189v). In the same vein, Cristóbal de Morales offers a literary rendering of one of these conversions in *La estrella de Monserrate* (1658). In a scene filled with supernatural occurrences, Ali looks on in amazement as three Christian captives break free from their shackles and a cloud miraculously transports them to the Virgin of Montserrat in Spain, prompting Ali to convert to Christianity *in situ* (46r–46v).

Some of the other Virgins the friar names in Lope's play also boast of miraculous conversions, bringing to the baptismal font even those Muslims who mocked Marian icons or rejected the power of images. In his *Anales de Madrid* ([1701] 1971), the early modern historian Antonio de León Pinelo records a conversion miracle linked to the Virgin of Atocha that bears some resemblance to Muley Xeque's change of heart. Significantly, it occurs in the same year as his baptism (Mariscal 1990, 158). The inhabitants of Madrid had taken the Virgin of Atocha out into the streets, asking her to send rain to their parched land, but a Turkish slave looked on in ridicule and scorned those who believed that the image would bring relief from the drought (fig. 14). As the rain finally poured down, this man who had once laughed at the Virgin's power came to trust her. Like the other miracles, this Muslim also chose to convert to Christianity and be baptized, spending the rest of his life in service to the Virgin.[30] Likewise, in Fray Gabriel de Talavera's book of miracles (1597), the Virgin of Guadalupe converts individuals with an inclination towards aniconism (fig. 15). Talavera recounts how one Muslim slave refused to enter churches or look at holy images until the Virgin Mary prompted him finally to gaze up at an image of her, validating her power in front of witnesses (1597, 301v–302r). The trope of conversion becomes apparent once more as the Virgin of Guadalupe is credited with this miracle.[31]

It was not so unexpected that images would stand out as protagonists in some of these stories of miraculous conversions, since religious images had often been celebrated for their didactic efficacy, including by the twenty-fifth session of the Council of Trent (Rodríguez G. de Ceballos 2009, 21). Post-Tridentine Spanish treatise writers on the subject regularly emphasized this same point. Following the ideas of the Italian cardinal Paleotti, Jaime Prades highlights the central pedagogical role of images to instruct both learned and ignorant individuals in the Christian faith in his *Historia de la adoración y uso de las Santas Imágenes* (1596) (Franco Llopis, 2010b, 90). Likewise, in his *Arte de la pintura* (1649), Francisco Pacheco underscores the usefulness of images over the written word as an instrument to bring one to Christian devotion: "So if the words that one reads or hears are so effective, to change our reactions,

Fig. 13. Juan Ricci, *Nuestra Señora de Montserrat*, seventeenth century.

Museu de Montserrat, Barcelona
Photo Credit: Album/Art Resource, New York

Fig. 14. Juan Carreño de Miranda, *La Virgen de Atocha*, c. 1680.
Museo del Prado, Madrid

Fig. 15. Frontispiece of Gabriel de Talavera's *Historia de Nuestra Señora de Guadalupe*, 1597.

Biblioteca Nacional de España, Madrid

those figures that breathe piety, devotion, modesty, and sanctity enter us all the more forcefully" (quoted in Martínez-Burgos García 1990, 101).[32] In this same discussion on the use and authority of religious images in the Catholic Church, Pacheco also highlights the crucial role of paint-ers, since their art has the ability to persuade others to turn to God: "But speaking of Christian images, I say that the main purpose is to persuade men towards piety and bring them to God" (1649, 143).[33]

In 1623, the Spanish Jesuit Father Martín de Roa defended the use and purpose of religious images in his *Antigüedad, veneración i fruto de las sagradas imágenes, i reliquias*. He compares the five senses, conclud-ing that vision is the most appropriate for spiritual matters, since "God teaches us about invisible things through visible ones" (42r).[34] He argues that images are much more effective than the spoken word, since their meaning can be transmitted instantly to one's soul: "The ease is in the fact that because of the colours, and exterior features, in a glance [the images] transmit meaning of a thousand things to one's soul, which if only heard would take a lot longer to enter. The eyes are so capable, and have so much resemblance to understanding, that with the admi-rable swiftness of just a glance they are able to comprehend innumer-able things, which the other senses only understand little by little, with great delay" (42v–43r).[35] Even though at the start of his book he criticizes Muslims, among others, for being aniconic, some of the most striking examples that he uses to articulate his point on the efficacy of images are precisely of Muslims who are said to be affected so forcefully by what they see. He recounts how it is specifically images of the Virgin or the cross that account for the conversion of a Muslim slave near Barcelona, an African king, and an adolescent Muslim girl in Melilla, all of whom chose to convert, not necessarily because of what anyone had told them, but simply because of their encounters with Christian icons (51v–51r, 52v–54r). Perhaps for this very reason, in *Don Quixote*, Zoraida's Christian slave tells her "to go to a Christian land *to see* Lela Marién" after teaching her about the Virgin Mary (Cervantes 2003, 347; emphasis added). The church in Vélez Málaga is significantly the first stop upon her arrival in Spain, where she immediately recognizes images of Mary. The didactic function of images is further emphasized in this passage as the renegade offers Zoraida a lesson in Marian iconology before they depart.[36]

In addition to linking Muley Xeque's future conversion through the Virgin of la Cabeza with other prominent images that were also associ-ated with miracles of conversion to Christianity, the friar connects the Moroccan prince and the sacred icon in Andújar with other Marian representations through a shared historical past. As this scene reveals, many of the images that the friar describes had been hidden during the

Islamic conquest of the peninsula, for safekeeping from the new arrivals: "Because many of them are from the time that you destroyed our Christian nation in Spain, when you made Muza a Spanish Nero. The Christians buried these sovereign images in the mountains; for they feared that on their relics they would put those barbarous hands" (Vega [c. 1593–1603] 2012, vv. 1949–58).[37] While addressing Muley Xeque, he attributes the possible mistreatment of these images both to the prince himself and to other Muslims who entered the peninsula before him, situating them on the same level and distributing the blame among them. The friar continues by citing Protestants' desecration of Marian icons, significantly suggesting some continuity through the iconoclasm of Muslims in Spain and English Protestants (vv. 1959–62).

Living in sixteenth-century Spain, Muley Xeque would have witnessed other images at religious celebrations during his travels around Andalusia. On at least one occasion before his conversion, archival documents record his presence at the festival of Corpus Christi in Carmona in 1590, where he would have seen religious images (*Libro de cuentas* n.d.).[38] In Lope's play, during his lesson in Marian iconography with the friar in Andújar, Muley Xeque recalls how Father Mendoza had already taught him a considerable amount about Marian icons, particularly the Virgin of Guadalupe (Vega [c. 1593–1603] 2012, vv. 1898–9). It is likely that the ecclesiastical figure mentioned in Lope's play is Francisco Sarmiento de Mendoza, bishop in the province of Jaen (1580–95) during the time when the historical Muley al-Shaykh was in Andújar.[39] In his seventeenth-century account of the prince's conversion, Salcedo Olid records how King Philip II wrote to this bishop and charged him with the task of indoctrinating Muley al-Shaykh in the Christian faith: "His Majesty also wrote to don Francisco Sarmiento, then bishop of Jaen, ordering him to come and instruct the prince in our holy law, as he did from June 15th when he entered Andújar, where he spent two and a half months teaching him Christian doctrine, visiting him two times a day at his house, until the end of August of that year, when the Prince of Morocco departed from this city to Madrid, where he was baptized" (Salcedo Olid 1677, 293–4).[40]

Historical documents also attest to Sarmiento de Mendoza's concern for the indoctrination of the Morisco community in his diocese, many of whom had been recently expelled from Granada after the War of the Alpujarras, in addition to the appropriate use and understanding of religious images by all of the Christian men and women in his episcopate. As images became more and more prevalent in popular religiosity, the bishop took great care to rectify any deviations from the Council of Trent's prescription of their use (Martínez Rojas 2004, 413–14, 436, 489–502). Muley al-Shaykh's regular contact with this ecclesiastical figure had the potential to influence his understanding of religious images, including the Virgin of la Cabeza, which plays a key role in Lope's play. The scene revolving around the topic of Marian icons has adequately primed Muley Xeque on the subject, and prepared him finally to encounter the Virgin of la Cabeza as it is paraded around Andújar. Even the prince himself notes the change that has taken place with regard to how he understands images when the Virgin finally comes to sight, as he exclaims: "With just cause, you call her sun, moon, rose, and star. I came here to mock her and I have developed an interest in her" (Vega [c. 1593–1603] 2012, vv. 2052–5).[41] It is significantly at this moment, in the presence of the image of the Virgin, that the Moroccan protagonist converts. His transformation on stage is further stressed by the prince's retinue, incredulous that a member of the royal family would convert to Christianity (vv. 2099–121). As Almanzor observes, Muley Xeque forsook his spot on the throne in Africa to live in Spain now as a convert, trading power for humility (vv. 2187–209). Such a radical change serves only to emphasize Mary's role in conversion. Like the many narratives that credit the Virgin with the power to convert, Muley Xeque's entourage acknowledges Mary as the primary source of his religious transformation on stage.

Even though Lope de Vega's play places the image of the Virgin at the centre of Muley Xeque's conversion, the Moroccan prince himself does not leave a written testimony of the reasons for his decision to convert. As one might imagine, Arabic sources chronicling the Saadian dynasty likewise make no mention of the prince's conversion, let alone his impression of the Virgin of la Cabeza (Oliver Asín 2008, 24–5). All the details of Muley Xeque's conversion thus are filtered through the pen of Christian authors such as Lope de Vega. As scholars have shown, some of these North African princes and high-ranking officials from other Islamic lands received certain benefits after their conversion that could have prompted them to make this decision (Alonso Acero 2006, 200, 260–84; Bunes Ibarra and Alonso Acero 2006, xxxviii, lvi–lvii). Their social status was improved, and some of them even received annual salaries, among other advantages. The newly named Felipe, Juan, and Diego de Persia, for example, each received 1,200 *escudos* every year from King Philip III upon their acceptance of Christianity (Alonso Acero 2006, 265; Bunes Ibarra and Alonso Acero 2006, lvi). Moreover, in the case of Muley al-Shaykh, there is evidence that, right up until the time of his change of heart, he had been persistently asking King Philip II and the Duke of Medina Sidonia to let him go back to North Africa. These requests were consistently declined by the Spanish king, leading Bunes Ibarra and Alonso Acero to speculate that these political circumstances ultimately might have influenced the prince's decision to convert, since he was unable to return to his homeland and reclaim his sultanate (2006, xxxvi–xxxvii).

Although it might be difficult to know the true motives behind Muley al-Shaykh's conversion, including the role of the image of the Virgin of la Cabeza, a few suggestive accounts attest to the prince's attachment to religious images beyond the one in Andújar. In the biography of Trinitarian priest Simón de Roxas (about whom Lope de Vega also wrote a *comedia* titled *La niñez del Padre Roxas*, 1625), Francisco de Arcos includes details about a visit Muley Xeque made to his church in Madrid. Roxas handed the prince a printed image of the Virgin, which he kissed. Significantly, the prince also called Mary the "mother of God," a polemical epithet for many Muslims and new converts: "He gave one to the Prince of Morocco, who was at the sermon, and he received it with great reverence on his knees and said 'Father Roxas, I confess to you Father that I do not deserve this mercy and favour of the mother of God.' And kissing her and putting her on his head, he continued: 'I will put it in gold to always carry it with me'" (Arcos 1670, 205).[42] Drawing on Gianolio di Cherasco's biography of Muley al-Shaykh, Oliver Asín suggests that, in 1602, the prince made a tour of different Marian shrines in the peninsula and that he often prayed before an image of the Virgin of la Soledad. He adds that the newly converted don Felipe de África frequently visited other Marian icons, such as the celebrated Virgin of Atocha in Madrid and the Virgin of los Remedios in the Convento de la Merced Calzada (Oliver Asín 2008, 186–7). Although these details lead Asín to affirm that "the prince was undoubtedly a man of sincere Marian devotion,"[43] I believe that Muley al-Shaykh's attachment to religious images in the years leading up to the expulsion of the Moriscos is much more complex than trying to qualify the "sincerity" of one's faith (187). As a number of contemporaneous cases reveal, individual responses to sacred iconography in early modern Spain and the Mediterranean world did not necessarily confirm religious creed. As we will see in Chapter 6, sacred symbols could also act as tools to mould identity, usually at a crucial moment when an individual needed to prove his or her religious beliefs, one way or another. In any case, in his will, Muley al-Shaykh requests that, upon his death (which occurred in 1621), money be sent to three churches of strong Marian devotion to keep oil burning in their lamps, in addition to donating his collection of tapestries representing Alexander the Great to a church in Italy.[44]

Beyond Conversion

Aside from prompting the prince's conversion, the presence of the image of the Virgin of la Cabeza is what facilitates the interactions and dialogue between Muslim and Christian characters. As we have seen, all of act 2 centres on representations of Mary from a principally Christian perspective, with the friar giving Muley Xeque a lesson in Marian iconography, especially of the image in Andújar that incites the Moroccan protagonist's religious transformation. However, Muley Xeque's servant Zaide,[45] who accompanies him in his travels of southern Spain, offers a few remarks on the image and festivities from a different point of view. Zaide describes the sacred landscape and celebrates the Virgin's shrine as a shared space: "Haven't you heard of this shrine which is said to be sacred by Christians, and even Moors, so rich in a thousand treasures which they offer to it?" (Vega [c. 1593–1603] 2012, vv. 1363–6).[46] He points out that it is not only Christians who celebrate the holy image, but that, according to him, Muslims also consider the shrine to be worthy of reverence. Shortly after, Zaide also draws attention to the three "Moors" who accompany the town mayor to the pilgrimage, whether voluntarily or against their will (v. 1413). In this way, at least in Lope's work, the celebrations in honour of the Virgin of la Cabeza are, remarkably, what bring together individuals of diverse backgrounds, including the Moroccan prince himself, albeit for different motives. In a similar manner, the Italian theologian Gianolio di Cherasco also describes how many people come together in Andújar during the procession of the Virgin of la Cabeza, some for pleasure and others for interest, including "Turks, and Moors, and others, taking advantage of the opportunity to make sales of various goods" (1795, 22).[47] Thus, the image also provides a social context and motive, which is not necessarily religious, for individuals with different beliefs to convene during the April festivities.

Granadan Moriscos also gather alongside Old Christians in some scenes that reveal the popularity of the Virgin in Andújar (Vega [c. 1593–1603] 2012, vv. 1684–877). While the Virgin of la Cabeza remains the motive for their gathering, the question of images and the tensions they could provoke in the Morisco community is never mentioned. Instead, their conversations expose a collective social situation where, at least for a moment, they participate on the same level. As they wait for the Virgin to pass by, the two groups set up tents in front of each other, sing together, and share wine. Although the Moriscos are the subject of some jeering from their Old Christian neighbours, the main conflict is limited to name calling between the Morisca Celia and an anonymous Old Christian woman. Unlike other plays penned by Lope, wherein he portrays

Moriscos as iconoclasts destroying images, these Moriscos from Granada do not talk or act in any way that would suggest a rejection of religious icons.[48] Certainly, as Usandizaga highlights, the Moriscos could have been at the celebration of the Virgin of la Cabeza to feign their faith in the form of *taqiyya*, if not to pay reverence to the image (2014, 245).[49] Yet, given the lack of comments about the image and religious context of the celebrations from the Granadan Moriscos, or any of the other characters, the focus of these scenes is not so much on the power of the Virgin, as in the rest of act 2 with Muley Xeque, but rather on the popular culture surrounding her presence during the festivities. Here, Lope represents how Mary puts people of diverse backgrounds in contact with the pretext of honouring the Virgin of la Cabeza. Pilgrims have journeyed to Jaen, Ecija, Baza, Cordoba, and Granada, and so have the thieves and rogues who make an appearance and add colour to the milieu. With this cultural backdrop and the mix of characters from different social classes, Lope paints a vivid portrait of the Andalusian festival, highlighting the popularity of the Virgin, or at least the social context that she provides, among individuals with different religious identities.

Even if the image of Mary did not end up converting followers of other religions or confirming their faith, as in these last few examples from Lope's play, the mutual respect shown to Marian icons in the Mediterranean world is validated in a variety of early modern accounts. Michel de Montaigne, for example, describes the statue of a Virgin in Loreto which was accompanied by numerous ex-votos and other offerings that others had left in her honour, including a large wax candle sent by a "Turk" when he found himself in a moment of desperate need (1962, 1248). In sixteenth-century Trapani, it was not infrequent for "Turks" and "Moors" to be granted safe conduct in order to visit the statue of a highly venerated Madonna there (Arnaldi 1990, 41). Even a curious *relación de sucesos* published in 1612 and held at the Hispanic Society of America describes how one of Muley al-Shaykh's close relatives – Muley Muhammad al-Shaykh al-Ma'mun, son of Ahmad al-Mansur – relies on an image of the Virgin Mary when he falls ill. Its author narrates how the Virgin of la Caridad cured his swollen legs and the gift he sent her in return for her healing, although it did not culminate in a conversion (Serato 1612, 3v).[50] All of these accounts serve to highlight the shared cult of the Virgin, in addition to the transformative power of Marian icons.

Still, some underlying tensions around the question of images persist in Lope's play. As almost no scholar has failed to notice, the festivities in honour of the Virgin of la Cabeza that precede the Moroccan prince's conversion take place during the years before the Morisco expulsion.

Around the same time that Muley al-Shaykh arrives in Spain and decides to convert voluntarily, Moriscos already had been forcefully baptized, and were soon to be exiled from Spain. A number of scholars, especially Felipe Pedraza Jiménez, have suggested that Muley al-Shaykh commissioned Lope's play about his life as a type of "cover letter" (2012, 18),[51] which would present his merits and the authenticity of his faith as a way to gain acceptance into the dominant Catholic society of that time. This would be especially important, as the expulsion of the Moriscos was quickly approaching. There is no doubt that the content of Lope de Vega's play could have been influenced by the fact that he knew Muley al-Shaykh personally: the playwright was likely in attendance at his baptism in the Escorial, and dedicated the sonnet "Alta sangre real, claro Felipe" to him, among other connections they shared (Oliver Asín 2008, 163, 186; Pontón 2012, 797–8). However, since there are no documents specifically attesting to Muley al-Shaykh's asking Lope to write the play on his behalf, the idea that Lope used the play to promote the Moroccan prince can only be considered a hypothesis (Pontón 2012, 798). Nevertheless, aside from how this play would have positioned the prince in the Catholic culture of seventeenth-century Spain, the fact that a religious conversion – provoked by a Marian icon – was staged publicly in the years leading up to the expulsion of the Moriscos would have been significant. Despite some unsuccessful attempts to convert Moriscos, and often to require them to respect religious images, Lope's representation of the prince's transformation on stage publicly confirmed the lasting influence of Catholic symbols.

Earlier, we saw how the question of images was a thorny issue for many Morisco communities. Although they were obligated to show the sacred icons respect, some deliberately rejected them in an attempt to define and conserve their Morisco identity, which frequently resulted in their being denounced by the Inquisition. After he had spent a couple of decades in the peninsula, some of that time alongside Moriscos, it would come as no surprise to Muley al-Shaykh that religious images pervaded nearly every aspect of daily life in Spain, and that not treating them with a certain amount of reverence could put him in a precarious situation. Although the prince was not a Morisco, as a recent convert to Christianity from Islam he might have been viewed as one in the eyes of some contemporaries. With this in mind, it is worthwhile to reconsider the prince's time at the pilgrimage to the Virgin of la Cabeza and his sudden change of heart in the presence of the Marian icon, at least as it is represented in Lope's play. To a certain extent, his association with sacred icons could determine how others perceived his religious identity, especially at a time when his Morisco contemporaries were being scrutinized.

Some historical documents attest to the precarious relationship that Muley al-Shaykh forged with some Moriscos in Andalusia before his conversion to Christianity. While he was residing in Carmona, he and some Moriscos from the region began to concoct a scheme to help the prince go back to North Africa, even though Philip II was not in favour of letting Muley al-Shaykh return home. Due to the prince's disquieting contacts with the Moriscos, the king first contemplates sending him to Portugal but finally decides to transfer him to Andújar, where there was less chance he would communicate with the Moriscos in Carmona (Alonso Acero 2006, 93; Oliver Asín 2008, 92–3; Bunes Ibarra and Alonso Acero 2008, xxx–xxxi). Yet, in the years leading up to Muley al-Shaykh's arrival in Andújar, the Morisco community in this region became a great concern for Francisco Sarmiento de Mendoza, bishop in the province of Jaen. Written communication between Philip II and Sarmiento de Mendoza about the New Christians in his diocese reveal that, despite the Moriscos' apparent assimilation, the bishop believed many were just feigning their Christian beliefs. He sought to teach them Christian doctrine, and eventually requested a second edition be published of Bernardo Pérez de Chinchón's *Antialcorano* in 1595 to help indoctrinate the Morisco community in that area (Martínez Rojas 2004, 489–502). As in other regions of the peninsula, Moriscos in Andújar were also rebuked for mistreating religious images and for not believing in Mary's perpetual virginity, among other offences. María de las Parillas and Ana de Andújar, for example, were among the Moriscos accused of making fun of Christian images in Andújar (Coronas Tejada 1991, 150–2, 187, 199).

After Muley al-Shaykh converts, he begins to show concern that others might associate him with the Moriscos, something he clearly would want to avoid in the years leading up to their expulsion. In 1596, just three years after his baptism, he writes a letter to the Holy Office of the Inquisition outlining his apprehension that his offspring would be mistaken for Moriscos, even though at this point he still had no descendants. The Inquisition responds to his uneasiness without making any promises: "it seems too early for your honour to be worried about this and to try to have so many things granted, given that so little time has passed since you received the baptismal water and have knowledge about the things of our Christian religion and it would be advisable to wait until you get married to see whom you marry" (quoted in Alonso Acero 2006, 95).[52] The authorities thus want to see whom he will marry before giving any guarantees about how his future children will be considered. In this regard, it is revealing that his one eventual descendant, Josefa de África, professed as a nun at the Monastery of Saint Paul in Zamora (Oliver Asín 2008, 211). Finally, after three decades in the peninsula,

Muley al-Shaykh departs for Italy, significantly in 1609, the year in which the official decree of the expulsion of the Moriscos was put into place. Although Gianolio di Cherasco believed that the prince's decision to leave was conditioned by his desire to visit Italy because of its important Christian heritage, Oliver Asín notes that the impending Morisco expulsion was most likely the key impetus behind Muley al-Shaykh's departure from Spain (2008, 195–7).

Lope does not represent Muley al-Shaykh's concern for the Moriscos' imminent expulsion in *El bautismo del príncipe de Marruecos* (Vega [c. 1593–1603] 2012), but instead reflects a similar fear in the words of the Muslim king in *La octava maravilla* ([c. 1609] 1917), a later play that includes many echoes of the Moroccan prince, as Valdés has shown (2001, 185).[53] The fictional Tomar, supposed king of Bengala, travels to Spain to admire the Escorial, but is shipwrecked and ends up as Baltasar's slave in the first act of the play. While talking to his new master, Tomar learns that all Moriscos will soon be expelled from Spain, and is taken aback when his preconceived ideas about diverse cultures living side by side in the peninsula are contradicted:[54]

> BALTASAR: So where are you from?
> TOMAR: I'm from far away, and although I'm not from Africa, I'm a Moor.
> Are you noble?
> BALTASAR: Noble and a knight from a lineage that has its roots in those who freed Spain from the Moors.
> TOMAR: So, Spain is free of Moors?
> BALTASAR: Yes, by the force of a Saint Fernando and another one that we call the Catholic.
> TOMAR: Well they told me that among you all lived the Moors.
> BALTASAR: Those are slaves, and one day they will also leave Spain.
> TOMAR: I regret being a Moor at this time.[55] (Vega [c. 1609] 1917, 259a–b)

The thought that some Muslims had already been banished from their homes, and especially that this process was not complete, provoked an uneasy feeling in the Bengalese king. As a self-proclaimed "Moor," Tomar would also form part of these Moriscos who were soon to be exiled. Sure enough, he too, like Muley Xeque, converts to Christianity near the end of the play because of his encounter with an image, this time of the Virgin del Sagrario in Toledo (275a–b).

The conversions of both Tomar and Muley Xeque via Marian icons in light of the Morisco question show how religious images allowed these characters to mould their identities and present themselves as newly converted Christians in early modern Spain, despite the uncertain circumstances. At a time when Moriscos were on the verge of being expelled, some specifically for their objection to Catholic icons, King Tomar and Prince Muley Xeque confirm for their audience the enduring power of their sacred images. For Lope, staging the conversion of his Muslim protagonists unmistakably portrayed the triumph of Christianity over Islam. Yet, beyond just representing this victory on stage, these plays also expose how sixteenth- and seventeenth-century authors negotiated their understanding of Muslims' relation to Marian icons. Although many Moriscos and North African Muslims might have objected to the prevalence of images in everyday practice, early modern writers such as Lope suggest that the power attributed to Marian icons ultimately could have offset any aversion to figural representations by bringing the religious "other" into the Christian fold.

More broadly, Lope de Vega also considers the place of the Virgin Mary. Tracing the presence of images of the Virgin in Lope's play about Muley al-Shaykh unveils how Muslim and Christian characters of diverse backgrounds come together, suggesting that admiration of Mary transcends religious and cultural frontiers. The fictional characters ultimately demonstrate a mutual respect for Mary, or at the very least a tolerance of the feminine figure, despite their initial reactions towards images representing her. Beyond the trope of conversion, Lope de Vega and other playwrights of early modern Spain also imagined surprising ways that Marian icons mediated between Christian and Muslim cultures in other scenarios, particularly on the battlefield. In the next chapter, I turn to a variety of these plays in order to shed more light on how the public of early modern Spain tried to make sense of Muslims' precarious relationship to Marian icons in the Iberian Peninsula.

5

Images of Mary on the Battlefield

In Francisco de Quevedo's picaresque novel *El buscón* ([1626] 2012), the protagonist Pablos stumbles across a troupe of travelling actors and decides to join them on their way to Toledo. After performing a play written by one of his fellow actors, he reflects on the current state of theatre, noting that "there is no author who does not write plays nor an actor who does not perform in dramas of Moors and Christians. I remember that in the old days, the only *comedias* worth listening to were those by Lope de Vega and Ramón" (162).[1] In this passage, Pablos's reflection subtly suggests that the quality of theatre has diminished in recent years since a whole new generation has begun to write and perform plays, regardless of their skill. More important, he also emphasizes the immense popularity of the *comedias de moros y cristianos* in early modern Spain. These three-act plays staged mock battles representing Christian-Muslim encounters that ultimately celebrated Christian victories during the so-called Reconquista of the Iberian Peninsula.[2] This cycle of *comedias* emerges in response to life on the frontier, following a sequence of conquest, battle, and reconquest, and is closely tied to the local culture of the particular town or city it commemorates (Carrasco Urgoiti 1996, 67–90). Yet, because of the Virgin Mary's prominent role in many of the legends and writings about the Christian conquest of the peninsula, the role of Marian icons in both Christian and Muslim cultures is inevitably staged in a wide variety of ways in these plays. In these dramas, images of Mary often play a leading role, either by coming to the rescue of Christian troops on the battlefield or in the staged concealment of a Marian icon during the Islamic period and her later recovery during the subsequent Christian conquest.

As we saw in Chapter 4, many sixteenth- and seventeenth-century Spanish authors were aware of the important place the Virgin Mary held in both Christianity and Islam. Yet some of the same authors who showcased

Mary as a point of union between cultures represented her in a different light in these *comedias de moros y cristianos*. The images of Mary that had once incited the conversion of the Muslim prince Muley al-Shaykh and the fictional King Tomar were now on the battlefield overlooking Christian and Muslim troops during the years of the Christian conquest of the peninsula. Amy Remensnyder has drawn attention to Mary's often overlooked role as an active and bellicose conqueror, urging us to balance our perspective of Mary in interfaith relations by bearing in mind that she was characterized by different authors not only as a compassionate intermediary figure but also as a proponent of warfare (2014a; 2014b, 49). This militant version of Mary is what comes to the foreground in the dramas of Moors and Christians in early modern Spain. This portrayal becomes even more complicated when we pay attention to the pervasive visual culture, particularly the Marian icons, in many of these plays. A close analysis of some of these dramas reveals how playwrights such as Lope de Vega, Calderón de la Barca, Rojas Zorrilla, and Fajardo y Acevedo negotiated their representations of Muslim attitudes towards images of Mary on stage. Instead of resorting only to the trope of conversion, with the Virgin Mary acting as a peaceful mediator, these playwrights offered new possibilities for how to portray the role of Marian icons in the development of Christian-Muslim encounters.

In this chapter, I trace the references to visual culture in four principal *comedias de moros y cristianos* in which the Virgin Mary, and images representing her, play a prominent role in the unfolding of how Christians and Muslims interact with one another: Lope de Vega's *La divina vencedora* ([c. 1599–1603] 1993), Pedro Calderón de la Barca's *Origen, pérdida y restauración de la Virgen del Sagrario* ([c. 1616–29] 1960b), Francisco de Rojas Zorrilla's *Nuestra Señora de Atocha* ([1645] 2014), and Antonio de Fajardo y Acevedo's *Origen de Nuestra Señora de las Angustias y rebelión de los moriscos* ([1675] 2000). As all of the titles indicate, the Virgin Mary in her different advocations is the protagonist of these plays. Organized chronologically, the first three plays are set in medieval Iberia, while Fajaro y Acevedo's *comedia* builds on the traditional plot and adjusts it to the Morisco context, reflecting more pointedly how these plays showcasing Marian icons could be understood within the politics of image worship in early modern Spain. These four plays form part of a larger corpus of *comedias de moros y cristianos* that emphasizes the Virgin Mary's place on the battlefield. Aside from the plays already mentioned, a brief survey of the titles of similar dramatic works reveals the dual nature of many of these plays – that is, they show how the presence of the Virgin is intimately aligned with conquest or local identity. These plays include *La soberana Virgen de Guadalupe y sus milagros y grandezas de España* (anonymous, 1605), *La conquista de Cuenca y primer* [*sic*] *dedicación de la Virgen del Sagrario* (Pedro Rosete Niño, 1663), *Nuestra Señora de la Victoria y restauración de Málaga* (Francisco de Leiva Ramírez de Arellano, c. 1672), *La Virgen de la Fuencisla* (Sebastián Rodríguez de Villaviciosa, Juan de Matos Fragoso, and Juan de Zabaleta, 1665), *Nuestra Señora del Mar y conquista de Almería* (Juan Antonio Benavides y Zarzosa, c. 1665–1700), *Nuestra Señora de la Candelaria y sus milagros y Guanches de Tenerife* (attributed to Lope de Vega, seventeenth century), and *La perla de Cataluña o Barcelona perdida y restaurada* (anonymous, c. 1782).[3]

The four plays I focus on in this chapter are by authors whose wider oeuvres also explore Christian-Muslim relations in the Mediterranean world more broadly.[4] Each of the theatrical pieces presents a unique outlook on Mary's role on the battlefield, and, more significantly for this study, the Marian icons are given serious consideration in each play for the ways in which their presence influences how Christian and Muslim characters respond to each other. The Virgin Mary and Marian icons intervene on the battlefield, sometimes immobilizing the enemy, at other times making characters invisible to aid their escape from their captors, and yet in others Mary herself appears miraculously to take part in the action.

This characterization of Mary as a miraculous warrior also needs to be framed within the rise in miracle books that were being printed in early modern Spain. One historian has labelled this period as "the golden ages and places of miracles in Christian history" because of the proliferation of accounts of miracles in the sixteenth and seventeenth centuries (Devaney 2019, 191). Early modern historian Jerónimo de Quintana, for instance, underscored how the Virgin of Atocha alone had performed more miracles than there are "sands of the sea, stars of the sky, and atoms of the sun" (192). Pages upon pages of miracle stories were published and reprinted in early modern times, highlighting how the Virgins of Montserrat, Guadalupe, and la Peña de Francia, among many others, were attributed an immense power to work miracles (Devaney 2019). Lope de Vega, Calderón de la Barca, Rojas Zorrilla, and Fajardo y Acevedo craft their plays within this culture of Marian miracles, choosing how to portray Mary's role in influencing Christian-Muslim encounters on the battlefield.

Even though Mary/Maryam is an important figure in Islam, the idea that she could perform miracles was problematic for many Muslims living in the peninsula and the larger Mediterranean world. In the seventeenth century, for example, an ex-Morisco exiled in Tunis ridiculed the notion that an image of Mary could be miraculous. According to this anecdote, after an image in Toledo began to sweat, the archbishop suggested that the image be covered to avoid catching a cold, at which point the ex-Morisco mocked his "madness and folly" (Epalza Ferrer 1985, 518; 1999, 180).[5] Centuries earlier, Muslims in al-Andalus also had rejected miracles that were attributed to the Virgin Mary. Aḥmad ibn ʿAbd al-Ṣamad al-Khazrajī (b. 1125) of Cordoba expressed disbelief in the miracle of the Virgin Mary descending from the heavens to place a holy chasuble on Saint Ildefonso in seventh-century Toledo (Epalza Ferrer 1999, 180; Granja 1968, 354). Medieval Muslim theologians and scholars of the Qur'an had long debated whether or not Mary/Maryam could perform miracles, but despite her special status, Qur'anic commentators such as Fakhr al-Dīn al-Rāzī (d. 1210) and Abū Hāshim al-Jubbā'ī (d. 933) reject belief in miracles attributed to Maryam (Lybarger 2000, 245–6).[6] So, the plays I examine here that show how a bellicose Mary, as well as images representing her, performed miracles on the battlefield and tipped the scales in favour of the Christian troops are particularly important in offering a broad perspective. As we will see, the authors of these popular *comedias de moros y cristianos* reveal the ways in which the early modern public was grappling with how Muslims responded to images of Mary and, more broadly, Mary's place between Christian and Muslim cultures.

Setting the Stage: Performing Conquest

Lope de Vega's play *La divina vencedora* ([c. 1599–1603] 1993) is an early example of the *comedias de moros y cristianos* that highlights the Virgin Mary's role on the battlefield. The action takes place in the middle of the thirteenth century, during Fernando III's military campaigns in Morón de la Frontera, and stars the Christian hero Meledón Rodríguez Gallinato, who relies on the divine intervention of the Virgin Mary to defeat the Muslim army and claim the castle of Chincoya at the end of the drama. The play stages Christian-Muslim skirmishes on the frontier, one of which even ends in friendship between the Christian knight Gallinato and the noble Muslim Cardiloro, thus recalling a similar alliance to that in *El Abencerraje y la hermosa Jarifa* (1560s) between Rodrigo de Narváez and Abindarráez.[7] In all other cases, Gallinato defeats his rivals, demands respect from his subjects, and captivates Muslim women through his position of power. However, amid a number of battles, disguises, and amorous affairs, Lope reveals that the true protagonist of the play is the Virgin Mary embodied in a Marian icon – the *divina vencedora*, or divine conqueror – who ultimately determines the fate of this military campaign in favour of the Christians.

The Virgin Mary's intervention is not fortuitous but, rather, depends on a type of *quid pro quo* in which Gallinato first rescues a Marian icon

to later petition for her support. In act 2, the named hero quarrels with
Zarabo, who is determined to burn an image of the Virgin Mary. Their
argument erupts into an impassioned altercation, ending with Zarabo's
death and Gallinato's saving the Marian icon from the flames. At the
end of the *comedia*, when three thousand Muslims are pitted against a
mere thirty-two Christians in the final battle for the castle of Chincoya,
Gallinato reminds the Virgin that he previously saved her from harm,
imploring that she now help the Christian army:

> Virgin of the Fortress, Lady,
> that I rescued from Granada
> captive among Muslim people!
> Lift up the sword also,
> fight, protect me now!
> Did I not take you out of captivity?
> Well, free me from captivity!
> Your image, is it not alive?
> Help me as long as I live![8]
> (Vega ([c. 1599–1603] 1993, 867)

As the same image that was rescued earlier by Gallinato is placed atop the
fortress, the king of Granada recognizes her as the "Mother of Christ,"
prompting the Muslim army to retreat and concede the victory to Gallinato's troops (870).[9]

In addition to staging the Virgin Mary's intervention in the battle, the
Marian icon also conquers the hearts of her rivals through religious conversion. In this sense, Lope's play represents the importance of visual
culture in Catholic practice, since the text suggests that the Marian
image is capable of prompting the conversion of the Muslim characters
on stage. This is most evident in act 2, when Gallinato gives his two Muslim captives, Zulema and Fátima, a wood box without revealing its hidden contents. Overcome by their curiosity, Zulema and Fátima open the
box and discover an image of the Virgin Mary, which instantly triggers
their conversion to Christianity. Zulema exclaims: "A Lady./For Muhammad's sake, wonderful encounter!/Everything trembles while looking at
her!/.../It seems that by looking/I have taken a liking to her" (829).[10]
The moment in which this conversion takes place is important, since the
two Muslim captives were fleeing a rather precarious and abusive situation that included being held as sexual victims by their Christian slave
owner, Gallinato. Despite these difficult circumstances, the image's aura
overwhelms them, inciting their conversion to Christianity. But did the
captives have any other choice than to convert? The two women had

just come face to face with Gallinato, the main source of their misfortunes, leading Zulema and Fátima to a dead end where Fátima herself
suggested obeying her master and returning to their miserable past life.
Their conversion was thus conditioned by their desperate situation, especially since the conversion generated compassion from their persecu-
tors. This same image sets in motion a series of miraculous conversions
as it overlooks the battlefield during the final conflict and influences the
combat in favour of the Christian troops. Among the new converts, the
noble Muslim, Cardiloro, surrenders to the Virgin and joins his comrades in praising Mary's everlasting power.

In contrast to the conversions incited by Marian icons discussed in the
previous chapter, the Mary of *La divina vencedora* shows another side to
the role of iconography of the Virgin in Christian-Muslim encounters.
As we saw in that chapter, the Muslim characters' religious transforma-
tions in those plays highlighted how images of Mary allowed these converts to mould their identities in the years surrounding the expulsion of
the Moriscos, while at the same time showcasing the miraculous power
of Marian icons to convert the "other," despite this group's alleged
tendency to reject figural representations. In *La divina vencedora*, as in
other dramas of Moors and Christians, religious conversions take place
on the battlefield in frontier zones straddling Muslim and Christian cultures, and they must be understood within this context. The conversions
usually presuppose the existence of victors and vanquished, and the
conversion usually occurs at the time of surrender. This position of dis-
advantage occupied by the defeated is reversed to some extent through
their conversion, which also represents the triumph of Christianity over
Islam. Tarife, the heir to the throne of the kingdom of Toledo in Lope's
El alcaide de Madrid ([1599] 1993), emphasizes this point. This Muslim
character finally converts to Christianity precisely after he is defeated
in a battle in which the Virgin of Atocha joins the Christian side, even
though he had already shown respect for a Marian icon beforehand,
when he was not in such a precarious situation (82, 99).

Many of the dramas of Moors and Christians also stage the concealment and later discovery of an image of the Virgin, usually tied to the
local culture of a particular city.[11] These plays typically juxtapose two
historical moments, beginning with the Visigoths' safe harbouring of a
Marian icon to protect it from profanation and ending with a shepherd's
unearthing of the image in the years following the Christian conquest.
Thus, the trajectory of the image weaves together a certain unity in the
plot of each theatrical piece (Carrasco Urgoiti 1996, 56, 60–1). In an
early example of this genre, the anonymous *La soberana Virgen de Guadalupe y sus milagros y grandezas de España* ([1605] 1970) recounts the

apparition of the Virgin of Guadalupe to a shepherd in Caceres, Spain, followed by the discovery of her image in a cave.[12] According to the legend, some Visigoth priests fled Seville with the image of the Virgin of Guadalupe after Muslims populated their territory. They hid the image with a bell and letter explaining her origin in the sierra of Guadalupe, where it remained for six centuries. It was not until the beginning of the fourteenth century, when the Virgin appeared to a shepherd out looking for his lost cow, that she revealed to him where to find the concealed icon (Crémoux 2000, 477–8; Christian 1981a, 88–93). Although the short drama loosely follows the legend, it also incorporates new miracles in what seems to be an attempt to make the tale more convincing (Crémoux 2000, 480).

The drama draws a number of parallels throughout that underscore the significance of the Virgin Mary and her image. At the start of the play, the strong Visigoth woman named Rosimunda refuses an offer to convert to Islam and marry a Muslim in exchange for her freedom, even though her husband Alarico has chosen to flee with the image of the Virgin to protect it, instead of his wife, from harm. Rosimunda appeals to the Virgin for help, and the Virgin miraculously makes Rosimunda invisible and allows her to free herself from her Muslim captors. Rosimunda's concealment from her supposed enemies foreshadows and parallels the Virgin's occultation from Muslim conquerors. Alarico and other Visigoths decide to hide the Virgin in the mountains to save her from the Muslims, with the hope that, in the future, when Spain becomes Christian again, the image could be recovered. Rosimunda's story ends here, but the Virgin herself later appears to a shepherd to show him where to find her image. Consequently, the Virgin drives the action of the play through her power to conceal and reveal.

The author of the play also hints at the parallel between the recovery of the image of the Virgin and the restoration of Spain as a Christian nation. The dialogue among the Visigoth characters marks a before and after for the Virgin that mirrors that of Spain. Through various references to exile in the Old and New Testaments, Teodoredo and Alarico suggest that once Spain returns to its former glory, so too will the Virgin emerge from her refuge. Thus, they hide the image of the Virgin of Guadalupe in the hope that the icon will come to light once Christian Spain is restored. The renewal of Spain is also represented through the shepherd's son, Francisco, who is miraculously resurrected by the Virgin's intervention. The last words he speaks in the play extol Mary's restorative power. With his phrase, "I am, Lady, who I was/and who, because of you, I will be again," and a reference to his own death and subsequent return to life, a clear parallel is drawn between the figure of the child and the loss and subsequent recovery of Christian Spain ([1605] 1970, 2005).[13] A return to origins takes place due to the intervention of the Virgin and her healing and supernatural powers. Despite the brevity and coarseness of *La soberana Virgen de Guadalupe*, these parallels draw attention to the continuity and influence of the cult of the Virgin through the staged concealment and discovery of the Marian icon, suggesting that Spain had and would continue to have a Christian heritage.

Visual sources also capture legendary moments related to the concealment and subsequent miraculous discovery of Marian icons in the Iberian Peninsula. This is the subject of Francisco de Zurbarán's painting *Saint Peter Nolasco Recovering the Image of the Virgin of El Puig* (1630), which illustrates how Saint Peter Nolasco, founder of the Mercedarian

Fig. 16. Francisco de Zurbarán, *Saint Peter Nolasco Recovering the Image of the Virgin of El Puig*, 1630.

Cincinnati Art Museum, Cincinnati
Photo credit: © Cincinnati Art Museum / Bridgeman Images

Order, discovered a highly regarded stone relief of the Virgin and Child in the thirteenth century (fig. 16). According to legend, it had been hidden alongside a Christian bell to protect it from Muslims, and only came to light just outside of Valencia in the hillside of El Puig when the Spanish village was being reconquered (Long 2009, 274; Baticle 1987, 109–11). Zurbarán significantly positions the relief of the Virgin of El Puig in the centre of the canvas, in the presence of Saint Peter Nolasco, who is clothed in the white robe of the Mercedarian Order, and King James I of Aragon, who is positioned to the right of the buried image. By foregrounding the Virgin closest to the viewer and by painting a fortress in the landscape that calls to mind the previously Islamic castle of El Puig, Zurbarán suggests that the period of Muslim domination of the Iberian Peninsula is just a distant memory, ushering in a renewed significance of the Virgin and the continuity of her cult in Catholic Spain.[14] These initial examples help set the stage and provide a blueprint for understanding the significance of Marian icons in the popular *comedias de moros y cristianos* that I explore throughout the rest of this chapter.

Buried Treasures

In the textual and visual sources recounting the legends of the Virgin of Guadalupe and the Virgin of El Puig discussed above, the concealed Marian icons are discovered by individuals of Christian heritage. This follows the common narrative of discovery of these hidden religious images in which a Christian, oftentimes a shepherd, unearths the object of devotion (Irigoyen-García 2014, 85–9).[15] Early modern authors who staged these discoveries in their plays also tended to adhere to this pattern, attributing the revelation of Marian images to Christian characters.[16] Calderón de la Barca's early play *Origen, pérdida y restauración de la Virgen del Sagrario* ([c. 1616–29] 1960b) provides a curious exception, since the playwright attributes the recovery of a concealed Marian icon to a Muslim character.[17] His *comedia* tells the story of the conquest and reconquest of the city of Toledo alongside the image of the patron saint of that city, the Virgin del Sagrario, which, according to legend, was hidden during the Muslim conquest and later miraculously reappeared when Toledo was under Christian rule. Each act in the drama corresponds to a different historical moment: the Visigoths' reign in Toledo, the Islamic period of the city, and the ensuing Christian conquest under King Alfonso VI. Despite the large temporal gaps between each act, Mary's presence on stage, embodied in the image of the Virgin del Sagrario, gives unity and meaning to the plot of the *comedia*.[18]

From the start of the play, the image of the Virgin del Sagrario is defined vis-à-vis the "other." While in the first act the description of the Marian icon is juxtaposed with Christian Visigoths and their iconoclast neighbours, in the following two acts Mary's image is characterized in relation to Christian-Muslim encounters. At the same time that the Visigoths' antagonists oppose religious imagery, Calderón draws a parallel by representing Muslims as aniconic characters in terms of figural representations of the Virgin Mary. Near the end of the first act, the alleged "heretics" Pelagio and Teudio plan to break the image into pieces by throwing it into a well. After plotting how to desecrate this religious representation, Teudio announces how this iconoclastic act would increase his honour, even though he never follows through with his scheme due to the Christian Visigoths' untimely arrival on the scene (Calderón de la Barca ([c. 1616–29] 1960b, 580b). During the Islamic rule of Toledo, the Christian characters fear that Muslims will defile the image, so they carefully bury the Virgin del Sagrario in a well. Calderón compares the situation of the Virgin del Sagrario to several passages from the Old Testament in which a precarious situation leads to a happy ending, equating the suffering and subsequent liberation of biblical characters with what he hopes will be the outcome for Toledo's Marian icon. Among the examples offered by the playwright, Queen Esther stands out as a woman who, despite being forced into a marriage of convenience, became queen and was able to save her family from exile. Likewise, the example of the exodus of the people of Israel, who after forty years of suffering finally managed to reach the Promised Land, offers a strong parallel for the subject of Calderón's play. The author thus suggests that the Virgin del Sagrario, although facing irremediable "captivity" during the years she is concealed in the well, will gain spiritual value because of these difficult circumstances (588b–89b).

As the image of the Virgin is defined in relation to the "other," the emerging character of the Virgin highlights her protective nature. Contrary to the Marian icon in Lope's *La divina vencedora*, who is physically present on the battlefield and lends a hand to the Christian troops, the Virgin del Sagrario in Calderón's play is portrayed more as a defender of the Catholic faith. In fact, Pelagio, one of the alleged heretics who intended to throw the image of the Virgin into a well, planned to do so precisely because of the image's power to defend Christianity. He describes the Virgin as a wall or fortress without which the Catholic faith in Spain would be neglected, thus imbuing the Virgin with both bellicose and spiritual attributes (580a). This defence of the Catholic faith can also be seen when the image refuses to abandon its Toledan countrymen in the face of advancing Muslim troops. While the Christian Visigoths try to safeguard religious images, taking them out of the city, the Virgin del Sagrario miraculously immobilizes Urbano so he cannot leave Toledo with her, since she does not want to abandon her followers (Calderón de la Barca [c. 1616–29] 1960b, 586a). The Marian icon thus acquires a special significance because it remains present, albeit dormant, in the bowels of the temple, hidden to preserve it from enemy hands.

Alongside the Virgin del Sagrario, Queen Constanza – the only other female character in the *comedia* – also adopts the role of leader and defender of the Catholic faith. Personified as a replica of the Virgin's own figure, Constanza takes on the position of guarding and protecting Christianity from its rivals. She appears on the scene defying the orders of King Alfonso VI and clearly resolved to recover what was once Toledo's most revered image. Constanza herself, in fact, proposes and instigates the assault on the mosque, becoming leader and spiritual inspiration, even for the Archbishop Bernardo de Sédirac. When the king learns that his wife has undermined his mandate allowing Muslims to continue practising their faith in the mosque of Toledo, Constanza is transformed into a character willing to become a martyr for her faith, as a consequence of her audacity in contradicting her husband. The affinity between the queen and the Virgin del Sagrario does not seem fortuitous, since Calderón accentuates the divine light that emanates from Constanza – the same light associated with the image of the Virgin throughout the play. The queen's radiant presence ultimately has a miraculous effect on the king, rousing him to change his mind and join his wife in the defence of the sacred space.

In addition to the visually significant Virgin del Sagrario, iconographic signs begin to multiply as Toledo moves from Visigoth to Muslim rule. Various characters substitute the symbol of the crescent moon for that of the cross, alongside the architectural conversion of the city. As Aben Tarif addresses the city of Toledo, he threatens to take the temple by force if it is not otherwise handed over to him, crowning the place of worship with symbols of the crescent moon as his way of appropriating the space (Calderón de la Barca [c. 1616–29] 1960b, 583b).[19] Later, in the last act, the audience witnesses the transformation of the great mosque into a church. Although King Alfonso VI promises Selín that the Muslims of Toledo can keep the best mosque for themselves, Queen Constanza has another view of how the city should stand. When she recalls how the Virgin del Sagrario was safeguarded and tucked away in some niche of this sacred space, she regrets her husband's promise to Selín and decides to take control of the situation. Constanza is determined to recover not only the religious space, but especially the Virgin del Sagrario that she believes is hidden within the mosque's confines (593b). The discovery of images, as Antonio Urquízar-Herrera suggests, was tied intimately to memories of the Christian conquest and to the "textual appropriation" of previously Muslim buildings. The sequence of loss and recovery of these images became a trope that helped legitimize Christianity's stake in these architectural spaces (Urquízar-Herrera 2017, 143). In Calderón's play, the visual reference of the concealed Virgin del Sagrario within the architectural remains allows Queen Constanza to assert her authority over the mosque and appropriate the Islamic space, emphasizing its continued Christian heritage by virtue of the Marian icon.[20]

With the mosque once again converted into a church, the Muslim Selín remembers his own version of this story, in which there is a treasure hidden within the confines of this newly converted space. This evokes another series of legends of the "treasure of the Moor," the folklore of Muslims' buried treasure in Spain. As José María Perceval explains, many of these tales of hidden treasure were an invention based on the alleged riches that the Morisco community clandestinely amassed and concealed underground. These legends, which became fixed in the collective imaginary, painted Moriscos unfavourably as greedy forgers of counterfeit money, a portrayal that would be used in anti-Morisco literature to help justify their expulsion from Spain (1987, 175–9).[21] In Calderón's play, as Selín laments the loss of the mosque, he reveals that he mourns this defeat not necessarily because he has had to relinquish his community's place of worship, but because he is forced to surrender the "enchanted treasure" hidden inside the temple (Calderón de la Barca [c. 1616–29] 1960b, 595b).[22] Giving credence to his account, King Alfonso VI implicitly associates Selín with these legends of buried treasure, fearing that "Moorish sorcerers" will seek retribution (599a).[23]

In addition to these negative stereotypes of Muslims and their purported craving for riches, François Delpech shows how these legends of buried treasure were sustained by fear that the Muslims who had previously controlled the territory would return to occupy these spaces. In contexts other than post-expulsion Spain, these types of legends were articulated through the existence of a supernatural entity, or referenced a time so distant that they did not fan any historical flame. By contrast, the Spanish case recovered an element that remained alive in the collective memory, and reactivated the fear of the possible return of Muslims to Spain (Delpech 2002, 568).[24] Yet, in *Origen, pérdida y restauración de la Virgen del Sagrario*, when Selín lowers himself into the cave to retrieve the treasure, he encounters an image of Mary holding her son. This surprise discovery of the Marian icon instead of buried riches suggests that the Islamic past that Selín seeks to recover has been erased from the collective memory. Although we might briefly consider that Selín's finding the image of the Virgin Mary evokes a shared past in which the Virgin Mary/ Maryam united Christian and Muslim cultures, this interpretation of his discovery of this object of devotion is complicated by the religious conversion provoked by the icon at the end of the play. Selín's conversion to Christianity after beholding the image, which he does not realize is a simulacrum of the Virgin Mary, more likely reflects Calderón's staging of the triumph of Christianity over Islam for his audience. Furthermore, by substituting the Virgin del Sagrario for the "treasure of the Moor" and expunging the memory of an Islamic past, Calderón emphasizes the continuity of Christianity in the Iberian Peninsula.

As I have already suggested, one unexpected aspect of Calderón's rendering of the legend of the Virgin del Sagrario's origin is that he attributes the recovery of the image to a Muslim. In the *comedia*, Archbishop Bernardo de Sédirac first hears a voice, revealing that there is a treasure hidden in the well, but Selín is the one who finally goes underground and discovers that the treasure is in fact the Virgin del Sagrario (Calderón de la Barca [c. 1616–29] 1960b, 596a, 599a–600b). Selín offers a long *descriptio puellae* of the female icon, realizing only at the end that the woman he is describing is actually the Virgin Mary (600a-b). As he emphasizes her supernatural beauty and extraordinary luminosity, juxtaposing her blonde hair with the dark colour of her face and hands, he is finally overcome by her splendour and decides to convert to Christianity.

In the other textual and visual sources that treat the discovery of the Virgin del Sagrario, there is no mention of Selín or any similar Muslim individual in the recuperation of the image. Some sources suggest that Archbishop don Rodrigo Jiménez de Rada found the Marian icon between 1215 and 1225 as the foundation was being laid for a new cathedral in Toledo, but medieval and early modern authors had no fixed consensus on the image's "inventor" (Moreno Nieto 1995, 42). As Elena E. Marcello (2004) has shown, Calderón drew on José de Valdivielso's poem *Sagrario de Toledo* (1616b) and his *Auto de la descensión de Nuestra Señora* ([1616a] 1983), especially for the first two acts, and on Rodrigo Jiménez de Rada's *Historia de los hechos de España* (*Historia de rebus Hispaniae*) ([c. 1243] 1989), particularly for the last act (Marcello 2004). Valdivielso's poem opposes the idea that the archbishop might have found the image, and hints instead that it was a shepherd, but his *Auto* is silent on this question (Valdivielso 1616b, 404r). Rodrigo Jiménez de Rada, on the other hand, dedicates a few chapters to the siege and conquest of Toledo and the subsequent transformation of the mosque into a cathedral, but does not include details about the discovery of the Virgin del Sagrario (1989, 247–52). Apart from these sources, in some of the poetry composed for a *certamen* (literary contest) celebrated in 1616 in honour of the restoration of the chapel for the Virgin del Sagrario, early modern poets competed with verses commemorating the Marian icon (Herrera 1617).[25] One octave penned by Luis de Góngora, "Era la noche, en vez del manto escuro," attributes the discovery of the image to an anonymous shepherd, as do other poets in the same literary competition (Herrera 1617, 41r). Finally, the visual sources depicting the iconography of the Virgin del Sagrario tend to focus more on the Virgin's descent to the church of Toledo to offer a divine chasuble to the Visigoth Archbishop Saint Ildefonso and, as far as I am aware, do not illustrate the moment of discovery of the image (Cavero de Carondelet 2019).

Early modern writers, as Javier Irigoyen-García has argued, "rewrote medieval legends of Marian apparitions so that the ethnicity of the foundational shepherd could be significant for the community of believers, linking his ethnicity to both the iconography of the Nativity and the myths of the *reconquest*" (2014, 89). In Calderón's play, instead of a Marian apparition, it is an image of her that Selín encounters. Given the tradition of shepherds – or at least Old Christians – as the protagonists in encountering these hidden Marian icons, it is suggestive that Calderón rewrites the legend of the Virgin del Sagrario in a way that initially might seem to *include* Muslims, especially since the *comedia* was composed in the years following the expulsion of the Moriscos from Spain. Given the contested accounts surrounding the Virgin del Sagrario's discovery, why does Calderón attribute the unearthing of the image to a fictional Muslim character whom he constructs in his play? The key is in Selín's description of the Virgin at the end of the play. It is striking that, in a play in which the protagonist is precisely the Virgin del Sagrario, the author waits until the end to offer a physical description of her and, above all, that this portrayal comes from Selín. This detailed Marian ekphrasis portrayed through the eyes of the defeated Muslim character further embellishes the Christian victory, and establishes a legitimacy in terms of the occupation of space, which is marked when Selín himself describes the ruins of the ancient Visigoths in the foundation of the temple. Following his description of the Marian icon, Selín prostrates himself before the king, surrendering to earthly authority in addition to the celestial with his impending baptism. The end of the drama is silent about Selín's whereabouts and the place of the Islamic legacy in the peninsula, although in Calderón de la Barca's Spain, the audience was already aware of the outcome and the tragic expulsion of the Moriscos.

Captive Portraits, Sacred and Profane

In Francisco de Rojas Zorrilla's *comedia* of Moors and Christians titled *Nuestra Señora de Atocha* ([1645] 2014), portraits of lovers and the Virgin

Mary take centre stage as they are taken hostage and exchanged multiple times. As the title suggests, his play stages the legend of the Virgin of Atocha, arguably one of the most important Marian icons in Hapsburg Madrid, rivalled only by the Virgin of Almudena.[26] As expected in this genre of drama, the play is set in medieval Iberia and presents Christian-Muslim encounters on the frontier, culminating with a final battle in favour of the Christian troops as a result of the Virgin's divine intervention. In this way, the unifying thread and main objective of the *comedia* is to celebrate the much-revered image of the Virgin of Atocha and her continued legacy in early modern Spain. Unlike the majority of other dramas of Moors and Christians in which the descriptions of visual culture principally highlight the influence of the Virgin on the battlefield, Rojas's play is unique in that it also narrates a parallel story featuring the fictional account of lovers that materializes in the desire and exchange of painted portraits. The playwright juxtaposes sacred and profane as portraits of the Virgin circulate alongside those of another woman. The portraits are at times even mistaken for each other, placing Christian and Muslim characters in contact with one another throughout the play. In this sense, Rojas's *comedia*, rich in artistic terms, can also be read as what Laura R. Bass has termed a "drama of the portrait" – plays that are part of an "age-old preoccupation with the powers, pleasures, and perils of the human simulacrum" (2008, 1).[27] The abutment of divine and human portraits in *Nuestra Señora de Atocha* invites us to ask what the circulation of these visual representations on stage can tell us about the intersection of religious art and interfaith encounters in early modern Spain.

The Marian icon in Rojas's *comedia* evokes some of the iconography of the Virgin of Atocha that depicts her as protector and defender of the city of Madrid. One of the treatises on the Virgin of Atocha written only a couple of years before Rojas's play and likely an influence on it is Jerónimo de Quintana's *Historia del origen y antigüedad de la imagen de Nuestra Señora de Atocha* (1637). The front page of this text depicts the Marian image atop Madrid's coat of arms, showing her as guardian of the city. Between this image and the escutcheon below her feet, a banner announces "by the protection of Mary shall you conquer," making Mary's bellicose character more explicit.[28] Jeffrey Schrader has linked this inscription with Constantine the Great, the first Christian emperor, who, before fighting in the Battle of Milvian, saw a vision in the heavens with a strikingly similar message: "By this sign shall you conquer" (2011, 501–2). Other iconography of the Virgin of Atocha on the front pages of treatises by Jerónimo de Quintana and Gil González de Ávila emphasizes these same attributes. In these cases, the engravers represent the Virgin at the top of the page, crowning the shield of the city, which suggests the Marian icon in her protective role, sheltering and defending the citizens of Madrid (Civil 1998, 36–41). Indeed, the Virgin of Atocha had long been tied to this warrior mentality. A number of legends recount her miraculous victories against Muslim armies, although it is difficult to know if these accounts emerged at the time of her triumphs on the battlefield or if they were constructed later (Schrader 2006, 28–9). In Rojas's work, after the image of the Virgin of Atocha is miraculously recovered, it joins Gracián Ramírez in battle to protect the city, and he declares her patron of Madrid ([1645] 2014, 2:vv. 2480–500).

Despite the obvious antagonisms based on superficial stereotypes and the combative nature of the Virgin that is manifested throughout the play, Rojas also shows that material objects, including portraits and effigies of the Virgin Mary, mediated between cultures and could be used for sacred or profane purposes. At the start of the *comedia*, Rosa, a Moorish princess and one of the leading characters, is infatuated with her captive, the gallant Christian don Fernando. He reveals that he is enamoured not only of one lady but of two – neither of whom is Rosa – and he intends to show her a portrait of his beloved Leonor, but mistakenly takes out a small painting of the Virgin Mary, based on the statue of Our Lady of Atocha. This error allows him to declare his love for the Madonna and explain the origin of the Marian icon, how she allegedly arrived in Iberia, and how she was concealed during the Islamic conquest and is still waiting to be restored to her former glory. As we saw in Chapter 2, many Moriscos criticized the conflation of the religious object with what it represented; similarly, Rosa does not understand how a simple piece of wood could be turned into a divine image. Her debate with don Fernando shows that it is not necessarily theological differences that separate the two characters, but a misunderstanding of the role of religious images in Catholic practice (Rojas [1645] 2014, 1:vv. 521–69). Although the sacred portrait holds little value for Rosa personally, she demands to keep the painting of Mary as a hostage, treating the canvas as if it were a human being. In a bizarre inversion of the *Abencerraje* story, the captive don Fernando pleads with his Muslim master, Rosa, for his freedom to go see his dear Leonor as long as he promises to return in a few days. Rosa expects that holding the portrait captive will guarantee his return, exposing another secular use for divine portraits. Don Fernando finally offers the portrait of Leonor in place of that of the Virgin, stating that, if he has the "original," he does not need the "copy."

Celín, Rosa's brother and the fictional king of Toledo in Rojas's play, also unveils the mediating role of images, treating them as a commodity to get what he wants instead of for their intended purpose. In this case, the captive portrait is one of Leonor, and Celín uses it to unleash desire and jealousy in other characters on stage. When Rosa realizes that her plan to get don Fernando to return has gone awry, she gives the hostage portrait of Leonor to Celín, believing that the woman's painted likeness will provoke more passion in the hands of a man. Indeed, rivals don Fernando and García, overwhelmed with envy, fight over the portrait (Rojas [1645] 2014, 2:vv. 1442–639). The portraits in Rojas's *comedia* are much more than just the painted simulacrum of Leonor, but could be better labelled as what Mercedes Alcalá Galán has called "erographies" because of their magnified capacity to seduce (2009, 105).[29] Due to the portrait's power to awaken desire, Celín is able to use the painting to lure his rivals in an attempt to capture them (3:vv. 2635–722). Celín himself is also overcome by these emotions, and seems to forget what led him to attract the attention of Fernando and García. Leaving aside his plan to capture them, he engages in a confrontation with Leonor's other suitors to decide who is the rightful owner of Leonor's painting and love.

Finally, when the outcome of the battle reverses the positions of Fernando and Rosa, Leonor's portrait acquires a renewed importance and plays a fundamental role in the interrelations among the characters. While Rosa gave don Fernando his freedom at the beginning of the drama, in the end it is don Fernando who helps rescue Rosa and Celín after the battle, in payment for his liberation. This gesture causes an outburst of gratitude in Celín, who feels obliged to return Leonor's painting to its owner, thus granting don Fernando the legitimate right to possess Leonor. This exchange of portraits among the characters entails an intangible benefit for all three: don Fernando, now free, can possess Leonor; Rosa can take revenge on García by not allowing him to retain the portrait; and Celín is now characterized in a more positive light because of his noble act in surrendering the portrait. This series of events is the culmination of a relationship among the characters that has always been articulated around material culture. Leonor's portrait and its circulation from one individual to another throughout the drama conditions the relationships among comrades and rivals, especially because of the desire that it arouses in the characters, provoking different outcomes (Rojas [1645] 2014, 3:vv. 3437–62).

As these last examples show, these portraits in motion acquire many more uses than those they were intended to perform. They exude human attributes, acting as a hostage, inciting jealousy and passion, and functioning as a surety, among other purposes. These multiple uses of portraits beyond their original purpose reveal the material exchanges that bring Christians and Muslims into dialogue on stage, despite their supposed animosity.

Setting aside some of the anachronisms and fictional inventions in *Nuestra Señora de Atocha*, the notion that material culture crossed cultural and religious boundaries is what most reflects the complex world of the early modern Mediterranean, whether or not this was the intention of the playwright. Lisa Jardine and Jerry Brotton have argued that the boundaries between East and West were "thoroughly permeable," revealing how portrait medals, tapestries, and equestrian art, among other objects of material culture, circulated beyond prevailing geographical and ideological divisions, even in moments of contention (2000, 8). These articles could incite "mutually recognizable readings" among all the actors involved, regardless of the location of these encounters (132). In Rojas's play, it would be difficult to ignore that it is precisely the religious material culture that produces moments of discord in the background details of the plot. Celín casually mentions to his sister Rosa that he has desecrated Marian icons in some twenty temples, and Leonor laments the damage done to a burned effigy of the Virgin and Son (Rojas [1645] 2014, 2:vv. 1329–30, vv. 1917–30). However, this is not the principal argument of the drama. Rojas's focus on the circulation of portraits, artistic questions of copy versus original, and sacred and divine art, with the Virgin of Atocha always at the centre, illuminates some moments of a shared material culture where the characters' emotions and values are more alike than some other early modern works on this Marian icon suggest.

The circulation of material culture in *Nuestra Señora de Atocha* evinces some compelling parallels between Leonor and the Virgin, in addition to demonstrating Rojas's presentation of the role of images in Christian-Muslim relations. Although they are two different paintings – human and divine – both portraits arouse similar emotions of awe in the beholder. When don Fernando unintentionally gives Rosa the portrait of the Virgin, she is overwhelmed by her own reaction and, perspiring, questions how the painting could provoke such a sense of astonishment (Rojas [1645] 2014, 1:vv. 611–15). Acknowledging don Fernando's mishap, Rosa recognizes that the portrait is a visual copy of the Virgin de Atocha, despite her ignorance of Marian icons in Catholic practice. Celín is also enraptured by the visual culture. He swiftly falls in love with Leonor by virtue of her portrait, unleashing an uncontrollable desire to possess the "original" (2:vv. 1551–639). The vocabulary the characters employ to describe their love for each painted woman criss-crosses between spiritual and sensual registers, further emphasizing the fusion between Leonor and the Virgin. As such, before don Fernando confesses to Rosa his feelings of passionate love for the Virgin, his servant Limonada describes his master's affection for the "dark-skinned" woman, referring to the colour of the Virgin of Atocha, and characterizes him as "abarraganado," implying that he has a carnal relationship with the Virgin out of wedlock (1:vv. 176–80).[30] On the contrary, Celín describes the portrait of Leonor as a "lost relic," elevating the figure of the human woman to a sacred sphere (2:v. 1516).[31]

These parallels between the Virgin and Leonor, between heavenly and earthly, suggest that the portraits are what fuel the action on stage, even if at times the circulation of material culture seems to overshadow the significance of the legend of the Virgin of Atocha. While Leonor's portrait stages the human relationships, the visual representations of Mary act to find a solution to these conflicts and to dignify her revered status, especially as a patron of the city of Madrid (Suárez Miramón 2009, 713). By juxtaposing the circulation and exchange of human and divine portraits, the *comedia* also invites the public to consider how the portrait of Leonor functions as a mirror of the Marian representations. Given the parallels between sacred and profane, and the fact that don Fernando views Celín as a potential "good" Christian, we could interpret the passion that Leonor's painting arouses in Celín in religious terms, correlating to what the image of the Virgin would have incited in its devotees. The fusion that occurs between devotional and romantic love helps to explain Rojas's characterization of Celín and his possible conversion to Christianity, precisely because Celín has been seduced by Leonor's portrait, the mirror image of the Virgin. Through this analogy, the author also manages to simplify the complexity involved in the conception of the divine image, staged in the work with the heated theological discussion held between Rosa and Fernando (Rojas [1645] 2014, 1:vv. 521–70). This comparison between divine and human image reveals some of the nuances involved in the worship of a divinity through a representation of its likeness, while also giving us some clues about the implications of the senses this devotional image can awaken in others, especially in enigmatic characters defined by their in-betweenness.

The descriptions and movements of the material culture in *Nuestra Señora de Atocha* shed light on some of the intricacies of interfaith relations in early modern Spain. Despite the palpable differences evident when the Christian characters are placed side by side with their Muslim counterparts, a close reading of the drama exposes that they ultimately share some of the same emotions and values. Still, it is undeniable that Rojas's *comedia* belongs to a series of other early modern texts on the Virgin of Atocha that show how her status is, in part, defined in contrast with the religious "other." Playwrights, poets, and religious and historical writers showcased both this revered status and the Marian icon's following in Madrid in the years leading up to Rojas's publication of this play.[32] These authors, including Lope de Vega, Salas Barbadillo, Francisco de Pereda, and Jerónimo de Quintana, highlight how the Virgin of

Atocha was hidden from Muslim conquerors during the Islamic period and restored during the Christian conquest.[33] In fact, "rescued" images such as this were one of the most characteristic types of Marian iconography in Madrid, marking their identity in relation to two of the alleged adversaries of the Catholic faith: Protestants and Muslims (Portús Pérez 2000, 65–78). In Rojas's work, this origin and legend also characterize the Virgin of Atocha. Leonor recounts how the image was hidden by the Visigoths, and in act 2 all of the Christian characters witness its reappearance outside the city walls. Following the discovery of the Marian icon, the Virgin protects the city of Madrid, marginalizing the Muslim characters on scene (Rojas [1645] 2014, 2:vv. 1859–2577). Rojas's *comedia* has received scant critical attention, and is not one of the better plays of Golden Age theatre. The work can be appreciated, however, because of the playwright's attention to visual and material culture, which helps unpack some of the anxieties surrounding the role of the image in Christian-Muslim relations in the Iberian Peninsula, or at least how writers conceived of these anxieties in their literary texts.

In Memory of the Moriscos

As we have already seen, in the *comedias de moros y cristianos* celebrating many of the most important Marian icons in early modern Spain, the majority of the action takes place during the Christian conquest of the Iberian Peninsula. Near the end of the seventeenth century, Antonio de Fajardo y Acevedo staged a play similar to those discussed in this chapter, but he trades in the medieval context of Christian-Muslim encounters for the situation of the Moriscos during the War of the Alpujarras (1568–71), offering a different angle from which to tackle the question of how playwrights imagined the role of Marian icons on the battlefield. In his *Origen de Nuestra Señora de las Angustias y rebelión de los moriscos* ([1675] 2000), Fajardo y Acevedo extols the Virgin of las Angustias, who was generally recognized as the patron of the city of Granada.[34] The image of this Virgin gained prominence during the War of the Alpujarras, in part because don Juan de Austria himself chose to kneel and pray before this Marian icon in 1569 during his military campaign, crediting her for the Christian victories during the war (Coleman 2003, 113). Even though the play was written a century after the conflict in the Alpujarras ended, the memory of the Moriscos was still much more recent in the collective imaginary than the legends of other miraculous Virgins that had appeared during the Christian conquest of the peninsula and dramatized in many of the plays in this chapter. Also, while the first-hand memories of the war had begun to fade, this play illustrates that the contention between Old Christians and Moriscos around the place of religious images in Catholic practice was still palpable in seventeenth-century Granada.

While framing the Virgin of las Angustias's prominence in Granada, Fajardo y Acevedo emphasizes attempts to desecrate the Marian icon from multiple perspectives. In act 1, Farax Abenfarax, one of the principal Morisco characters and very loosely based on the historical individual of the same name, voices his grievances incited by Philip II's repressive decree against Morisco cultural practices and plans to take revenge, in part, by profaning the religious images in the Alpujarras ([1675] 2000, 1:vv. 791–802). Later, when the characters are in full revolt, Abenfarax appeals to his coreligionists, inciting them to enter the chapel and defile the image of the Virgin of las Angustias, less to take revenge on the Christians than for the mere pleasure of destroying images and offending the Divine (2:vv. 1561–6, vv. 1629–42). Although Abenfarex's actions are excused somewhat because he has been manipulated by the devil and is not acting fully on his own volition, Fajardo y Acevedo also characterizes Moriscos as aniconic in other moments of the play. Corroborating these ideas from another perspective, María laments the destruction in the Alpujarras to her Morisca acquaintance Zoraya, animalizing the Moriscos as "bloodthirsty wolves" and deploring the sacrilege of destroying sacred images (3:vv. 1711–24).[35] Even in 1669, just a few years before Fajardo y Acevedo composed this play, one passerby in Ugíjar recorded his testimony of the religious symbols allegedly profaned by Moriscos. One of the images in question was a stone cross on the path to Berja with a crucified Christ on one side and the Virgin of las Angustias on the other, both of which, according to the witness, had been desecrated during the uprising in the Alpujarras (Barrios Aguilera and Sánchez Ramos 2001, 306). Nearly six decades after the expulsion of the Morsicos, both the fictional and testimonial examples surveyed here suggest how the memory of Old Christian-Morisco relations were still defined through the surrounding visual culture of their time.

Fajardo y Acevedo's play takes into consideration how the Christian characters appropriate images of the Virgin of las Angustias on the battlefield. In one of the most graphic examples, don Juan de Austria contends that his troops will be victorious by bringing a standard with the portrait of the Virgin into battle. He finishes his military harangue by evoking the particular iconography of the Virgin of las Angustias, "by whose divine blades/of seven swords, everyone/we will put to the sword" ([1675] 2000, 3:vv. 2676–8).[36] In this way, don Juan recalls the Marian iconography of the seven swords piercing her heart to represent her anguish and transforms it into something much more bellicose and fitting for the battlefield. Moreover, don Juan includes the standard with the Virgin as the last of a long list of other contenders in the War of the Alpujarras, effectively characterizing her as the most important warrior. Covarrubias's definition of *estandarte* (standard) helps shed some light on the meaning that Fajardo y Acevedo gives this object in his play. The lexicographer points out that, when Roman emperors carried a standard before them into war, the soldiers "respected, revered, and worshipped it as a divine thing," often placing a religious symbol on the banner (Covarrubias [1611] 2006, 845).[37] Thus, the connection between the Virgin and combat is made visually explicit for the public of Farjardo y Acevedo's *comedia*.

The principal Moriscos in the play also recognize the significance of the Marian iconography on the standard. Near the end of the conflict, don Fernando de Válor (Aben Humeya) concedes victory to the Christian troops and acknowledges the Marian icon's role in his defeat:

> María de las A[n]gustias
> is the cause of this outcome,
> because when seeing the standard
> with its sovereign effigy,
> the arm lacked strength,
> and the sword lacked exuberance.[38]
> (Fajardo y Acevedo [1675] 2000, 3:2917–22)

Even Farax Abenfarax, the same Morisco who earlier intended to profane sacred images and who is still consumed by the devil, admits that the Virgin of las Angustias has influenced the conflict in favour of the Christians (3:vv. 2910–12). Fajardo y Acevedo's play ends with the founding of a brotherhood in honour of the Virgin and, notably, don Juan de Austria and his half-brother King Philip II's membership in it. The audience is left with a final image of the Virgin of las Angustias, who is celebrated for her victory in Granada (3:vv. 3059–116).

Fajardo y Acevedo further emphasizes the Christian triumph over Islam with the embellished conversion of don Fernando de Válor at the end of the play. Despite the fact that an earlier and better-known dramatic work, Calderón de la Barca's *Amar después de la muerte* ([1633] 2008), makes no reference to his conversion back to Christianity, four decades later Fajardo y Acevedo represents him on stage as an individual propitious to change.[39] When the conflict in the Alpujarras intensifies, don Fernando de Válor changes his name to Aben Humeya, emphasizing his Morisco identity, as other sources also indicate (1:vv. 955–7). Later, when the battle changes course in favour of the Christians and he finds himself in a position of surrender, this same character converts to Christianity (3:vv. 2927–38). The iconography of the Virgin of las Angustias is important in his conversion, since the Marian icon with the seven swords piercing her heart appears to him in a dream, inciting him to leave behind his Islamic practices and instead adopt the Christian faith (3:vv. 2318–40). Early modern authors such as Luis de Mármol Carvajal, Diego Hurtado de Mendoza, and Ginés Pérez de Hita briefly include a few lines about don Fernando de Válor's conversion in their texts, but do not attribute it to the divine intervention of the Virgin or to the power of Marian icons.[40] In Fajardo y Acevedo's play, the graphic staging of don Fernando de Válor as the wayward sheep returning to the Christian fold influences how the Virgin's celestial battle revolves around this figure, especially considering his Christian past and his ambiguity in this regard. The Virgin's earthly battle is unleashed on the same battlefield, with don Juan de Austria's invoking the Virgin through a Marian ekphrasis on the standard, which leads the Christian troops to victory against the Moriscos. In this sense, the Virgin conquers both heavenly and earthly realms.

A close reading of *Origen de Nuestra Señora de las Angustias* alongside the other dramas examined in this chapter suggests that not much had changed between the early *comedias de moros y cristianos*, such as Lope de Vega's *La divina vencedora*, and this late seventeenth-century drama: the Virgin Mary still holds the role of "divine conqueror" as she tilts the scale in favour of the Christian characters in the play. Alongside this portrayal of the Virgin, the "other" is defined by their reception of Marian icons, which often prompts a conversion to Christianity at the end of the play. Nevertheless, in Fajardo y Acevedo's *comedia*, the memory of the Moriscos is still vaguely present, and influences the meaning of the Marian image on stage. The way that individuals responded to religious images had real consequences in sixteenth-century Granada. Don Fernando de Válor's brother-in-law, Diego de Rojas, was just one of the Moriscos accused of profaning religious images during the War of the Alpujarras. His Inquisition case reveals that, after finally showing some remorse, his sentence was lessened and he was condemned to perpetual rowing in the galleys for his actions committed against sacred images (García Fuentes 1981, 100). In Fajardo y Acevedo's play, don Juan de Austria likewise promises to punish the rebels who desecrate Catholic objects of devotion, among other offences ([1675] 2000, 3:vv. 2599–610). Born nearly two decades after the expulsion of the Moriscos began, Fajardo y Acevedo could not have had any first-hand knowledge of this cultural minority himself, and his play shows that he is carried away by his imagination and freely uses historical sources. Yet, at its core, the play brings to the surface some of the lingering anxieties about the place of Moriscos and their relation to Catholic religious culture in early modern Spain.

As we have seen, the Virgin Mary/Maryam represents a powerful connection between Islam and Christianity. The early modern authors studied in this chapter used their writing as a tool to negotiate how to represent Muslims' reception of Marian icons and the ways in which these images had a bearing on how Christians and Muslims interacted with one another. These playwrights proposed that the figure of Mary is intimately tied to conquest and local belonging. Even if some of her miracles still result in religious conversions on stage, she is not always represented as a compassionate intermediary figure; the Marian icons that prompt conversion in these plays are more closely linked to the surrender of the "other." Likewise, buried and recovered images of the Virgins del Sagrario and of Atocha, among others, are represented as the protectors and defenders of Spain's cities, thus marginalizing the Muslim characters and defining them by their reception of Marian icons. In the following chapter, I move beyond this context of the Iberian Peninsula to the broader Mediterranean world to show how Marian icons, among other sacred images, also starred as protagonists in some extraordinary accounts of captivity. By examining how these images circulated among slaves, captives, renegades, merchants, and redeemers, my aim is to show how various writers narrated this coexistence between individual and image, thus exposing the intricacies of cross-cultural relationships in the Mediterranean.

6

Captive Images and Forged Identities

In his *A la muy antigua, noble y coronada villa de Madrid* (1629), Jerónimo de Quintana describes the capture of a sculpted image of the Virgin with her son in her arms that Fray Diego de Ortigosa had ransomed in 1618. According to Quintana's account, Muslim corsairs raided the coast of Tenerife and siezed a chest containing an image of the Virgin Mary as booty. Once the image was taken to Algiers, a renegade and a "Turk" threatened to burn the image and commit other "sacrilegious affronts" before a captive Christian witness (418v).[1] Eventually, a Trinitarian friar arrived just in time to reach an agreement and ransom the image for six *reales*. The friar brought the Marian icon to Madrid, where it was displayed in the Convent of the Calced Trinitarians and known as the Virgin of Ransom. Similar to other redeemed religious images, this figure of the Virgin was paraded around the streets of Madrid alongside hundreds of other ex-captives in a procession headed by ecclesiastical authorities (González Dávila 1623, 252). The numerous accounts of this particular image's captivity and safe return to Spanish soil attest to her popularity in seventeenth-century Spain.[2] More important, this story suggests that human and material lives were undeniably interlaced in the borderlands of the Great Sea, as images of Christ, the Virgin Mary, and the cross, among other devotional objects, were taken captive and ransomed alongside the many men, women, and children who lost and recovered their freedom in this space.

As the image of the Virgin Mary travelled between social contexts, it acquired new meanings through each displacement. This recurring exchange of hands and the geographical, cultural, and religious crossings that took place certainly contributed to the peculiar condition of the image, since its value and the desire to possess it varied with each transaction. Arjun Appadurai has proposed that examining the "social lives" of objects through "regimes of value" illuminates new forms of knowledge (1986, 3–63). In this way, the diverse fictional and historical captivity narratives that embed material vestiges of the Mediterranean world can provide a nuanced perspective on how images influenced interactions between individuals of different religious affiliations and what these encounters reveal about interfaith relationships during the early modern period.

In this chapter, I explore this other side of Mediterranean captivity, in which religious icons were taken captive and circulated in North Africa, paying attention to how various writers of the period narrated this coexistence and interaction between individual and image. I also delve into the effects and responses that these sacred items elicited in all of the diverse people involved. Aside from the material exchanges of captive images, I examine sacred objects in works on captivity more broadly, to consider how some individuals in delicate situations, such as martyrs and renegades, used and abused these devotional objects to fit their own particular circumstances at any given time. By contextualizing the images in a variety of works from different genres, I illustrate the ways that many individuals used and manipulated these devotional objects to finesse their outward identity. Although Spanish captivity narratives and treatises have been examined from many angles, the written descriptions of religious images are often relegated to the margins or ignored in these texts.[3] Yet, since human and material lives were so intertwined, "we have to follow the things themselves," as Appadurai posits, "for their meanings are inscribed in their forms, their uses, their trajectories. It is only through the analysis of these trajectories that we can interpret the human transactions and calculations that enliven things" (1986, 5). Thus, by paying close attention to the role of images in these texts, especially their close connection to the human experience of captivity, we see how the displacement of Catholic devotional objects to Islamic lands was intimately connected to the quotidian life of human captives and others inhabiting this space. Ultimately, a focus on the descriptions of captive images and the circulation of sacred objects throughout the Mediterranean in these texts exposes the intricacies of cross-cultural relationships coupled with anxieties about identity in early modern Spain.

Captive Images between Two Worlds

Before turning to some of the literary texts on North African captivity, it is important to consider how early modern authors chronicled the circulation of images in and around the Mediterranean, keeping in mind, of course, that some of these accounts might not necessarily present a faithful reflection of reality, but instead might have been driven by ideological motivations. Within a framework in which the divine and the human come together in striking ways, images and humans were embroiled in the same precarious circumstances, as various early modern authors illustrate in their works. Antonio de Sosa, for example, alludes to some images that were taken captive along with humans from Christian galleys by the famous Calabrian renegade 'Ulūj 'Alī. The images were later burned in 1579 by order of the renegade Hasan Veneciano.[4] According to Sosa, Veneciano demanded that "[they] carry to his door the three aforementioned images, and in a small square that is in front, by order of the Marabouts, they hacked these images to pieces and burned them in a great fire,"[5] all because these sacred objects had been blamed for causing a drought that had devastated the region (Haedo [1612] 1927–9, 1: 159).[6] The human captives were also held responsible for the parched land, and were prohibited from attending mass as a result. In addition to confronting restrictions on exercising their religious practices, then, these men and women also grieved the destruction of the captive images, a punishment based on public humiliation and physical harm that would be more characteristic of a human penalty. This points to the Christian tradition in which God became man to suffer a martyrdom for the benefit of human beings, just as these sacred figures endured a martyrdom that could have been inflicted on any of the Christian slaves. This humanizes the captive devotional objects and places them in the same earthly realm as the human captives.

Other authors, such as Jaime Bleda (1600b, 398–403), one of the apologists of the expulsion of the Moriscos, and the chronicler Gaspar Escolano (1879–80, 1:508b–509a) recount the captivity and eventual ransom of a crucifix alongside other Christian captives in Algiers. According to Escolano, in 1539, "the Muslim corsairs from Algiers took a Christian ship, and when they reached port with it and were going through the clothes, they came across a largely formed crucifix" (1:508b).[7] Some Christian merchants from Valencia who were in Algiers negotiating the ransom of their captive sisters found out about this crucifix. Treating it as if it were a human captive, they also attempted to salvage the figure by offering to pay what a human captive would cost for its ransom (1:508b). According to Bleda's and Escolano's accounts, the Algerians who had the crucifix were not satisfied at first with the amount the Valencian brothers offered to rescue the object. Believing that they would receive more profit from its ransom, they decide to set the price according to its weight. What appears to be a lucrative deal for the crucifix's Algerian captors, however, results in a miracle: the scale is not offset until there are only thirty coins left, a suggestive amount that clearly evokes the coins Judas Iscariot received in his betrayal of Jesus. The rescue culminates with the image's return to Valencia, where it appears in a devout and solemn procession in celebration of its safe arrival.

In 1625, Fray Antonio Juan Andreu de San Joseph gave an account of this same captive image, describing the miracles associated with its ransom in great detail. He recounts the journey of the captive image between Algiers and Valencia, while also describing the parallel experience of human captives Ursula and Madalena Medina, who were abducted off the Levantine coast by Muslim corsairs. After four trips to Algiers, the captives' brothers, Andrés and Pedro Medina, finally manage to ransom Ursula and her son alongside the captive crucifix. Madalena, however, is not as fortunate as her sister, and is forced to remain in Algiers in possession of the cadi, who refuses to negotiate the ransom of any other female captives (Andreu de San Joseph 1625, 273). The Valencian painter Jerónimo Jacinto de Espinosa captures the Medina brothers' ransom negotiations in a 1623 painting, focusing on the moment when the crucifix is miraculously counterweighted by only thirty coins (fig. 17).[8] Here, the representation of Christ is strikingly realistic, and by not including either of the Medina sisters in the painting, the artist underscores that the ransom of greatest value for the public is that of the rescued image. The human captives, thus, are relegated to the margins.

Notably, some of the redeemers who ventured to the other side of the Mediterranean with the hope of rescuing Christian captives added descriptions of sacred images that were rescued alongside individuals who were released from bondage. Fray Raphael de San Juan, for example, was one of a few redeeming friars from the Order of the Holy Trinity who left written records of images on their lists of ransomed captives. He reveals how, in 1642, in addition to 156 captives rescued in Algiers, an image of the Virgin was also salvaged; some years later, in 1674, another Marian icon that had been gravely damaged by North African Muslims was ransomed in Tétouan and Salé alongside 128 captives (San Juan 1686, 103–4). Likewise, the Trinitarian friar notes that, along with 211 captives freed from slavery in 1682, they also "redeemed seventeen holy images, with all the ornaments, crosses, and sacred vessels, which the Moors had taken from the fortress in La Mámora" (104–5).[9] Among these objects of worship was the sculpture of the Christ of Medinaceli, one of the most esteemed captive images, which is still devoutly venerated in Madrid today.[10]

The work of the friar Gabriel Gómez de Losada presents some essential features of the peculiar relationship between religious images and individuals in captivity in North Africa. As Gómez de Losada acknowledges in his prologue, one of the principal purposes in writing his treatise *Escuela de trabajos* (1670) is to portray the cruelty that Christian

Fig. 17. Jerónimo Jacinto de Espinosa, *El milagro del Cristo del Rescate*, 1623.

Private collection, Valencia

Photo credit: Francisco Alcántara Benavent

captives suffered in Algiers. Together with this objective, he also tries to persuade others to partake in the redemption of captives and contribute money to this cause. In addition, he offers practical recommendations for professional redeemers who, like him, travel to North Africa with the intention of negotiating the ransom of Christian captives. For these reasons, the friar recounts his own adventures travelling to Algiers in 1664 and a second trip in 1667. His text mirrors those of other religious writers such as Antonio de Sosa, Pierre Dan, and Jerónimo Gracián, who describe the circumstances of captivity based on their personal experiences in North Africa. Gómez de Losada borrows many ideas from Antonio de Sosa's *Topografía e historia general de Argel* (Haedo [1612] 1927–9), despite his contention in the prologue that he is not familiar with any text similar to his own (Pallares Garzón 2012, 103). What is original, and not addressed in Sosa's work, however, stems from Gómez de Losada's involvement in rescuing an effigy of Christ in Algiers. This sacred figure, which circulated among Muslims, Christians, and Jews, becomes the central protagonist in the last book of his treatise, which he titles "On the best rescued captive."[11]

Gómez de Losada informs his readers about this captive effigy while recounting one of his redeeming efforts in Algiers. According to his written testimony, the sacred object was on a boat in transit from Italy, but was captured by Turkish corsairs before reaching its destination and brought to Algiers, where it was sold three times: "once in the Divan, where they sell what the Turks seize; another time when the Turk sold it to the Jew; and the third time when I bought it from him" (1670, 537).[12] Given that one of his stated motives for writing his treatise is to portray the immense cruelty experienced by Christian captives in Algiers, it might seem surprising that the Turkish corsair who captures the effigy does not figure more prominently in this part of the narrative. Instead, Gómez de Losada attributes a relatively minor role to this individual, and the Turk remains unnamed. Perhaps the Mercedarian friar's lack of first-hand knowledge or credible testimony accounts for Gómez de Losada's limited description. Yet, for this Turk, the religious statue is of sufficient value to steal and later sell alongside other humans and goods taken captive in Mediterranean waters, highlighting a shared culture of material exchange that exists despite the religious differences of those who participate.

Gómez de Losada's first encounter with the effigy of Christ occurs while he is negotiating the ransom of several Christian captives. The Jewish individual who initially purchases the image spontaneously offers the sacred representation to Gómez de Losada, exclaiming, "Father, stop and buy this Christ that is yours from me, for whatever you want, since

I'll give it to you cheaply" (1670, 502).[13] Astonished that this object of worship was not more highly valued, since, in his opinion, "he who leaves what he is selling at the discretion of the buyer is a sign that he either doesn't know its value or that he values it little,"[14] Gómez de Losada accepts the Jew's offer and purchases the effigy of Christ for thirty-two silver *reales*. Although the author makes an obvious allusion to the thirty coins Judas Iscariot received,[15] he adapts his account to make it more credible by setting the price at four eight-*real* coins, adding up to thirty-two silver *reales*.

As the captive effigy of Christ circulates among Christians, Muslims, and Jews, the figure is transformed into a material object of desire. Before the effigy is finally ransomed by the Mercedarian friar, the object's desirability multiplies with each transaction in the narrative. The escalating desire to acquire the image crystalizes once a certain Antonio López attempts to plunder the captive effigy. Having promised to bring the image back for a woman from his home town, he poses as a redeemer with the pretext of helping Christian captives return to Spain, and travels from Cartagena to North Africa. The woman's strong desire to possess the figure impels her to offer any sum of money for it, inciting others also to bid on the effigy, with each offer superseding the previous: the first bidder offers four hundred eight-*real* coins and a painting, a second volunteers a sum of ten thousand *reales*. From having little value on a secluded street in Algiers, the image, especially after enduring captivity, becomes more and more desirable.[16]

The material exchanges of the effigy of Christ in many ways parallel the experiences of human captives along the shores of the Mediterranean Sea as their ransoms are negotiated before they finally return to Christian lands. For Gómez de Losada, the image of Christ endures the same hardships that many men and women confined to North Africa suffered, thus humanizing the sacred figure and imbuing it with the same sentimental attributes as other captives. The effigy of Christ is not merely an object of worship; Gómez de Losada's treatise nearly transforms it into a real human captive. The vocabulary used to describe the different adversities faced by the statue highlights this parallel, mimicking the words used to portray the experience of human slavery: the effigy of Christ is "taken captive," "sold," "mistreated," "insulted," and finally "ransomed." The effigy's earthly and heavenly features are intimately joined when it arrives at the royal court in Madrid and participates in a procession alongside the other redeemed captives as if it were one of them: "The procession took place very solemnly in the Court and with an audience, which was never seen again, with the captives and the most Holy Christ as the principal one rescued" (1670, 511–12).[17] If the captive is sometimes

understood as an *imitatio Christi*, made to suffer the same hardships
endured by Christ during his Passion, this image, in effect, becomes the
model captive because it not only imitates Christ in its fortune but also in
its physical appearance.[18] Gómez de Losada suggests this clear relationship between the captive image and Christ's suffering before addressing
any other issue and prior to revealing the particulars of his fourth book:
"And for the subject of this chapter we have to enter into a meditation
of the sacred Passion of Jesus Christ, and at any moment of it we shall
find him not only with very intense and harsh pain, but also extremely
insulted, full of humiliation, shame, and disgrace" (497–8).[19] The Passion of Christ is one of the most earthly moments associated with the
divinity, since elements such as suffering, thirst, and fear, among others,
come into play. Thus, by showing that the effigy of Christ has also gone
through the same adversities, Gómez de Losada underscores the image's
human qualities.

Martyrs and the Cross

This close association of the captive image with Christ's suffering and
crucifixion often becomes more evident during acts of martyrdom,
endowing the already tragic episode with more drama and emotion. In
both of Cervantes's plays that take place in the city of Algiers, he presents
the audience with an episode of martyrdom where an image of the cross
takes centre stage. At the end of the first act of *El trato de Argel* ([c. 1582]
1996), the young captive Sebastián recounts the martyrdom he has just
witnessed, explaining that it occurred in retaliation for a death sentence
given to a Morisco in Valencia and his subsequent burning at the stake.
When the Morisco's relatives learn about this tragic outcome, their thirst
for revenge incites them to burn a Christian in the same way.[20] The individual chosen to pay for this death is a Valencian priest, who has a cross
notably woven onto his clothes and placed on his chest:

> They seized this one in a great haste
> to carry out their deed,
> because they saw that on his chest
> he was wearing the cross of Montesa,
> and this sign of victory
> that made possible his good fortune,
> if it caused his death on earth,
> it gave him glory in Heaven;
> because these blind men without light,
> who have seen such a sign on him,

planning to kill Christ,
kill the one who wears his cross.[21]
(1:vv. 531–42)

Although it is unlikely that the priest was chosen as the scapegoat solely due to the religious emblem on his chest, the act of executing a religious figure who was prominently boasting a Christian symbol on his clothing contributes an added layer of meaning to the scene. More than a retaliation against a specific individual, the action transgresses a boundary to achieve a more ambitious and profound reprisal: attacking the beliefs of an entire society. Lope de Vega rewrites this same episode in his play *Los cautivos de Argel* ([c. 1599] 2017), although his version has more tragic undertones and includes additional gruesome details.[22] In Lope's *comedia*, the image of the cross and the priest share the limelight during the act of martyrdom, except that this time the cross does not appear on the martyr's clothes but, rather, is marked on his chest with a knife. The captive Sahavedra recounts the scene, fusing individual harm with violence against an entire religion:

> He looked, in fact, at the cross,
> and wanting the enemy
> to make the same one on his chest
> as what he worshipped on his garment,
> he made another (alas,
> I'm made of stone, so I say this!)
> with a sharp knife,
> a knife that was a brush.
> The blood gave colour,
> the canvas his blessed chest,
> and so, a cross, was left on him
> of bright red paint.
> If you want to see him, look at him,
> at the divine priest,
> offering to Christ his soul
> who is host of the sacrifice.[23]
> (3:vv. 2001–16)

These elements certainly taint the scene with the macabre and intensify the act of martyrdom, but they also bind the fates of the cross and the captive priest. This scenario, in which an object of worship and an individual experience a similar outcome, arises in similar passages in Gómez de Losada's treatise on captivity, giving us a better idea of how different early modern authors chose to describe the nuanced relations among images, captivity, and martyrdom.

These types of retaliation, in which there is a *quid pro quo* on opposite shores of the Mediterranean, were sometimes carried out specifically on sacred images, in addition to human figures, as in the case of Fray Miguel de Aranda. Gómez de Losada recalls how Genoese privateers captured a renegade corsair in Algiers in 1666 and, as punishment for his acts of piracy and his disobedience to the Catholic faith, sentenced him to be burned at the stake. When this news reached Algiers, authorities were ordered to go to places of worship to burn all the images and sacred objects they found (1670, 368). In this instance, some Christian captives in Algiers discovered the intended fate of these objects of worship and were able to keep them in a safe place to prevent them from being reduced to ashes, thwarting any revenge. Yet, in all these cases, image and individual share a common destiny, with certain similarities and analogous values.

Turning now to Cervantes's play *Los baños de Argel* ([1615] 1983), some of the images of worship that appear in different scenes emerge precisely during episodes of martyrdom, or in relation to diverse passages associated with the Passion of Christ. This is the case with the renegade Hazén, who kills Yzuf in a fit of rage to take revenge for the ruthless cruelty the latter had shown towards his fellow countrymen. In retaliation for this crime, and in addition to Hazén's announcing his Christian faith publicly, the *cadi* is forced to order his impalement, which Hazén himself transforms into an act of martyrdom and atonement for his past faults. At this precise moment, the Cervantine renegade "takes out a wooden cross,"[24] producing a scene so graphically charged that it adds more value to Hazén's death by transforming it into a pious sacrifice (1:vv. 667–881). This snapshot in which a renegade grasps a wooden cross, captured so aptly by Cervantes in his play, allows the reader to see the close connection between the renegade's desired martyrdom and the sacrifice that is represented in the icon he embraces. Antonio de Sosa recalls a similar case in his *Diálogo de los mártires de Argel* (1612), describing how renegades from different nations plotted a rebellion against their master, Hasan Veneciano, which they planned to carry out during their sea voyage.[25] Their motive for the revolt coincides with Hazén's in *Los baños de Argel* – namely, the extreme cruelty that some renegades display towards others. One of the renegades dissociates himself from the attempted uprising and reveals the plans to his master, and the rebellion does not reach fruition. As a reprimand, Hasan Veneciano orders the death of all the conspirators. Among them is the renegade Yusuf, who, during an intense moment of his martyrdom and after losing his ability to speak, "with the fingers on his right hand continuously made the sign of the cross" (Haedo [1612] 1927–9, 3:159).[26] Just as Cervantes presents the renegade's martyrdom in *Los baños de Argel*, here Sosa associates a martyr with an image of the cross in one of the more dramatic moments.

Cervantes imbues acts of martyrdom in *Los baños de Argel* with special visual significance precisely because of the religious imagery that he connects with them. At the end of the second act, the dialogue between Juanico and Francisquito highlights how the two children reaffirm their faith in Christianity and recite various prayers while playing together. When the *cadi* arrives on the scene and discovers what is taking place, the tension heightens, and the children are forced to explain why they are saying their prayers and to whom they are addressed. The *cadi* takes these circumstances as a personal affront, urging the children to renounce their Christian faith. Yet, before recounting the outcome of the two young boys' forced conversions, Cervantes intercalates a scene depicting the Easter celebration officiated by Christian captives and, significantly, observed by other Muslim characters.[27] As a prelude to what his own son Francisquito later will embody, the father of these two children witnesses this ceremony commemorating the Passion of Christ. Francisquito's suffering in Algiers is a clear reflection of the Passion of Christ, but Cervantes emphasizes this by creating a visual representation of the anguish this character undergoes: "He is tied to a column, / made to look like Christ, / from head to toe / in his same red blood."[28] The spectators are thus presented with a human embodiment of Baroque imagery and an image of Christ during the Passion ([1615] 1983, 3:vv. 352–5).[29] The representation that Cervantes captures here is just one moment during the martyrdom of an innocent child who is tortured to death simply because he professes his Christian beliefs. Yet this is the only concrete image we have of his act of martyrdom. Thus, in addition to associating the suffering and death of the child with the Passion of Christ, in this rendering the human martyr becomes a sculptural figure of Jesus during the events leading up to his death. This vivid representation of Francisquito at the time of his martyrdom evokes the religious iconography of the Christ child with the crucifix, linking the childhood of Jesus with his Passion and death. Alonso Cano captures this same association in one of his sculptures representing a young Christ carrying the cross on his shoulder (fig. 18).[30]

As we have already seen, some of the religious images that appear in these works are transformed into privileged witnesses of the martyrs' torment and add value to their suffering and death. All this torture that transpires in captivity invites a recurring analogy with the Passion of Christ,

Fig. 18. Alonso Cano, *Niño Jesús nazareno*, 1657.

Iglesia de San Fermín de los Navarros, Madrid
Photo Credit: Album /Art Resource, New York

and the possibility of considering these images that represent Jesus at this moment in his life evinces an inexorable division between European Christian authors and Muslim writers from North Africa (Matar 2009, 40–1). As Nabil Matar suggests, this is one likely reason that there are relatively few traces of Arabic writing on the subject of captivity during this era. For Christians, however, a captivity in which one's own suffering and humiliation could be compared to the torment that the central figure of Christianity underwent hundreds of years earlier would surely be an incentive to describe their experiences. And the many examples of Baroque imagery depicting the Passion of Christ – imagery that is evidently not prominent in Islamic art – would have served as an additional inspiration for many of these same authors.

In the case of captive images exposed to torture, the very object gains value as it experiences captivity and other adversities in this Mediterranean space. Returning to the fourth and final book of Gómez de Losada's treatise, for example, we see how the effigy of Christ becomes more valuable precisely because of its passage through captivity in Algiers. Its circulation between the shores of the Mediterranean and the series of affronts and difficulties it endures gives the effigy a particular worth. Without bearing the suffering and torture, this image of Christ would be simply another religious image, and, as the author suggests, it would not represent so vividly and effectively the suffering the effigy itself embodies. For this reason, the trials that the image suffers in Algiers give it more value and admiration, and this prompts the author to share the misfortunes and miracles associated with this effigy, "to rouse the devotion of the faithful, which should be strong, knowing the origin of its freedom, the wonders and miracles it has brought about after being among Catholics" (1670, 496).[31] It is also this experience that allows the image the possibility of evoking the Passion of Christ, especially because of its "resemblance with its original" (538).[32] To emphasize this point, Gómez de Losada explains how some of the most renowned painters have tried to replicate the revered figure but always without success. According to the Mercedarian friar, even the best artists of the court who have tried to copy the image could not capture in their works whatever it was that so vividly represented Christ (538).

Renegades and Frontier Figures

If images embedded in early modern texts on captivity allow martyrs to align their own suffering more closely with that of Christ, in the hands of renegades devotional objects take on a more active role, allowing these individuals to mould their fluid identities depending on their fluctuating circumstances. Bartolomé and Lucile Bennassar estimate that at least 300,000 individuals of Spanish origin, as well as individuals from other places in the Mediterranean, converted from Christianity to Islam between 1550 and 1700 (1989, 168).[33] Renegades were so abundant that, according to Antonio de Sosa, "[they] outnumber all the other Moorish, Turkish, and Jewish neighbours of Algiers, because there is no Christian nation in the world without renegades in Algiers" (Haedo [1612] 1927–9, 1:52).[34] As Bartolomé and Lucile Bennassar, Isabel Braga, María Antonia Garcés, Steven Hutchinson, and Lucetta Scaraffia, among others, have emphasized, these renegades are often personified as frontier figures, living between two worlds and religions, capable of passing from one place to another if their circumstances compelled them to do so. But this movement from one shore to the other required a more exhaustive transformation than simply adopting a new religion. These individuals often acquired new names, changed their attire, embraced new cultural practices, and sometimes learned a new language. In many cases, these new behaviours and customs allowed the renegades to straddle two worlds and move fluidly between both cultures.

In recent years, renegades have been the object of many rigorous studies, but the effects and meanings that religious images incited in the hands of these frontier figures have not yet been taken into full consideration.[35] The interaction of these individuals with a symbol as distinctive and intimately tied to Christianity as the cross adds new subtleties to an icon that originally was conceived to have a single and common meaning. In the hands of renegades, the cross takes on different significance depending on how and for what purpose it is used. By examining the complex relationship between renegades and the power of images, we can see how, in the particular context of the early modern Mediterranean, objects of religious devotion can be manipulated as tools to mould identity and external appearance according to each individual's circumstances.

The Cervantine renegade in "The Captive's Tale" offers a productive starting point to address this question, as this character's experiences underscore the malleable roles of Christian images in North Africa (Cervantes 2003, 1:37, 39–42). In this episode, the only religious images that appear are significantly tied to the two frontier characters whose identities raise the most doubts: the renegade from Murcia and the Algerian Zoraida. After the captive captain receives the first of Zoraida's letters, the Murcian renegade renders it in Spanish and learns of the clandestine plan to leave Algiers. Now that Zoraida has expressed her longing and willingness to go to Christian lands, the captives finally see a real opportunity to abandon their life in Algiers and escape from captivity.

Mindful that the letter was directed to one of the captives and eager to take part in this endeavour, the renegade tries to gain the trust of the group of captives in order to join them in their flight. To reinforce his commitment to them and prove his loyalty, the renegade resorts to a religious image hidden beneath his clothing:

> the renegade realized the paper had not been found by chance but had really been written to one of us, and he implored us that if what he suspected was true, that we trust him and tell him so, and he would risk his life for our freedom. And saying this, he pulled out from under his shirt a metal crucifix, and with many tears he swore by the God that the image represented, and in whom he, though a sinner, believed completely and faithfully, that he would be loyal to us and keep secret anything we wished to tell him; he thought, and could almost predict, that by means of the woman who had written the letter, he and all of us would obtain our freedom, and he would find himself where he longed to be, which was reunited with the body of Holy Mother Church, from whom, like a rotten limb, he had been separated and severed because of his ignorance and sin.[36] (Cervantes 2003, 1:40, 347–8)

At this emotional moment, when the renegade grasps the crucifix, the relationship between renegade and captive is solidified, establishing a commitment that both of them need.

This image of the cross is used by a character whose mere status as a renegade requires him to prove his Catholic devotion. Only moments earlier, Zoraida had warned Ruy Pérez de Viedma not to trust Muslims. Thus, any possible connection between the renegade and Islam could call his honesty and loyalty into question and put him in a delicate situation.[37] For this reason, the material used for the renegade's cross is not fortuitous. Relying on a crucifix made of metal evokes a solid and enduring promise, casting out any possible anxiety over the renegade's Catholic beliefs or honesty. The comparison between the renegade's strong affirmation and the strength of the crucifix is significant, especially when juxtaposed with the small cross made of reeds that Zoraida displays out of her window. Even though the captive openly declares his friendship with the renegade, he still appears to harbour some reservations about the renegade's loyalty, since he initially chooses not to disclose the origin of Zoraida's letter: "before I told him everything, I asked him to read the paper for me, saying I had found it in a crack in the wall of my cell" (1:40, 347).[38] Coincidentally, the content of this passage also addresses the allegiance or distrust that some characters feel towards others. Thus, the firm union between the two occurs only after the renegade displays the metal crucifix while publicly declaring his intentions, at which point the captive agrees to divulge all of the details to him: "The renegade said this with so many tears and displays of so much repentance that we were all of the same opinion and agreed to tell him the truth, and so we revealed everything to him, hiding nothing" (1:40, 348).[39] There is no doubt that the use of this symbol as a graphic display of his intentions gives the renegade enough credit to gain the trust of his countrymen and the good fortune to join their group.

The renegade's use of a crucifix is particularly striking if one considers that, in "The Captive's Tale," the renegade and the enigmatic Zoraida – two characters whose identity and affiliation are marked by some uncertainty – are the only ones directly linked to religious images. While the renegade relies on the cross to display publicly his beliefs and ally himself with Ruy Pérez de Viedma, the possession of religious images in the early modern Mediterranean can also generate questions about its owner's identity. Shortly before the renegade reveals his metal cross, the captives witness a small reed cross protruding from Zoraida's window. Instead of clarifying her religious identity, it creates more confusion for the group of captives:

A small cross made of reeds was dangled from the window and immediately pulled back in. This confirmed that a Christian woman was probably a captive in that house and was the one who had done us the good turn, but the whiteness of her hand and the bracelets we saw on it disabused us of the thought that she was a slave; then we imagined she must be a renegade Christian, for they are often taken as legitimate wives by their masters, who consider this good fortune since the men esteem them more than the women of their own nation. In all our speculations, however, we were very far from the truth of the matter.[40] (Cervantes 2003, 345)

The captive recognizes that symbols can conceal their intended meaning depending on the context in which they are used. In this case, the single exhibition of a reed cross first causes the captive to affirm the Christian identity of the woman holding it out of her window. But after his initial reflection and later speculation that she could instead be a renegade, Ruy Pérez de Viedma finally admits that they had been misguided in their assumptions. The episode thus reinforces the malleable nature of religious icons in captivity narratives, where an image such as the cross possesses different meanings in the hands of each character, urging us to question the use and abuse of religious images in this context.

Despite the doubts that Zoraida's reed cross generates in the other characters, the Algerian woman has much more in common with the renegade than the beginning of "The Captive's Tale" seems to suggest. As Steven Hutchinson notes, "after *reneging* ... Zoraida situates herself in same in-between space as the Murcian renegade, who shows evident signs of wanting to leave exile and return to his native land and religion" (2011, 158; emphasis in original).[41] Zoraida is also a renegade, although her act of apostasy has a shorter route than that of the Murcian renegade, a route that goes in only one direction and seems to have no return. Despite the differences between the two characters, both find themselves in a comparable position at the beginning of the episode. Each is pursuing a similar goal that requires them to use intermediaries to carry out their intentions, especially since their conversion and longing to reach Spain forces them to consider every action carefully. These frontier figures who have renounced their faith are the only two to make a public and striking use of the cross, not necessarily for spiritual motives, but instead because this tool allows them to travel to the other side of the Mediterranean. In this sense, Miguel Ángel de Bunes Ibarra's study exploring renegades' psychology of conversion underscores the common mistake of reducing their conversion solely to a religious context, noting instead other, more useful factors for understanding their transformation, such as the economy, politics, and power. In particular, Zoraida's conversion does not seem to have purely religious motives, since, as we have seen so far, the symbol of the cross raises more doubts, rather than confirming any exemplary spiritual conversion. We must remember that Zoraida tragically abandons her father, leaving several open wounds that tarnish her conversion. Thus, throughout "The Captive's Tale," the two frontier characters, marked with suggestive ambiguities, are the only individuals associated with religious icons, icons that initially seem to have only one clear and concise meaning. Yet, through these two individuals, it becomes clear that images can incite different interpretations and have multiple meanings, especially in the in-between spaces of the Mediterranean borderlands.

Guillén de Castro also addresses these issues in his play *El renegado arrepentido* (Castro y Bellvís [c. 1592–1600] 1925) through the protagonist and renegade Osmán and his manipulation of Catholic devotional objects.[42] Osmán publicly proclaims his acceptance of religious images in an attempt to prove himself a "sincere" Christian, even though he had previously renounced his faith. He decides to turn his back on Christianity after he believes that his father, King Honorio, has unjustly imprisoned him and taken away his succession to the throne. He flees his father's land, is captured by Hazén Bajá, and is handed over to King Cosdroé. After six years in captivity, Osmán decides to renege to gain more power, and he later becomes the favourite of the Muslim monarch.

Following a number of cruel plans to have his father humiliated and killed, the renegade takes out a cross and has time to reflect on his decision to convert to Islam, finally deciding to spare Honorio's life. This whole accumulation of contradictions concerning Osmán's spiritual beliefs generates some doubts about his identity, especially when trying to define his allegiance to one religious group or another. It is Osmán himself, however, who reveals to the audience his inner intentions, relying for this purpose on an image of the cross. Not surprisingly, at this moment of the play, the renegade takes the icon out from under his shirt in an attempt to strengthen his argument:

> For my witness I choose you:
> you well know, Holy Virgin,
> what the image of the crucifix
> could do with me.
> I never saw you crucified,
> that I did not cry and crying
> they found me, you know when,
> kissing your side.
> And for more proof,
> *He pulls out a small crucifix from his bosom, and continues:*
> You, my sweet company,
> if I was careless one day,
> say it here, I will forgive you.
> You know well that I reneged,
> and that I remembered you,
> to have you as God,
> because I took you out from blasphemy.[43]
> (Castro 223a; emphasis in original)

This attachment to the cross, both physically and figuratively, allows Osmán to maintain this inner desire and publicly affirm his religious beliefs, while strengthening his statement in the eyes of the spectators and the other characters. Despite his sharp rupture with his former lifestyle, Osmán clings to his past through his connection with this Christian icon, a key element for both the character's development and the work itself.

Only a few pages later, the now-repentant renegade is confronted by Christ on the cross, who asks him to give an account of his life and explain the good works he has accomplished. Of the four deeds that Osmán describes, three directly relate to his actions towards religious images and the reactions these objects elicited in him. Most significant is his interaction with a Muslim seafarer who had stolen a golden image of Christ with the intention of burning it. Anguished at the thought of the harm that would be done to this sacred object, Osmán buys the stolen image and later uses it to help a poor widow ransom her captive son. In this particular case, it is (curiously) the renegade who gives the image a certain role, rescuing it and using it for the benefit of other Christian individuals. His actions emphasize the self-interested character of the renegade, relegating spiritual intentions to the margins and instead focusing on the material use of images. Furthermore, his decision to renege on his Christian faith is more dependent on his desire for power than on any acceptance or rejection of religious beliefs. In fact, as Steven Hutchinson stresses, "[r]eligious belief seems rarely to have been the prime motive of converts in this geohistorical setting. What one sees again and again is that while the question of belief was transcendent for Christianity and Islam, it was not always so important for the people who practiced these religions" (2012c, 59). Then, for the repentant renegade in Guillén de Castro's play, his behaviour towards images is not necessarily an example of his religious intentions. Rather, how he *acts* towards them is more important than what he *believes* about them.

Inquisition cases corroborate some of the aspects of renegades' use of religious images to shape their fluid identities captured in fiction by Cervantes, Guillén de Castro, and other early modern authors. The Frenchman Guillaume Bedos, also known in Tunis as Arráez Xabán, was taken captive by Muslim corsairs when he was only ten years old. According to Inquisition records, after his capture he went on to renege on Christianity and began to follow Islamic practices and doctrines. Two decades later, Guillaume was taken captive again, this time by a Sicilian galley, and brought before the court of Palermo in 1619, where he chose to reaffirm his faith in Islam publicly instead of converting back to Christianity. Initially, he not only rejected the worship of images but even went on to mock them. On 11 February 1620, the priest Filippo Polidoro, prisoner of the Holy Office, testified against the captive, mentioning Guillaume's rejection of religious iconography, and declaring that the renegade "made a mockery of the Christians worshipping the images, saying that it was a sin" (*Proceso de fe contra Guillaume Bedos* 14r).[44] That same day, another prisoner of the Holy Office, Don Andrea Lo Restivo, admitted that Guillaume "also denies the adoration of the images, saying that they should not adore Christ, nor the saints, nor any relic" (16r).[45] However, when Guillaume was finally condemned to death and on his way to the gallows, he suddenly decided to kneel before an image of the Virgin, an action that helped him reconcile with the Church and diminish his sentence (Bennassar and Bennassar 1989, 65–88; Bennassar

1992, 119–23). Could this sudden and perplexing change in his actions towards religious images have been a way to feign his belief at a critical moment in his life? In this case, it is also striking that *Le dictionnaire des inquisiteurs* (*Repertorium inquisitorum*, Valencia, 1494) records how, in the view of the inquisitors, there was a strong connection between blasphemy and the treatment of religious images:

> The inquisitor can intervene if it can be shown that the blasphemer denies God by word and deed. And what about the one who would efface the image of God, or of the Blessed Virgin, or of a saint, or who would destroy them, or who would throw them on the ground, or who would paint images or write the name of God in places where their presence would be an affront to divinity. What can be said? For whoever acts in this way, the revenge will be hard, severe punishment, regardless of the condition, dignity, and degree of the offender.[46] (1981, 112–13)

Although it is difficult to know with certainty, it seems more than likely that Guillaume changed his behaviour towards images to mitigate his punishment, and undoubtedly the act of kneeling before an image of the Virgin saved him from imminent death. Beyond the integrity of his actions, what does seem evident is that the religious image played a fundamental role in some renegades' acts of repentance while facing Inquisitional authorities.[47]

In this sense, it is also significant that, during their confessions to the Inquisition or to their families, some renegades declared how they carried a Christian image with them, even when they supposedly had reneged on their Catholic faith. Jacobo de Maqueda, for example, attested to the Inquisition that he had always carried a rosary and a picture of the Virgin Mary, in addition to presenting some letters claiming that he had never really abandoned Christianity (Gonzalez-Raymond 1992, 119). The Portuguese renegade Gaspar Fernandes also testified before the authorities that he "worshipped images with signs of being a Christian" (Braga 1998, 96).[48] In a similar vein, the Spanish renegade Mateo Castellano documented some of the events that took place during his captivity in a letter intended for his Christian wife in the Canary Islands, suggestively mentioning that he carried a picture of Christ and Our Lady of the Rosary (Bennassar and Bennassar 1989, 444). For these renegades, the act of associating themselves with religious images during their stay in North Africa was not accidental, especially if they had to present themselves to the Inquisition or reconcile themselves with family members.

The English captive Richard Hasleton offers a Protestant counterpoint, revealing how the question of images could surface during an

Inquisition trial of a former captive in Islamic lands. Although he was not alleged to be a renegade, this Englishman lived as a captive in Algiers for five years until 1587, when the galley he was rowing was shipwrecked on the island of Formentera. Hasleton initially was sent to the neighbouring island of Ibiza, where he was imprisoned and interrogated about an alleged crime of defamation against the Spanish monarch and the Church of Rome. Because Hasleton kept silent in front of Spanish authorities, he was later sent to Majorca to be presented before the Inquisition. There, during his trial, Hasleton chose to highlight the vast weight put on Catholic veneration of religious images and his contrasting view to this practice. According to the English captive, his rejection of sacred objects of worship in the face of Inquisition officers was reason enough for them to berate him and call him a "Lutheran" (2001, 77). As he explained, they began by offering him a tablet with religious iconography and later ordered him to kneel down and venerate other images set before him, all of which he vehemently refused to do. The officers continued by handing him a cross that he was urged to worship, inciting Hasleton to spit on the inquisitor's face. As his narrative develops, Hasleton highlights other instances in which he sharply disagreed with these authorities on the subject of icons.

Although many of the real and fictional renegades examined above align themselves with the cross to associate themselves publicly more closely with Catholic practices, other renegades use these very same images with contradictory motives. By damaging sacred representations and openly publicizing their actions, these renegades try to demonstrate outwardly their rejection of an important part of Catholic culture. In Gómez de Losada's *Escuela de trabajos*, for example, he gives an account of a repentant Portuguese renegade who, at one point during his long stay in Algiers, was driven to burn an effigy of the Virgin in order to win the favour of his Muslim neighbours: "And to make the Turks think that he was like them, he did this great sacrilege of hurling the most holy image of Our Lady onto the fire" (1670, 366).[49] In this passage, the renegade uses the object of worship for a specific purpose contrary to its intended meaning, as it allows him to distance himself from his past and identify with what, at that moment, was more convenient for him. In a letter written from Algiers in 1550, a Spanish captive in North Africa describes a similar incident. In his account, a group of captives who had been waiting to be rescued from Algiers began to lose hope that they eventually would be ransomed, so they opted to renege on their Christian faith. To demonstrate their resolution and rid themselves of their status as captives, they decided to resort to the symbol of the cross, as the letter explains: "The first thing they did in the king's house was to make a cross on the ground and spit on it and trample over it and shout that they were Moors, denying the true Jesus Christ as God" (172).[50] This use of crosses or other sacred representations with contrary intentions also formed part of the way in which several renegade women converted to Islam. Ana, a renegade of Russian origin, could only deny her religion after stepping on "a cross, spitting on it three times and throwing it into the sea."[51] Other women gave similar accounts of how they had to repudiate the Christian symbol to be accepted as followers of Islam (Bennassar and Bennassar 1989, 338).

The image of the cross that the Cervantine renegade displayed so intentionally in order to strengthen his ties with the captive Ruy Pérez de Viedma is the same image other renegades used with a radically different purpose, as these last examples demonstrate. Like the letters of safe conduct that renegades could use or abuse, given their circumstances, religious images allowed these frontier figures to mould their outward identity as they adapted these sacred objects to their individual situations. When Ruy Perez de Viedma turns to the renegade for help translating Zoraida's letters, he reveals just how some renegades take advantage of the letters signed by other captives:

> because certain renegades, when they intend to return to Christian lands, take with them signed statements from important captives testifying, in whatever fashion they can, that the renegade is a moral man, and always has treated Christians well, and desires to escape at the first opportunity. Some obtain these declarations with good intentions; others use them as a possible defense when they come to plunder Christian lands: if they happen to be shipwrecked or are taken prisoner, they show their declarations and say that these papers prove their intention to remain in Christian lands, which was the reason they came on a raid with the Turks. In this way they avoid the initial violence of their captors and reconcile with the Church, and no one does them any harm, and at the first opportunity they return to Barbary to be what they were before. There are others, however, who obtain and use these papers with good intentions and remain in Christian lands.[52]
> (Cervantes 2003, 346)

Therefore, objects such as letters signed by captives could be used for profoundly different purposes, but both would lead to a benefit sought by the bearer. Only after the Cervantine renegade wields the crucifix, his safe conduct, do the other captives begin to confide in the renegade and allow him to join them in their journey back to Spain.

Given these examples, the behaviour of the Murcian renegade in "The Captive's Tale" at the moment when he arrives on the Spanish coast is especially relevant. Once in Vélez Malaga, his first stop is at a church, where he instructs Zoraida on how to understand the religious icons. Significantly, this occurs right before the renegade presents himself to the Inquisition (Hutchinson 2011, 158).[53] Could the renegade's actions help mitigate any consequences as he appears before Inquisitional authorities and reintegrates into the Catholic Church? In this sense, it is striking that the renegade focuses particularly on an image of the Virgin Mary when he gives Zoraida a short lesson on the meaning of the images. According to the captive's testimony, neither the renegade nor Zoraida alludes to any other Christian iconography that would have been in the church in Vélez Málaga. Remarkably, there is no mention of any representation of Christ in the church, and the only references to images are of Lela Marién, the same figure that Zoraida had evoked several times in Algiers. As we saw in Chapter 4, Cervantes and other early modern Spanish writers were certainly aware of the prominent place that Maryam/Mary occupies in the Qur'an, and thus it does not seem unintentional that it is only a Marian icon that is referenced when the renegade enters the church with Zoraida. Using images of the Virgin Mary to find a point in common between Christians and Muslims in Spain is something that the first archbishop of Granada, Fray Hernando de Talavera, tried to implement with the approval of Queen Isabel I as he attempted to evangelize to the Moriscos living in that kingdom (Pereda, 2007, 249–373). The Morisco community, however, widely rejected this imposition of images, including those of the Virgin Mary, although images of the Virgin were opposed to a lesser extent than those representing Christ (Pereda 2007, 350–6; Franco Llopis 2010a, 96–7). Although Zoraida is clearly not a Morisca, the text is silent with regard to this Algerian woman's reaction to the renegade's lesson on religious iconography, and the account never reveals to what extent she accepted or rejected the images, only indicating that she "understood" them (Cervantes 2003, 1:41, 513).[54]

The renegades of the early modern Mediterranean era, skilled at passing between the two sides of the sea and capable of modifying their language, name, clothes, and religion, took advantage of sacred objects such as the cross or the Virgin Mary to facilitate travel to both shores. Once in the hands of renegades, religious images acquired different values and meanings beyond any purely religious use, exemplifying how the same icon could be used by people of diverse cultures, beliefs, and circumstances. All the examples presented here, and especially the case of the Murcian renegade in "The Captive's Tale," help us to understand the particular role of images that circulated in the Mediterranean world and how these objects of devotion could provide substantial benefits to renegades, in particular, since their identities were marked by the ambiguity of being caught between two worlds.

Unorthodox Perspectives

Throughout this chapter, we have seen how various texts depict the unique coexistence of and interaction between individuals and images in Mediterranean captivity, as well as how the diverse members of this world responded to and were affected by icons in this shared space. Some early modern Spanish authors, however, portrayed an entirely different scenario in their captivity treatises and other narratives, exposing sometimes "unorthodox" perspectives on images. The Spanish Protestant Cipriano de Valera's *Tratado para confirmar los pobres cautivos de Berbería* ([1594] 2004) addresses the subject of captivity and cross-cultural encounters with Muslims in North Africa, much like the treatises of other Spanish religious writers, including Fray Matías de San Francisco, Fray Francisco San Juan del Puerto, Gabriel Gómez de Losada, and Fray Jerónimo Gracián de la Madre de Dios (Bunes Ibarra and Alonso Acero 2004, 28). These authors all share a similar concern for the Christian captives confined to North Africa, fearing that they might renege on their faith and convert to Islam. Cipriano de Valera, however, is particularly apprehensive about Christian captives' encounters with another religious group in North Africa. For him, Spanish Catholics – or Papists, as he names them – are much more problematic for the Protestant captives who carry out their quotidian activities alongside them.[55] Throughout his work, he continuously refers to Catholics as "our adversaries,"[56] while juxtaposing his intended audience as the "true Christians."[57] Even though Valera directs his treatise towards the Reformed captives in North Africa and recognizes their situation as prisoners in Islamic lands, he does not focus on their hardships and suffering, as many other authors and religious redeemers do. As Beatriz Alonso Acero and Miguel Ángel de Bunes Ibarra note, it is quite obvious from Valera's writing that he does not have any first-hand experience of life in captivity. Certainly, for this reason, his text does not incorporate the brutal descriptions of captives' torture and pain that so many other works of this nature include (2004, 29).

Given that Valera is more concerned with his readers' ability to maintain their belief while living alongside Catholics, Muslims, and Jews in North Africa than with the daily torment and adversities they face as captives, the content of his treatise focuses on the basic principles of Protestant theology while highlighting his criticisms of the Church of Rome. Among the issues that concern him is the veneration of religious images, as he accuses Catholics of not adhering to the Ten Commandments by creating and worshipping other gods: "Of these Ten Commandments our adversaries, as the traitors and betrayers that they are towards the God who raised them, have completely eliminated the second, which is against images" ([1594] 2004, 158).[58] He further highlights the excessively prominent role of the pope and the creation of the cult of saints, including any figural representations of them: "They are not content invoking the saints, but they invoke their images, their statues, or rather, their idols" (49).[59] Contrary to the accounts of such authors as Gómez de Losada and Andreu de San Joseph, which extol the miraculous crucifixes rescued from captivity, Valera warns his readers about these icons, and urges them to recognize the symbolic meaning of the cross without worshipping it: "I made this comment about the cross in passing, so that no one takes this as an excuse to worship a wooden or silver cross; for to do so is superstition and idolatry" (156).[60] This Protestant treatise on captivity clearly was not meant to portray the horrors and gruesome details that many of those enslaved in North Africa experienced. Rather, it was intended, at least partially, to demonstrate the flawed practices of Catholics. In doing so, Valera signals how some of the anxieties surrounding religious and cultural identities come to the foreground, particularly within the context of captivity, by magnifying the place of images in cross-confessional encounters.

In the anonymous sixteenth-century dialogue *Viaje de Turquía* ([c. 1557] 1980), it is specifically the space of the Muslim "other" wherein comparisons and criticisms of religious practices, including the veneration of sacred objects, transpire. Divided into two parts, the colloquy involving three friends – Juan de Voto a Dios, Mátalascallando, and Pedro de Urdemalas – relates the experience of the Spanish ex-captive Pedro in Istanbul, depicting the various customs and practices he observed in the Ottoman Empire. Through this exposition of daily Turkish life, a parallel is drawn with Spanish ways, revealing what the author believes to be some of the latter's weak points. There is an evident critical tone towards the numerous outward demonstrations of Catholic faith, and, by virtue of this, Pedro calls into question the efficacy of such things as relics, pilgrimages, alms, and hospitals.

During the second day of the dialogue, the three interlocutors exchange views on their interpretations of the Turks' religious beliefs and traditions. To address Juan's questions about the churches in Istanbul, Pedro underscores the ornamentation inside their mosques: "Some mosques are well done, except that they neither have saints nor altars. They really abhor figural images, considering them a great sin" (*Viaje de Turquía* [c. 1557] 1980, 389).[61] Later, Pedro emphasizes that, even though they revere one God, they reject any type of figural image that could represent him: "Yes, and there is not more than one, and only that person is to be worshipped, and from this comes the idea that they abhor the images that in church, home, or any other place they are not allowed to have, not even portraits or adornments" (391).[62] While Pedro insists on calling attention to the question of images, he is prudent not to go too far in his criticisms, since Mátalascallando has already reproached him for having Lutheran ideas when he suggested throwing relics into the river (124–5).[63] Yet, as much as Pedro might find fault with the exterior nature of Catholic rituals while praising some of the practices of the Turks, he never hesitates to refer to Islam as a false religion, and is even willing to die as a martyr for his faith instead of renouncing his beliefs (Delgado-Gómez 1987, 55–6).

In the same Erasmian fashion, Alfonso de Valdés's *Diálogo de las cosas ocurridas en Roma* ([1527] 1956) shares many of the criticisms of Catholic religious imagery found in *Viaje de Turquía*. Although the dialogue is intended as a defence of the Emperor Carlos V from accusations regarding the Sack of Rome, Valdés also uses it as an attack on the corruption and excesses of the Catholic Church. The *Diálogo* does not focus on Mediterranean captivity, as do the many other texts discussed in this chapter, but the work contributes an added layer of meaning to the nuanced relation between images and captives. In the second part of their debate, Latancio offers examples of how some Christian practices do not line up with Christian doctrine, particularly the act of relying on images to rescue captives from foreign lands:

> For what reason do you think that one person leads the other to believe that a wooden image will rescue captives and that it returns sweating all over, but only to entice the common people to offer things to that image of which they will later take advantage? And he or she does not have fear of God to deceive people in this way. As if Our Lady, in order to ransom a captive, needed to take a wooden image with her! And being a ridiculous idea, the common people believe it because of the authority with which it is said.[64]
> (Valdés [1527] 1956, 137)

This critique of the way images linked to ransoming captives could be used to achieve personal objectives contradicts precisely what authors such as Gómez de Losada and Andreu de San Joseph underscore in their own works. For Valdés, religious images have no place in ransom missions, even if, in the popular imaginary, stories circulate about a particular image's power. Like the *Tratado para confirmar los pobres cautivos de Berbería* and the *Viaje de Turquía*, Valdés's work uncovers how religious debates about the use and role of sacred objects crossed geographic and cultural borders, and were inserted into larger conversations about captivity in the Mediterranean world.

At this point, it is useful to contextualize some of the works examined in this chapter and to reflect on the authors' intentions for writing these texts on the theme of captivity. Aside from the last few texts discussed here, many other accounts were written to be used principally as propaganda and to raise public awareness about the importance of rescuing captives, which evidently required adequate funding. These narratives were written with a deliberate purpose, and so it is critical to question the way these authors conceptualized the value attributed to the icons described in their works, taking into consideration how the circulation of these images throughout the Mediterranean might have a special significance in this particular context. If the supposed value of some of these sacred figures depended on their experience of captivity or the degree to which they were subjected to cruelty by their adversaries, emphasizing this contempt becomes a necessary component to add weight to this idea, whether the details of each account are accurate or not.

Despite their inclination to document the hostility to which these images were subjected in North Africa, at other times these same authors present a peaceful coexistence between religious images and members of different religions and cultures. A sizeable portion of Gómez de Losada's writings portray the taunting and affronts that some religious objects sustained in Algiers, but, at certain times, paradoxically, he also describes the respect that other sacred images were shown. This is especially true of the Holy Sacrament, as when he explains, "some female Turks and Moors sometimes gave them wax candles, so that they would burn in front of the Holy Sacrament, and other such particular things, on which a long treatise could be written" (1670, 371).[65] Following along the same lines, Jerónimo Gracián, in his *Peregrinación de Anastasio* ([c. 1613] 2006), also illustrates how images were used and valued in North African captivity, offering diverse examples of the treatment of religious objects by their supposed adversaries.[66] Yet, in contrast to some examples that he offers describing the maltreatment of the cross in Tunis, Gracián includes another anecdote about how a Christian icon is treated more benevolently by a Muslim.[67] The story outlines how, after Gracián had explained the meaning of the crucifix to a "big drunken Turk"[68] named Resuán, this individual "gave a coin or two for the lamp's oil and he became very angry if he found it put out"[69] every time he passed by the image (103n3). His testimony reveals the different values and uses that these religious objects could acquire within the wide variety of genres treating themes related to captivity.

As this chapter has illustrated, the lives of images and human captives were intertwined within the context of Mediterranean captivity. A careful examination of writings about captivity reveals the complexities of how religious images were manipulated and used according to one's own motives in the frontier spaces between Spain and North Africa. An initial reading of many of these captivity accounts draws attention to the adverse reception of Catholic icons in Algiers, Tunis, and other Mediterranean corsair locales. Yet, a closer look at these texts suggests that captive images and other sacred objects circulating between the shores of the Mediterranean at times coexisted among individuals of diverse religious and cultural backgrounds. Ultimately, many of these historical and literary works on captivity show how the written descriptions of images included in these texts are inscribed with much more meaning than just their symbolic value. The objects acquired new significance once they were embedded within the realm of captivity, especially in the hands of martyrs and renegades. In texts about martyrdom, religious iconography of the cross allowed martyrs to align their suffering with that of Christ, and make meaning out of their experience for the public of the time. Works about renegades, on the other hand, show how these individuals used sacred images to mould their identities and more closely position themselves with either Christianity or Islam, depending on how they treat the images at any given moment. In different circumstances, Spanish Protestants or other writers with Erasmian influences employed the backdrop of captivity to criticize the use of images in Catholic practice. Fundamentally, the trajectories and material lives of the religious images that travelled between the Iberian Peninsula and North Africa tell novel stories about Christian-Muslim relations and a life shared in common with the sacred images that incited their attention.

Conclusion

This book began with the story of the coveted effigy of Christ that circulated among Muslims, Christians, and Jews in Algiers and throughout the Mediterranean. Tracing the circulation of this image allows us to follow some of the ways in which individuals of diverse beliefs and practices encountered one another. With each movement, this image took on new meanings, but it also allowed some individuals to reaffirm or shape certain aspects of their own cultural and religious identities. Fray Cristóbal Bas adds another piece to the story of this image's trajectory as he sketches out its afterlife once it is redeemed and returned to Spain.

In 1670, Bas preached a sermon on this ransomed effigy of Christ on one of the Fridays during Lent at the Convent of Our Lady of Mercy in Madrid.[1] In the sermon, he tries to return the image to its "original" meaning as an object of Catholic devotion. Addressing the congregation, he specifies how they should understand this image, how they should look at it, and how their emotions should align while contemplating it (Bas 1670, 1–5). Nevertheless, the storied history of the effigy is still marked by its cross-confessional encounters in Algiers. In particular, Bas's sermon stresses the effigy's status as a captive and how it suffered alongside human captives, in order to show the redemptive power of God through this image (5). Even as the image has been returned to its place of origin, Bas cannot divorce it from its prior trajectory throughout the Mediterranean. Thus, the image still serves as a barometer for how Christians and Muslims encountered each other in the early modern world.

The case of this ransomed effigy of Christ reaffirms much of what I have endeavoured to show throughout this book. *The Arts of Encounter* has sought to reframe our understanding of Christian-Muslim relations in early modern Spain by uncovering the significant role of religious images in interfaith encounters described in a range of literary genres, which I read alongside a wide assortment of other early modern sources. As I have argued, the power of images omnipresent in everyday life influenced how early modern writers chose to portray relations between Christians and Muslims. These authors lived and wrote surrounded by the religious visual culture of their day, and, as I have suggested, they understood Christian-Muslim relations in visual terms. Due to the overwhelming presence of crosses, images of the Virgin Mary, and effigies of Christ, among many other objects of devotion, these manifestations of religious visual culture populate the drama, poetry, and narrative fiction of early modern Spain, yet sometimes get relegated to background details and unintentionally taken for granted precisely because of their ubiquitousnes. Throughout this book, I have proposed that, by paying attention to the visual cues in the texts, a more nuanced understanding of Christian-Muslim relations emerges.

It has not been my intention to take these literary genres as an unequivical rendering of exactly how religious confrontations or mutual understanding always took place – although they often provide important details about the ongoing exchanges among a variety of groups – since each author will have had their own bias and motivations for writing. However, a close reading of these texts tells us much more about how these writers perceived cross-confesional relations and, as a result, the way in which these ideas were shared with a wider public. They present a valuable perspective on how early modern society grappled with religious identity and what was at stake for individuals by aligning themsleves in particular ways with the pervasive visual culture that surrounded them. Literary texts complement the other textual and visual sources I examine – including historical chronicles, Inquisition cases, religious treatises, miracle books, travel memoirs, captives' testimonies, letters, autobiographical accounts, paintings, and engravings – by enrichening discussions on the role of religious images in interfaith relations. Many of the writings I explore in this study show that the contentious question of religious images went far beyond how they were actually accepted or rejected and unveiled some of the anxieties about what it meant to belong to different religious and cultural communities.

Several common threads connect the writings I examine throughout this book that have significant implications for understanding Christian-Muslim relations in the early modern world. One thread is the multivalient meanings and uses that writers attribute to religious images within different social and cultural contexts. Images of the cross, Jesus, and the Virgin Mary, among other "idols" and imagined "Islamic" iconography or even Arabic characters appear on both shores of the Mediterranean in a variety of written sources. We tend to attach fixed meanings to many of these images, such as the cross, because they are intimately tied to a certain religion and are intended to have a single, common use as an object of religious devotion. Despite what many early modern authors might have claimed about these images, their writings actually reveal the multiple ways the same image could be used, attesting to the fluidity of their meanings. These writings show equally that the cross could be a marker of "true" Christian conversion, but that it could also assert its authority over an entire cultural minority – as the apologists used the cross to justify the Moriscos' expulsion from Spain. The multiple trajectories of images of the Virgin Mary are even more surprising given the revered place of Mary/Maryam in both Christianity and Islam. Writers credit images of Mary for the conversion of a Muslim prince, while, at other times, Marian icons are more closely aligned to conquest and local belonging, exerting military force against their perceived enemies. Yet in other instances, these same images incite desire or respect by individuals of diverse religious faiths for reasons that have nothing or little to do with their professed religion.

In many ways, the multiple trajectories and lives of the images that run through this book also help to highlight the malleability of religious identity in the early modern world. Whether directly or indirectly, many of the writers examined here suggest that Christian and Muslim identities were not rigid, but varied along a broad continuum. In fact, many of the fictional and real Christian and Muslim individuals who come in contact with each other are defined by their very in-betweenness, as figures who live at the crossroads of porous religious and cultural boundaries. These forced converts (Moriscos), renegades, captives, martyrs, merchants, corsairs, redemptionist friars, and diplomats, among others, display different attitudes and behaviour towards religious images depending on the social pressures and their particular circumstances, needs, desires, or beliefs. In writings both by and about Moriscos, the diversity in their responses to religious images could be attributed in part to pressure from religious authorities or the imminence of their expulsion. But it also depended on how certain authors wished to characterize this group, including how some Moriscos used writing as a vehicle to resist forced image worship. On the other shore of the Mediterranean, renegades and martyrs could use these same images in contrasting ways to affirm their religious affiliations publicly when they found themselves in precarious situations. These and many of the other cases I have explored suggest that these writers, and, by extension, a sizeable part of the early modern public, understood and defined people by the way they responded to religious images. References to the visual material culture in their texts helps to delineate the multiple ways a variety of

groups continuously came in contact with each other, including under
circumstances of forced friction or mutual respect.

Although my sources focus on the context of early modern Spain,
the texts also have taken us to other parts of the Mediterranean world,
underscoring how parallel discusions about religious images transversed
imperial and cultural boundaries. In particular, important connections
between Moriscos and Protestants, among other groups, become more
apparent by placing texts about Spain, North Africa, and the greater
Mediterranean world in dialogue with one another. Likewise, the power
of these images to evoke strong feelings or indifference, devotion, rage,
and conversion did not discriminate based on where they were located
geographically. These images, which coexisted alongside individuals of
diverse backgrounds, cultures, and faiths, leading to encounters among
different groups of people, predisposed how early modern authors
would take up these themes in their literary works. Despite some significant divergences, this approach still suggests a certain unity of the
kind that Braudel and Horden and Purcell outline in their respective
histories of the Mediterranean. In general, as I hope many of the examples in this book have demonstrated, references to the material visual
culture are crucial for tracing how Christian and Muslim communities
perceived each other. By putting these images "on display," to use W.J.T.
Mitchell's term, we are in a much better place to begin to see how cross-
confessional encounters were perceived and expressed in print (2002b,
166). Ultimatly, *The Arts of Encounter* offers an approach that I hope
will open up new avenues for examing how writers moulded the role
of images in cross-cultural relations to enrichen our understanding of
interfaith relations in early modern Spain and the Mediterranean world.

Notes

Introduction

1 Gómez de Losada narrates the history and circulation of this effigy of Christ in the fourth book of his captivity treatise, *Escuela de trabajos* (1670), which I discuss in more detail in Chapter 6. The Mercedarian friar Cristóbal Bas preached a sermon on this same captive image of Christ, which is recorded in his *Dispertador espiritual y oración evangélica del Redentor redimido o santo Cristo del Rescate* (1670). The list of the 211 ransomed human captives is included in the final folios of the *Libro de redención de cautivos hecha en Argel en 1667 por los Padres mercedarios Pedro de la Concepción, Gabriel Gómez de Losada y Juan de Luque*. On Algiers as a Mediterranean corsair capital, see Garcés (2011).

2 For a summary of the vast array of early modern Spanish texts that include Muslim characters and related themes, see Mas (1967). In the case of Cervantes's oeuvre, Francisco Márquez Villanueva (2010), among many others, has analysed the principal scenes with Christian-Muslim encounters. For Lope de Vega's works, Thomas E. Case's *Lope and Islam* (1993) outlines the prolific playwright's many pieces that deal with relations between Christian and Muslim characters.

3 Felipe Pereda (2007, 2019) and Borja Franco Llopis (2008a, 2008b, 2010a, 2011b, 2014, 2019) have approached similar issues in their illuminating studies from the discipline of art history. See also Cynthia Robinson (2013), who has addressed this question in an earlier time period, focusing particularly on fourteenth- and fifteenth-century Castile, also from an art historical perspective. On the question of captive images in the Mediterranean world, see the cited research by art historian María Cruz de Carlos Varona (2011).

4 On the important roles of religious images in early modern Spain, see especially María Cruz de Carlos Varona et al.'s edited volume (2008), Palma

Martínez-Burgos García (1960) and Amanda Wunder (2017), in addition to the illustrated exhibition catalogue *Sacred Spain: Art and Belief in the Spanish World* (Kasl et al. 2009), provide a useful introduction to many of the debates around images in sixteenth- and seventeenth-century Spain.

5 "todo parece indicar que la admisión de las imágenes en el culto constituyó una de las líneas infranqueables que separaban a los cristianos de los musulmanes y que con esta misma línea se marcaba muchas veces la frontera, si no de su convivencia, sí por lo menos de la permeabilidad de su intercambio cultural"

   On the problem of images, see also Franco Llopis (2010a, 2011b, 2011–13, 2017) for a broader understanding of how followers of Islam in the Iberian Peninsula understood religious images. Cardaillac also offers some interesting examples of how the Moriscos reproached the cult of the images of the Catholic Church (2004, 301–4).

6 This image, known as the Christ of Medinaceli, was later ransomed and returned to Madrid, where it is still highly venerated today. For more on this image, see Carlos Varona (2011).

7 "despojos de su triunfo"; "en odio de la Religión Christiana"

8 See also the extensive bibliography on this issue cited by Pereda (2007, 341–2n198), as well as Gruber's recent edited volume, *The Image Debate* (2019).

9 On the presence of Muslim communities in seventeenth- and eighteenth-century Cartagena, see Torres Sánchez (1986).

10 "ponen las ymágines de los sanctos en sus casas a la cabecera de la cama para que al echar y al levantar se acuerden dellas"; for more on Bernardo Pérez de Chinchón, see Pons Fuster (2014).

11 See the cited studies by Pereda and Franco Llopis.

12 "un palo"

13 See Pereda (2007, 398–402) and Franco Llopis (2010a, 2011).

14 David Freedberg has called this intent to see certain religions as having no images at all the "myth of aniconism" (1989, 54–81). See also Oleg Grabar (1987) and Mika Natif (2011) on this issue.

15 "وبداخل المسجد أنواع الصور والصليب وصور الملائكة جبريل وميكائيل وعزرائيل وإسرافيل وغيرهم، وصور الأنبياء في الطبقة العليا يحيى وزكرياء ومريم بولدها عيسى على عضدها، ومهد عيسى، وغير ذلك من تلاعب الكفرة. وقد قلع المسلمون لما دخلوها صور الصليب كلها وبعض الصور غيرها، وتركوا بعضها. وبهذا البلد مساجد حاولوا فيها شبه هذا المسجد الأعظم، لكن عجزوا عن ذلك"

16 "Están esta Nuestra Señora y el morabito de tal suerte que ni los turcos cuando llegan a esta isla maltratan la imagen de Nuestra Señora ni los cristianos al morabito"; Contreras offers a similar description of this shrine in Lampedusa in his *Vida del capitán Contreras* ([c. 1630–1641] 1982, 45). For more on this shared space, see Arnaldi (1990).

17 "cristianos, moros, turcos, galeotes, bogadores, oficiales, corsarios, mercaderes y otra infinita gente"

18 These challenges with terminology have led prominent scholars such as L.P. Harvey and Luce López Baralt to title their respective books about the descendents of Muslims from the Iberian Peninsula as *Muslims in Spain, 1500 to 1614* (2005) and *La literatura secreta de los últimos musulmanes de España* (2009), avoiding the problematic category of "Morisco" on their cover pages, despite still using the term in various contexts within their works.

19 For a comparison of different cases of Protestant and Morisco iconoclasm in early modern Europe, see Cardaillac (2004, 119–41) and Franco Llopis (2011b, 2011–13).

20 "los cristianos papistas"

21 "los cristianos luteranos"

22 Jews' reception of religious art in medieval and early modern Spain also developed along a parallel path to that of Moriscos and Protestants, but falls outside of the reach of this study, since the authors of the narrative fiction, theatre, and poetry, in addition to the other non-fictional sources, that I examine here rarely, if at all, mention these connections. However, cases like the profanation of the Christ of Patience in Madrid (c. 1630) were contemporaneous with many of the Christian-Muslim encounters I study throughout the book. On the Christ of Patience, see Alpert (1997). For broader implications of Jews' reception of religious images, see Pereda (2007) and Glazer-Eytan (2019).

23 "moro y luterano"

24 "las cruzes eran espantajos y que no se avían de reverençiar … y que las ymágenes hera todo compuesto y que no servían de adorar ni reverençiar sino solamente tener en cuenta de Dios"

25 "Comúnmente entre los fieles católicos llamamos imágenes las figuras que nos representan a Cristo Nuestro Señor, a su benditísima Madre y Virgen Santa María, a sus apóstoles y a los demás santos y los misterios de nuestra Fe, en cuanto pueden ser imitados y representados, para que refresquemos en ellos la memoria; y que la gente ruda que no sabe letras les sirven de libro"

26 صنم. The Hans Wehr Dictionary defines the word as "idol, image" (616). On its meaning, see also Lane (1984, 2:1735–6). *Wathan* (pl. *awthān*) is another Arabic word used to describe figural images as idols, but the authors that I examine did not use this term in their works. On some differences between *wathan* and *ṣanam* and their usage in the Qur'an, see Monnot (2019).

27 صورة. Hans Wehr labels the term as "form, shape; pictorial representation, illustration; image, likeness, picture; figure, statue; replica; copy, carbon copy, duplicate; version, form, draft (of a proposal, etc.); manner, mode" (619). On its meaning, see also Lane (1984, 2:1744–5).

28 For more on these images, see especially the section of Chapter 1 titled "Of Crescent Moons and Other Images" with the associated bibliography.

29 "ídolo de Mahoma"

30 On the existence of some "Islamic icons" in early modern Spain, see Franco Llopis and Moreno Díaz del Campo (2018, 120–3).

31 Several important monographs in English have been published in recent years, among them: Green-Mercado, *Visions of Deliverance: Moriscos and the Politics of Prophecy in the Early Modern Mediterranean* (2019); Hershenzon, *The Captive Sea: Slavery, Communication, and Commerce in Early Modern Spain and the Mediterranean* (2018); Hutchinson, *Frontier Narratives: Liminal Lives in the Early Modern Mediterranean* (2020); Irigoyen-García, *Moors Dressed as Moors: Clothing, Social Distinction, and Ethnicity in Early Modern Iberia* (2017); Johnson, *Affective Geographies: Cervantes, Emotion, and the Literary Mediterranean* (2020); Kimmel, *Parables of Coercion: Conversion and Knowledge at the End of Islamic Spain* (2015); and Lee, *The Anxiety of Sameness in Early Modern Spain* (2015).

32 See especially Felipe Pereda (2007, 2019) as well as Borja Franco Llopis (2008b).

33 On the trope of passing in Spanish literature, see Barbara Fuchs (2003) and Christina H. Lee (2015).

34 Mercedes García-Arenal has proposed an expanded and more integrated approach to studying Moriscos within the larger context of the Mediterranean (1992, 493). See especially Mercedes García-Arenal and Gerard A. Wiegers's edited volume (2013) and the recent English translation (2014). Steven Hutchinson (2012b) also draws attention to the importance of studying Cervantes's Morisco characters within a broader Mediterranean framework.

1 Moriscos between Cross and Crescent

1 "hereges apostatas, y proditores de lesa Magestad"

2 For more on the anti-Islamic propaganda espoused by the Catholic apologists of the expulsion, see especially Magnier (2010, 119–36).

3 For examples of Morisco polemical writings about the crucifixion, see Cardaillac (2004, 258–67).

4 Rafala is the only Cervantine character from the Morisco community associated with the symbol of the cross throughout Cervantes's oeuvre. The only minor exception is the Morisco Ricote in Cervantes's *Don Quixote*, who possesses coins marked with Christian crosses. For more on Ricote's coins, see Leahy (2016). However, many other Cervantine frontier characters associate themselves with the symbol of the cross in Cervantes's works, some of which I discuss in more detail in Chapter 6: (1) Christian converts: in *Los baños de Argel*, Zahara pretends to not understand the significance of the

cross laced between the beads on her rosary ([1615] 1983, 3:vv. 2883–911);
in "The Captive's Tale" intercalated in *Don Quixote*, the Algerian Zoraida
displays a reed cross out her window, which leads the captive Ruy Pérez
de Viedma immediately to associate her and the cross she holds with the
religion that it symbolizes (1978, 1:40, 487). (2) Renegades: in the same
episode, the renegade from Murcia relies on a small crucifix kept close to
his heart as a measure of his trustworthiness (1:40, 490); in *Los baños de Argel*,
the renegade Hazén holds up a wooden cross in an attempt to redeem all his
past sins while being martyred ([1615] 1983, 1:vv. 667–881). (3) Christian
captives: the Christian captive Catalina de Oviedo in *La gran sultana* exhibits
an ebony cross in the Great Turk's seraglio ([1615] 1999, 1023), while in
El amante liberal, the Christian captive Leonisa takes out a small cross from
under her clothes in the house of her mistress Halima in an attempt to
externalize her Catholic faith ([1613] 1980, 169).

5 "bien merecían ser desterrados del mundo"

6 "Que por las graves injurias que los moriscos hazían al Santíssimo Sacramento,
   y a la Sacratíssima Cruz estava nuestro Cathólico Monarca obligado a echarlos"

7 "Hazían los pérfidos moriscos mofa y escarnio del Santíssimo Sacramento,
   como se ha dicho, a todos los domingos y fiestas, oyendo Missa injuriavan
   todas las Cruzes de los caminos y de las salidas de sus lugares: estos delictos
   pues los sacaron de España, sin que pudiessen quedar en ella: *Expulsi sunt,
   nec potuerunt stare*"

8 "Podemos ya yr por este Reyno sin temor destos enemigos; gozamos de ver
   las Santas Cruzes libres de tantas injurias que ellos les hazían"

9 "guerra contra las Cruzes"

10 Marcos de Guadalajara y Xavier, like the other apologists, intentionally
   highlights the idea that the Moriscos were concocting a plan with their
   Turkish neighbors, even though, as Francisco Márquez Villanueva explains,
   this was only a "conspiratorial myth" (1998, 141–66).

11 "desseavan salir con triumpho de poder de los christianos"

12 These two accounts of pictorial representations of Muhammad that
   Guadalajara y Xavier recalls are especially striking when keeping in mind
   the aversion to figurative representations – although not generalized –
   in Islam. See Oleg Grabar's chapter "Islamic Attitudes toward the Arts"
   in his book *The Formation of Islamic Art* (1987, 72–98) and the collection
   of essays edited by Gilbert Beaugé and J.-F. Clément (1995). For some
   exceptions of figural representations in Islamic art, see Eva Baer (2004).
   Gaspar Escolano also includes a similar account of an old Morisca woman
   prognosticating the future, this time with six eggs decorated with the cross
   and the remaining six with the symbol of the crescent moon. The outcome,
   however, is the same (1879–80, 2:823a).

13 "Que no emprendiessen novedad, porque sería su perdición"
14 "dos cirios tan yguales, que no pesase el uno mas que el otro un solo cabello"
15 "Mal va nuestra empressa, perdidos somos, los christianos han de vencer"
16 See Chapter 2 for my analysis of Morisco accounts of Catholic religious images as idols.
17 "sus menguantes lunas"
18 "otras çiertas señales como la luna esculpida e pintada"
19 "las personas y las cosas se conocen por las señales que tienen y se juzgan ser de aquel cuyas señales traen"
20 "una media luna de paño azul del tamaño de una naranja"
21 Within a broader context, Hildburgh (1942) studied the symbol of the crescent moon as an amulet in Spain.
22 "Lo que es muy digno de consideración en esta visión milagrosa es que aquella rutilante muger tenía la luna debaxo de sus pies, significándonos claramente que vendrá día, en que (como la vido el evangelista) la Iglesia Christiana escogida de Dios, pisará y tendrá postrada a sus pies la pompa y Magestad de los mosulanos [sic] turcos, que son la luna desvariada, según que ellos se la atribuyen a sí mismos"
23 For more on Luis de Alcázar's influence on Pacheco and the iconography of the Immaculate Conception with the crescent moon, see Reeves (1997, 193–6).
24 One possible exception could be Nicholas de Lyra's *Postilla super totam Bibliam* (1472), which circulated widely in the sixteenth and seventeenth centuries. He interprets the woman standing on the moon in Revelations as "the Church militant and its victory over heresy" and uses an example of the seventh-century Byzantine Christian emperor Heraclius's victory over the Persian King Heraclius to illustrate his point (Ostrow 1996, 234).
25 "un Maomica de oro, digo, sobredorado, con la luna a sus pies, el Alcorán en la mano y otras diversas circunstancias que agravavan el casso"
26 "De una Cruz que apareció sobre la Luna"
27 See Manuel Ruiz Lagos's introduction to Gaspar Aguilar's poem for a succinct discussion of the *Cofradía de la Cruz* (Ruiz Lagos 1999, 32–40).
28 "una cofradía, o hermandad de christianos viejos, que cuydassen de guardarlas y levantarlas a lugares tan eminentes, que no pudiessen llegar aquellos sus enemigos a maltratarlas"
29 During the preparations for forming the *Cofradía de la Cruz*, Jaime Bleda went to the Inquisition to receive its approval. The Holy Office refused to endorse this organization since the general inquisitor, Cardinal don Hernando Niño de Guevara, would not allow a mass denouncement of all the Moriscos, as Bleda was planning (1618, 961a).

30 "por medio de la mesma Cruz"

31 Bleda recalls this miracle some years earlier in his *Breve relación de la expulsion de los moriscos del reyno de Valencia*, which he includes in his *Defensio fidei* (1610, 596). For more on the cross of Caravaca, see Villanueva Fernández (1999) and García Arenal and Rodríguez Mediano (2010, 218–22). I discuss this cross in relation to the Moriscos and the Sacromonte in Chapter 3.

32 "como diziéndonos el Cielo con tal prodigio que el báculo poderoso de Christo nuestro salvador, que es su victoriosa cruz, con su virtud insuperable nos dexava ya essentos de las assechanças de infieles domésticos, y se quedava libre de las blasfemias continuas dellos llevándolos delante de sí a hechallos por essos mares, barriendo nos la tierra de su pestífera contagión para que libres del mal exemplo de sus infidelidades y escándalos intibiadores la adorasen todos los fieles con mayor fervor y puridad"

33 For an overview on the collection of paintings depicting the expulsion of the Moriscos, see Jesús Villalmanzo Cameno (1997). See also Bernabé Pons (1997-8); Dopico Black (2003); and Gerli (2016a).

34 "Tenía el lienço (que sería de tres palmos a lo largo, dos y medio de ancho) una sala espaciosa, un venerable viejo vestido de una alba blanca y no ceñida que tenía sobre los ombros y cabeça una muceta azul, un moro assentado a sus pies, con quien parece comunicava algún negocio grave, y una çarabatana cuadrada de color de pino que el uno de sus orificios estava encaxado en la pared y el otro al oydo del viejo. Según parece por lo que resultava del dicho processo y común fama y estimación de toda la Andaluzía que el viejo era Mahoma"

35 "no veneran ni honran la figura toda de Mahoma, sino su Zancarrón: que es un braço adornado, conforme la posibilidad de cada uno, de pedrería, anillos y otras riquezas"

36 José María Perceval studies the image of the *zancarrón* in detail in various texts of the time period, including the works of Lope de Vega and Quevedo (1997, 204–7). More recently, Antonio Sánchez Jiménez has traced references to the *zancarrón* in Lope de Vega's dramatic work (2019, 191–209). Albert Mas (1967, 2:290) and Louis Cardaillac (2004, 311–12) also dedicate a few pages to this topic. Furthermore, Borja Franco Llopis analyses three Inquisition cases in which Moriscos are accused of possessing and worshipping not only a relic of the Prophet, but an entire figural representation of Muhammad (2010a, 97–9).

37 See Aznar Cardona for his nuanced use of the *ampsa* (1612, 2: 50v). Moriscos' association with the *ampsa* has been analysed by several scholars, such as Cardaillac (2004, 312) and Perceval (1997, 211), while referencing these texts. However, the etymology of the term remains to be studied.

"sacavan para adorar, una mano retratada del pérfido Mahoma, a que llamavan Ampsa"

38 "que en su ley tomaban un zancarrón de borrico y le ponían enhiesto y se hincaban de rodillas todos los moriscos delante de él, y que un morisco, que no nombró la dicha Inés, dijo que se vestía como clérigo y decía misa delante del zancarrón"

39 Márquez Villanueva, among other scholars, contextualizes the discourses of the *xadraque* Xarife, relating them to the texts of the apologists of the expulsion (1975, 292). More recently, Gerli has placed Xarife's prophecy in a broader dialogue with the polemics surrounding prophecies in early modern Spain, especially Morisco *jofores* (Gerli 2016b).

40 "¡Cristiana, cristiana y libre, y libre por la gracia y misericordia de Dios!"

41 "buena torre tenemos, y buenas y ferradas puertas la iglesia, que, si no es muy de propósito, no pueden ser derribadas ni abrasadas"

42 José Manuel Martín Morán (2004, 566–7) and Steven Hutchinson (2012b, 189–90, 199) have highlighted precisely how the only two Moriscos who are conceded a voice throughout the episode are the Christian Moriscos, Rafala and her uncle Xarife, thus censoring the perspective of the majority of the crypto-Muslim Moriscos who are preparing to leave their homes in the kingdom of Valencia and set sail with Turkish corsairs.

43 "Lo mismo hicieron [los moriscos] en la iglesia y casa del cura, donde degollaron un muchachuelo que le servía; y pisando y arrastrando por el suelo los sagrados ornamentos, acuchillaron las imágenes de los Santos y cortaron de un alfanjazo la cabeza a un Crucifijo … Y acaeció, para confusión dellos, que habiendo puesto fuego al altar de la iglesia del palacio, se quemase todo el retablo y escapasen las imágenes solamente"

44 See Domínguez Ortiz and Vincent for other examples of image destruction after the War of the Alpujarras (1978, 277–9).

45 "[Los cristianos] recogiendo sus mujeres e hijos, se metieron en la iglesia y se hicieron fuertes en la torre del campanario. Luego acudieron los moros de Bayárcal y de los otros lugares comarcanos, y robando las casas de los cristianos, fueron a la iglesia, y hallando poca defensa, porque los nuestros se habían recogido en la torre, entraron dentro, y con cruel rabia deshicieron los altares, rompieron las aras y los retablos, y saquearon cuanto había dentro, y arrastraron y trajeron por el suelo todas las cosas sagradas … Y por más escarnio asaetearon y acuchillaron las cruces y las imágenes de bulto, y poniendo los pedazos de todo ello y de los retablos en medio de la iglesia, le pegaron fuego y lo quemaron"

46 For more on the cult of the Holy Innocents and its popularity in medieval Europe, see Wasyliw (2008, 29–38, 46–8).

47 "Cobraron estos animosos soldados con este pregón nuevo brío para morir en defensa de la fe; y, confiando poco en sus fuerças, por ser débiles y flacas,

se aprovecharon de las divinas y, bueltos a una imagen de la sacratíssima Reyna de los Ángeles, destroçada y medio quemada por aquellas infernales manos, empeçaron a decir a bozes: 'Reparadora de nuestra cayda, remedio de nuestras miserias, esperança de nuestra gloria, patrona y abogada de los afligidos, socorrednos y amparadnos, Señora, en este riguroso trance, para que nadie de nosotros falte a la obligación que tenemos'"

48 For further study, see Franco Llopis (2008a, 2010a, 2011b) and Pereda (2007), who have examined the relationship between Moriscos and religious art. The former centres principally on the geographical region of Valencia, while the latter focuses on Granada.

49 "una cruz e imágenes de santos, en sus aposentos, todo el año, con mucha decencia y veneración"

50 For more on the attempts to convert Moriscos through religious art in Valencia, see especially Franco Llopis (2019).

51 "Cuando iba a visitar esta gente llevaba imágenes de papel, de aquellas estampas viejas que entonces se tenían por buenas; dábales a unos y a otros. Enseñábalos en cuánta reverencia las habían de tener, y por ser punto tan vedado en su Corán tener imágenes, decíales cuán engañados estaban en aquello y qué consideración habían de tener en esta adoración, mostrándoles cómo no se comete en ella ninguna idolatría, pues son para levantar el corazón y despertar la memoria de aquello que representan, y adorar en ellas lo representado, que es Dios, su Madre y sus santos"; see also Pereda (2007, 272) and Franco Llopis (2008a, 389), who cite this same passage.

52 In *Instrucción de Talavera a los vecinos del Albaicín* (c. 1500), the archbishop of Granada requires of the Moriscos "that you all have in your homes and in decent and clean places images of our Lord or of the holy cross or of Our Lady the Virgin Mary or of some saint" ["que tengáys en vuestras casas en lugares onestos y limpios alguna ymájines de nuestro Señor o de la Santa Cruz o de Nuestra Señora la Virgen María o de algund santo o santa"]; see Pereda (2007, 276).

53 For more on Moriscos' domestic devotions and their religious material culture, see Franco Llopis and Moreno Díaz del Campo (2018, 107–25).

54 Although Alonso de Contreras's account cannot always be trusted, L.P. Harvey verifies that his description of Hornachos does include many authentic details, including some of the individuals mentioned. For more on the Morisco town of Hornachos and Contreras's involvement there, see Harvey (2005, 369–77).

55 "Y fue que entrando en otras primero, decían era enviado del obispo de Badajoz a ver las casas si tenían imágenes y cruces, y como yo era ermitaño creyéronlo, y fue causa que vinieron santeros con estampas de papel a Hornachos, que se hicieron ricos, y no había puerta que no tuviese dos o tres cruces, que parecía campo de matanza"

56 "ni imagen ni cruz en casa"
57 "hizo oración a las imágenes y luego se abrazó con su tío, besando primero las manos al cura"
58 "El escribano ni adoró ni besó las manos a nadie, porque le tenía ocupada el alma el sentimiento de la pérdida de su hacienda"
59 It is worth noting that scribes were often appointed as officers of the Inquisition, responsible for denouncing any unorthodox practices among the Moriscos; see Flores Arroyuelo (1989, 103) and Romero Múñoz's notes to his edition of the *Persiles* (1997, 552n35) for more on scribes' role in villages heavily populated with Moriscos. In this Cervantine passage, it is precisely the scribe who, at least when compared with Rafala, could be held accountable for displaying little interest in the Catholic images. In early modern Spain, scribes were also generally required to prove their status as Old Christians, although this was not always the case (Marchant Rivera 2010, 210–11). Thus, the figure of the scribe with his preoccupation with material possessions, is carefully positioned next to the New Christian protagonist more concerned with spiritual matters. This contrast serves to focus more attention on the Morisca Rafala.

2 Text against Image in Moriscos' Literary Culture

1 This book, composed by al-Ḥajarī, is a summary of his full travel account and is now lost. For more about this fascinating Morisco, see Wiegers (1992, 2017); Harvey (1959); and Bernabé Pons (1996).
2 See especially chapter 1 of Mary Elizabeth Perry's *The Handless Maiden* (2005, 19–37), as well as her articles "Patience and Pluck: Job's Wife, Conflict and Resistance in Morisco Manuscripts Hidden in the Sixteenth Century" (2003) and "Morisco Stories and the Complexities of Resistance and Assimilation" (2012). See also Barletta (2005); López Baralt (2009); and García Arenal (1992).
3 Throughout this chapter, I intentionally use both images and idols to refer to Catholic objects of adoration. As W.J.T. Mitchell argues, idol/idolatry is not a separate category of objects but rather a name used as a way of talking about "object relations," highlighting that "one and the same object (a golden calf, for instance) could function as a totem, fetish, or idol depending on the social practices and narratives that surround it" (2005, 188).
4 On the complexities of categorizing Morisco literature into specific genres, see Valero Cuadra (2000, 49–54).
5 For more examples of how the term *ʿabīd al-aṣnām*, or "idol worshippers," was used to refer to Christians in Spain, see Eva Lapiedra Gutiérrez (1997,

316–20). See also the Morisco *jofor*, or "prophecy," in which ʿAlī Ibnu Jābir Alfārasiyo announces the future triumph of Islam over the "adoradores de los ídolos" ("idol worshippers") or Christians in Spain, (López Baralt 2009, 222). Even Diego Hurtado de Mendoza explains, in his *Guerra de Granada*, that "idol worshippers" ("adoradores de los ídolos") was the name Moriscos gave to priests, since in their view images were equivalent to idols (1852, 85b).

6 Very little is known about the mufti of Oran. For more on his identity, see Stewart (2006).

7 See the Aljamiado and Arabic transcriptions of the mufti of Oran's fatwa included in Harvey (1964, 172, 175), where Catholic objects of worship are referred to as idols ("ídolaš" in Aljamiado and "*aṣnām*" in Arabic).

8 "Si a la hora de la oración se os obligase a ir a adorar los ídolos de los cristianos, formaréis intención de hacer la *tacbir del alihram*, y de cumplir vuestra oración; y vuestra mirada se dirigirá hacia los ídolos cuando los cristianos lo hagan; mas vuestra intención se encaminará a Dios, aunque no estéis situados de cara hacia la alquiba, a la manera que hacen oración los que en la guerra se hallan frente al enemigo"; *Takbīr al-iḥrām* is the exclamation of the Arabic words *Allāhu akbar*, meaning God is great, at the beginning of the prayer.

9 These scholars have identified at least four extant copies and/or translations of the fatwa in Arabic, Aljamiado, and Spanish, although the original document has not yet been found. For a copy of the Arabic text, see Harvey (1964, 174–8). For the complete Aljamiado version dated to 1563, see Harvey (1964, 171–4), or the partial and modernized version of this text in García Arenal (1975, 44–5). For the later Aljamiado version dated to 1609, see Cantineau (1927, 6–10). María del Mar Rosa-Rodríguez has located and published an early seventeenth-century Spanish version (2010, 165–74). See Luis Bernabé Pons's bibliographic entry on "The Mufti of Oran" for a complete record of all manuscripts (2014b, 67–72).

10 "descreencia, idolatria y falsedad"

11 For the Arabic *qaṣīda* and English translation, including an introductory essay, see Monroe (1966, 281–303).

12 While Alonso del Castillo attests in his *Cartulario* to providing a Spanish translation of Ibn Daud's Arabic writings (1852, 41–59), the letters might have been composed by Castillo himself (Harvey 2005, 209). Ibn Daud's letter is also included in Mármol Carvajal's *Historia del* [sic] *rebelión y castigo de los moriscos del reino de Granada* ([1600] 1991, 3:9, 85a–86b).

13 "Metieron a las gentes en su ley e les hazen adorar con ellas las figuras, apremiándoles a ello, sin osar ninguno hablar en ello. ¡O quántas personas están afligidos entre los que no creen! Llaman a las gentes con campana para adorar la figura, e mandan a la persona yr presto a su ley revoltosa"

14 I quote from Nabil Matar's partial English translation of this text included in his book *Europe through Arab Eyes* (2014, 194–200), but have also consulted the full Arabic transcription included in al-Turkī (1967, 25–63). Here, the Arabic word used for "idols" is "*aṣnām*" (29).

15 On the importance of Arabic in Islam, see especially Hegyi (1972); and Bernabé Pons (2009, 66–84; 2010).

16 "como cosa santa"

17 For other examples of the significance of the Arabic script in different time periods and geographic regions, especially to Sufi mystics, see Annemarie Schimmel's study on *Calligraphy and Islamic Culture* (1984, 77–114).

18 "denota alttuwra, ke eš Allāh alto en todo fecho; no ay a Él iwwal ni aparssero; eš Allāh alto en nonbaradíyya, eš Allāh alto en todo poderíyyo, eš Allāh alto en ešensiyya i toda koša šeñala šuw altuwra; no ay koša ke desiyenda en šuw nonbaradíyya"

19 See William A. Christian Jr.'s article "Images as Beings in Early Modern Spain" (2009), in which he demonstrates how several images acquired a unique aura incited by miracles or spectacular circumstances associated with them.

20 Annemarie Schimmel refers to the following passages in the Qur'an: 96:3–4, 68:1, 85:21–22, 82:10, 50:16, 17:73, 10:62, 34:4 (1970, 1). She expands on many of these Qur'anic references to writing in her book *Calligraphy and Islamic Culture* (1984, 77–114).

21 "besaban y adoraban el libro del Alcorán por cosa santa"

22 "ay una imagen de las que pintan, alçando el sacerdote la ostia y del un lado y del otro de la ostia están unas labores pintadas que parecen lazos, y son letras arábigas bien hechas y formadas y dicen del un lado –No ay otro Dios– y del otro –sino Dios–, que es la sentencia que an usado y usan oy los mahometanos y arrianos para negar la divinidad de Jesucristo nuestro Señor y todos los sacramentos, y esto lo saben assí muy bien los moriscos de aquella ciudad"; see also Bernabé Pons's illuminating interpretation of this passage (2007, 65).

23 On Morisco Aljamiado literature as Islamic texts, see Bernabé Pons (2010). Bernabé Pons, Galmés de Fuentes, and Montaner Frutos, among other scholars, have organized Aljamiado literature under different rubrics for categorizing the genres. For a helpful summary of these and relevant bibliography, see Valero Cuadra (2000, 49–54).

24 For an in-depth comparison of the Aljamiado story with similar European and Arabic legends, see Pino Valero Cuadra's comprehensive introduction to *La leyenda de la doncella Carcayona* (2000).

25 In this chapter, I quote from Pino Valero Cuadra's edition (ibid.), based on the Aljamiado versions. For a study and copy of the legend written in Spanish with Latin characters, see Galmés de Fuentes (1957).

26 "[¡Ye padre!], haz lo que querrrás [*sic*], que no tornaré de lo que estoy ni
dexaré la obedencia por la desobedencia, ni el jaleqador por el [jaleqado,
ni el *al-ŷanna*] por *ŷahannam*, ni dexaré a[da Allāh] por las ídolas"

27 See especially Valero Cuadra (2000, 66); Bernabé Pons (1998, 328); and
Perry (2005, 19–37). For an alternative reading of how this Aljamiado story
was also used by Christians, see Quinn (2013, 101–33).

28 See also Valero Cuadra's introduction to *La leyenda de la doncella Carcayona*,
where she shows how Aljamiado stories, such as this one, allowed Moriscos
to preserve and transmit their religious identity, actively resisting the
oppressive Christian culture (2000, 151–6; 226–9).

29 "rey de los romanos"

30 See also Anwar G. Chejne's *Islam and West: The Moriscos* (1983, 76, 193n).

31 Luis del Mármol Carvajal relates how the Morisco translator Alonso del
Castillo was asked to write a forged letter in Arabic directed towards Morisco
rebels in the Alpujarras. In the letter, Castillo warns that the "rumís," or
Christians, in Spain will eventually expel Moriscos from their land: "The
Rumís [Christians] will expel you out of it in various groups to the roughest
parts of their lands" ("Sacaros han los rumís della en diversas juntas a las
partes más ásperas de sus tierras") ([1600] 1991, 8, 10, 227a). Alonso del
Castillo includes his own Spanish translation of the letter in his *Cartulario*
in which he renders the term "rumís" as "romanos," offering the following
explanation: "'The Romans will expel you out of it in various groups to
the most rough parts of their lands:' you should understand Romans as
Christians, and from that you should understand as those from the good
places of Andalusia" ("'Sacaros han los romanos della en diversas juntas a
las parte más ásperas de sus tierras:' los romanos entiende xpianos, e della
entiende de los buenos lugares de Andaluzia") (18).

32 "";¡Ye padre!, antes demando perdón a[da Allāh], mi señor y tu señor. Dexa
[d]el servicio de las ídolas, aquéllas que no oyen ni veen, nuecen y no
aprovechan"

33 In the Inquisition case of Miguel Vencuay, for example, he states "that
the Christians while revering the cross adored a stick" ("que los cristianos
reverenciando la cruz adoravan un palo") (quoted in Franco Llopis
2011b, 119). For additional Inquisition cases presenting Moriscos'
denunciation of Catholic images see Pereda (2007, 398–402) and Franco
Llopis (2010a).

34 The anonymous story of 'Umar ibn Zayde is edited by Federico Corriente
Córdoba and included in *Relatos píos y profanos del manuscrito aljamiado
de Urrea de Jalón* (1990, 69–80). Allāt and al-'Uzzā together with Manāt,
mentioned here and in other Morisco narratives, were the principle deities
associated with idolatry during pre-Islamic times. For more on these idols
see Hawting (1999, 130–49).

35 ""¡Yā padre!, tú vives en la desyerror i en la mentira, ke la ídola Alāta
w-Al'uzzā no tiene ningún poder ni saber ni provecho, ni daña ni defiende"

36 Ottmar Hegyi has transcribed and published ms. 4953 under the title *Cinco
leyendas y otros relatos moriscos* (1981). I cite from this edition.

37 See also Barletta (2005, 105–11), who expands Hawkins's framework for
reading Morisco-Aljamiado miscellanies.

38 Ottmar Hegyi transcribes the Morisco version of the text in his book *Cinco
leyendas* and renders the protagonist's name as Tamima Addār (1990, 160–
84). For more about this figure and an English translation of the text see
Lourdes María Álvarez (2007).

39 For other examples, see *Libro de dichos maravillosos*, edited by Ana Labarta,
especially the introductory section, "La magia de la palabra" (1993, 0.34–
0.35). In a broader context aside from the Moriscos in early modern Spain,
see Schimmel (1984, 84).

40 On the literary motif of idols and idolatry in legendary *maghāzī* literature,
including a brief mention of it in the *Libro de las batallas*, see Bellino (2018).
Of the battles recounted in the *Libro de las batallas* (ms. 5337), idols are an
important element of the plot in the first seven narratives.

41 "presente quando ciertas personas leyan en un libro cosas de mahoma y
su perversa seta especialmente como mahoma avia ganado y señoreado
muchas tierras y otras cosas y de oyr leer lo suso dicho Francisco de
Espinosa se holgaba mucho"

42 While there is no written evidence from Muhammad's time, the ninth-
century historian al-Azraqī narrates how Muhammad destroyed 360 idols at
the Ka'ba in Mecca, with the exception of a picture of Jesus and Mary, which
he preserved (Natif 2011, 42–3; Hawting 1999, 14; al-Azraqī 1969, 1:165–9).
Muhammad's destruction of idols at the Ka'ba was a popular theme, and is
retold in a number a Morisco writings, such as *La batalla de Badri i Hunayn*
included in the *Libro de las batallas* (Galmés de Fuentes 1975b, 184–212) and
Libro de las luces (Lugo Acevedo 2008).

43 "وهم يتوسلون بالرهبان والاصنام, ونحن نتوسل بسيد الانام الى موجب ذو (كذا) الجلال والاكرام, وهم
عازمين (كذا) على الجزائر, والله تعالى هلكهم وينصر دينه وهو نعم الناصر"

44 For more on the diverse uses of Morisco *jofores* throughout the early modern
Mediterranean, see especially Green-Mercado (2013, 2018, 2019).

45 This prophecy is included in ms. 11/9414 (formerly ms. T-18), fols.
128r-132v, at the Biblioteca de la Real Academia de la Historia in Madrid.
Cardaillac has edited these pages and includes them as an appendix (2004,
413–18).

46 "serán vencidos los adoradores de las ídolas i los komedores del puerko; no
kedará sino ell addin (*ley*) del alīçlām"

47 "los adoradores de las ídolas y komedores del puerko"

48 On Moriscos who did identify as Christians, see especially Dadson (2007).

3 Granada and the Poetics of Sacred Space

1 I am grateful to Luis Bernabé for his suggestion that I look at the crosses on the Sacromonte hillside in relation to wider debates about Moriscos and the symbol of the cross.

2 The discovery of the lead books on the Sacromonte was preceded by another related account in 1588. When workers demolished the minaret of the old mosque in Granada to construct the new cathedral, they came upon a lead box with a parchment that boasted a letter written by St Cecilio, the patron saint of Granada, among other objects. There is a vast and rapidly expanding bibliography on these forgeries. For a succinct summary of the affair and critical bibliography, see Bernabé Pons (2014a). A. Katie Harris's monograph (2007), Barrios Aguilera and García-Arenal's two edited volumes on the subject (2006, 2008), and García Arenal and Rodríguez Mediano's *Un oriente español: los moriscos y el Sacromonte en tiempos de Contrarreforma* (2010; 2013 for the English translation) are essential reading on the topic.

3 Harris also returns to the Sacromonte's sacred landscape in later publications. See her Spanish translation (2006), chapter 5 of her monograph (2007, 108–48), and "Sacred landscape" (2017, 30–42). For complementary perspectives on Granada's Christian transformation, see Calatrava (2000, 2006); Coleman (2003); García Arenal (2015); and Orozco Pardo (1985).

4 In addition to the aforementioned sources describing the proliferation of crosses on the Sacromonte, I have also consulted Coleman (2003, 199–201); Gila Medina (1992); Hagerty (1980, 33); and Harris (2007, 5–6, 162).

5 "vista tan hermosa, que causava en los virtuosos gozo espiritual, y los coraçones más distraydos deshazía en devoción"

6 "Al valor divino y fuerte de unos soldados, que fueron tales que al mundo vencieron y sujetaron la muerte, y a sus despojos ganados con tal fuerza y tanta luz, levantaron esta Cruz otros piadosos soldados. A la memoria y ejemplo de aquellas piedras famosas cuias columnas preciosas fueron de Dios bivo templo en el monte donde vieron tanta gloria y tanto bien, de piedra esta Cruz, también los canterios ofrecieron"; Gallego y Burín includes the inscriptions on the pedestals of four of the surviving crosses on the Sacromonte in his footnotes (1996, 393–4n11–14).

7 For more on Moriscos' particular uses of the "seal of Solomon," see Fernández Medina (2012); and Roisse (2006).

8 While many scholars reference Góngora's sonnet "Al monte santo de Granada" in their investigations on the lead books, further research on the poetry composed about this event is still needed. To date, Emilio Orozco Díaz and José Ignacio Fernández Dougnac are the scholars who have most

thoroughly examined this poetry, especially that of Agustín Collado del Hierro. See Orozco Díaz (1965, 2000) and Fernández Dougnac (2007, 2008, 2011).

9 "unas canciones al Monte Santo desta ciudad"

10 The *Poética Silva* does include one short poem by Pedro de Granada Venegas praising the Virgin Mary (Osuna 2000, 1:221).

11 "de cruces coronado"; I cite from Ciplijauskaité's edition of Góngora's *Sonetos completes* (1982, 232), but have also consulted the notes in Orozco Díaz's *Los sonetos de Góngora* (2002, 155–8) and Harvey's English translation (2005, 399–401).

12 "con tiernos ojos, con devota planta"

13 "este"

14 "espira luz"

15 "trofeo"

16 "fuerza santa"

17 Despite the few contemporary studies on Alonso de Bonilla, other early modern writers recognized his skill, principally for religious poetry; for more on Bonilla see, Chicharro Chamorro (1988).

18 I quote from Cruz Cruz's recent edition (Bonilla [1614] 2004, 332).

19 "Suele la tierna y regalada planta / de alguna flor, de codicioso olfato, / rendir tributo generoso y grato, / si en buena tierra se traspone y planta. / Pero después que su beldad quebranta / la ignominia cruel del tiempo ingrato, / corresponde semilla en vez de ornato, / y sobre lo supremo se levanta."

20 To the best of my knowledge, there is only one extant copy of Fernández de Ribera's *Canción al Monte Santo*. I consulted the copy housed at the Biblioteca Capitular y Colombina in Seville (1617, 30–1-3 [3]). On Archbishop Castro's support of the lead books, see Barrios Aguilera (2006); Drayson (2016, 114–34); García Arenal and Rodríguez Mediano (2010, 31–3); and Harris (2007, especially chap. 2).

21 Part XI of Fernandez de Ribera's *La asinaria* treats the "piteous Morisco expulsion" ("morisco destierro lastimoso") (MS 1473, fols. 119–29). Only a portion of the poem has been published in Carlos Petit Caro's 1947 edition, but this does not include the verses on the Morisco expulsion. I have consulted the manuscript located at the National Library of Spain in Madrid (ms. 1473). Perceval notes that Fernández de Ribera was an eyewitness to the expulsion of the Moriscos from Seville (1997, 223n).

22 "O Agricultor de esta Eredad ignota, / Que da fruta divina, / I hojas de plomo para libros brota"

23 On Granada's geography as a metaphor in Bermúdez de Pedraza's *Antigüedad y exelencias de Granada*, see Calatrava (2006, 426–8).

24 "Al alto cielo dirigir, divino / Monte, podrás loçano / El cuello ecelso i la serena frente"

25 "Pirámide"

26 "segundo venerable Elías"

27 "La gente mas estraña / más barbara i remota / vivas lágrimas vierta, porque creas / su compunción devota"

28 While the engraving is commonly referred to as "Bautismo de los moriscos," as it is in the catalogue description at the Museo Casa de los Tiros in Granada, recent scholarship has shed light on the details that this scene represents. Pérez Galdeano (2016, 42) explains that, in 1606, Muslims from Fez fled to Spain because of the plague, and some of them converted to Christianity. Later, Archbishop Castro publicly baptized these converts with the Sacromonte in the background, which is what the lower portion of this engraving represents. Franco Llopis and Moreno Díaz del Campo also give a similar description of the scene, and offer an illuminating interpretation of this engraving, noting how Heylán erases all traces of the converts' ethnic and cultural heritage (2019, 328–31). I am grateful to Borja Franco Llopis for these references.

29 "manos Sarrazenas"

30 I examine these narratives in more detail in Chapter 5.

31 "están diseñados de manera hábil para que cada lector, cristiano o musulmán, pudiera reconocerse en ellos de acuerdo con sus propias creencias"

32 As García Arenal affirms, there is essentially no question that Moriscos Alonso del Castillo and Miguel de Luna are the authors of the *plomos*. Alongside these authors, however, she believes that they did not act alone and likely were in touch with the Morisco elites of Granada (García Arenal 2006). On Miguel de Luna's project to present an alternative vision of Spain's Islamic past, see Márquez Villanueva (1981; 1998, 45–97) and Bernabé Pons's critical introduction to Luna's work (2001, vii–lxx).

33 See Fernández García et. al. (2003) for a compilation of texts and documents from 1517 to 2001 that mention the Cross of Caravaca. In Pozo Martínez's bibliography of the first accounts of the Cross of Caravaca, he lists Antonio de Guevara's *Segunda parte de las epístolas familiares* (1541) as the first source (2017, 153).

34 "Cosa muy recebida es, assí entre los hombres doctos, para la averiguación, y calificación de cosas antiguas, la autoridad de las letras, pinturas, caracteres, y cifras, que en piedras, retablos, y paredes nos dexaron esculpidas los antepassados, para la noticia de cosas grandes, y memorables, que por no ser dados tanto al escribir, como aora, las dexaron con sola esta creencia: las quales tienen tanta fuerça en mostrar las verdades de las cosas

passadas, y sucedidas, que no se pueden averiguar por escrituras, que no hay quién en esto ponga duda"

35 García Arenal and Rodríguez Mediano offer evidence of how Jerónimo Román de la Higuera and Miguel de Luna might have benefited from their involvement in shaping Corbalán's *Historia* (2008; 2010, 218–22).

36 "Árabes, semejantes a las que acá llamamos Góticas"

37 "Con este cavallo ensalzé la Ley de Dios, y vencí sus enemigos en batalla muchas vezes. En que nos muestra aver tomado las armas en favor de la Religión Christiana. Y las historias de Castilla, y Aragón nos lo dizen, que fue acompañando al Rey Don Fernando el Santo, quando ganó a Sevilla, y al Rey Don Jayme quando tomó a Valencia"

38 On the historical Abū Zayd, king of Valencia, who also converted to Christianity but seemed to veil it from the public for some time, see the succinct entry and bibliography in Gerli's *Medieval Iberia: An Encyclopedia* (2003). This entry suggests that the Muslim king converted to Christianity after his defeat, which adds an extra layer of meaning to the king's transformation and Robles Corbalán's rendering of it in his *Historia* (1615, 10).

39 See Szpiech (2012, 328–34) for a study of the Muslim anti-Pauline tradition in Iberia.

40 In crafting the story of the Cross of Caravaca, Pozo Martínez believes that Jaime Bleda drew on an earlier account by the Dominican Alonso Chacón's *De Signis Sanctissimae Crvcis* (1591). For more on the extensive bibliography on this cross in the early modern period, see Pozo Martínez (2017). Villanueva Fernández, in turn, has shown how later accounts, such as that of Robles Corbalán, have influenced the literature on the Cross of Caravaca (1992).

41 "la santa Cruz que es su açote, los acabó de echar desde allí"

42 Corbalán was familiar with at least some of Jaime Bleda's works, since he mentions his writing on the Cross of Caravaca to support his own narrative (Robles Corbalán 1615, 52v).

43 Archivo Histórico Nacional, sección Inquisición, legajo 197, expediente 5. Mercedes García Arenal has brought this case to light and has studied it extensively. See García Arenal (2010) and García Arenal and Rodríguez Mediano (2010, 192–6). I am grateful to Luis Bernabé for bringing this case to my attention.

44 "no hay en España mejor moro"

45 "ques maldad y traición lo que han inbentado de adorar imagines de palo y de piedra"

46 The lead books have been the object of many studies over the past few decades, although, as Remensnyder notes, little focus has been placed on the Virgin (2011, 552). Bernabé Pons offers a useful summary of the significance and debates surrounding the lead books, including an updated

bibliography on the topic (2014a). More broadly, Harris's important study on the lead books demonstrates how these forgeries influenced the new collective identity of Granadans (2007).

4 Marian Images of Conversion

1 "Reza, reza, Catalina, / que sin la ayuda divina / duran poco humanos bienes; / y llama, que no me espanta, / antes me parece bien, / a tu Lela Marién, / que entre nosotros es santa ... Bien la puedes alabar, / que nosotros la alabamos, / y de ser Virgen la damos / la palma en primer lugar" (*La gran sultana* [1615] 1999, vv. 1738–44; 1749–52).

2 For an overview of the role of the Virgin Mary, Maryam in the Qur'an, in Islam see: Abd-El-Jalil (151); Cuffel (2003); Neuwirth (2014, 328–58); Pelikan (1996); Schleifer (1997); and Smith and Haddad (1989). On the specific context of Mary and Islam in the Iberian Peninsula, see Epalza Ferrer (1999, 161–90); Franco Llopis (2014); Pereda (2007, 339–73); Remensnyder (2014a, 175–205); and Robinson (2013, 160–5).

3 "حبّ ثلاث نسوة مطهرات مذهب / عائشة التي لعا الفخر العظيم الرتب / برأها الرحمن من فدية أهل الكذب / وقبلها فاطمة ذات العلى والنسب / وأبدا بأزكى منهما ربّة بيت النصب"
   I am grateful to Tariq Jaffer for his insight on my English translation.

4 For more on the Mancebo's treatment of the Virgin Mary, see Narváez Córdova (1976).

5 For editions of these legends, see Vespertino Rodríguez (1983, 300–25), which is also included in Guillén Robles (1885–6, 1:117–58) and Pareja (1960). For criticism on these texts, see Schleifer (1993).

6 See Wood's (2019) study on the inclusion of the Latin Ave Maria prayer in this hadith. For more on the importance of Mary in this hadith, see Vespertino Rodríguez (1978).

7 For a summary of research carried out on this topic, see Alonso Acero (2006, 21–3). See also Henry de Castries's (1928) article-length study on the Christian conversion of the latter two Moroccan princes.

8 In addition to Lope de Vega's play about Muley al-Shaykh, which I closely examine in this chapter, Calderón de la Barca represents the life of the newly converted Balthasar de Loyola in *El gran príncipe de Fez* (1960a). Colombo (2013) has studied this figure extensively in Calderón's play, in addition to letters and an autobiography written by the convert. For more on the popularity of Calderón's representation of this Moroccan prince in the New World, see Hesse (1955).

9 To distinguish between the historical individual and the fictional character, I use "Muley al-Shaykh" while referencing the historical person and "Muley Xeque" while discussing Lope's *El bautismo del príncipe de Marruecos* (Vega [c. 1593–1603] 2012).

10 See Luis Cabrera de Córdoba (1998, 3:365–6); Antonio de Escovar (1909, 2:204); Antonio de León Pinelo ([1701] 1971,150); Jerónimo Quintana (1629, 347v); Jerónimo de Sepúlveda (1924, 148–9). For more on these historical sources and their relation to Lope's play, see Oliver Asín (2008, 127–30); Pontón (2012, 803–4).

11 For more on the problem of the Incarnation, a doctrine that Alfonso X knew was not part of Islamic beliefs, and Mary as "Mother of God," including in this *cantiga*, see Remensnyder (2014a, 189–90); Epalza Ferrer (1999, 174–5).

12 Other *cantigas* (99, 183) also relate Muslims' reaction to images of the Virgin Mary, but they do not always end in their conversion to Christianity. For more on the varied representation of Muslims in Alfonso X's *Cantigas*, see García Arenal (1985).

13 For more on San Francisco de Borja and the important role of art in his evangelization campaigns, see Franco Llopis (2010c, 2011a).

14 Felipe Pereda (2007, 352–6) and Borja Franco Llopis (2010a, 96–8) have studied how images of the Virgin Mary were sometimes harmed by Moriscos, although to a lesser extent than images of Christ or the cross.

15 I am grateful to Carlos Fernández Peñafiel at the Parroquio de Nuestra Señora del Martirio in Ugíjar for his assistance in obtaining a digital image and permission to use this painting.

16 In his *Historia eclesiástica de Granada*, Justino Antolínez de Burgos describes Moriscos' assault of the figure of the Virgin and how the humans tortured alongside her found renewed inspiration in their martyrdom from her example ([1611] 1996, 262–3). Contemporary historians Francisco A. Hitos (1993, 181–90), Manuel Barrios Aguilera and Valeriano Sánchez Ramos (2001, 147–51), and José Carlos Vizuete Mendoza (2012) provide additional details on the desecration of the Virgin del Martirio during the War of the Alpujarras and her reappearance in early seventeenth-century Spain.

17 "Y ansí mismo [su hijo] llorava quando contaba a esta testigo que en la yglesia de Uxíxar a una ymajen de Nuestra Señora le avían echado una soga a el quello y la avían arrastrado y echado en el fuego y, con menospreçio, se avían sentado encima de su sacratísimo rrostro"

18 "su menosprecio y odio de nuestra sagrada religión"

19 Another *relación*, published two years earlier, shares the same concern with Moriscos bringing images from Spain to North Africa. Here, the king of Algiers forbids expelled Moriscos to bring any religious images with them, unless they represent the Prophet Muhammad (Ángeles 1610).

20 The title is only recorded as *Tragedia del rey don Sebastián y bautismo del príncipe de Marruecos* in the index of the *Oncena parte* in the *princeps* edition (1618). In other editions, the work is referred to as *El bautismo del príncipe*

de Marruecos. For more on the title, see Pontón (2012, 800n16); Usandizaga (2014, 220n5). On the dating of the play, see Pontón (2012, 798–800).

21 For more on the play's structure and unity, see Belloni (2014, 89–90); Pontón (2012, 805–6); Usandizaga (2014, 223–5).

22 For a succinct summary of the battle and the key players, see García Arenal (2009, 6–21). For a brief account of the motives for Muley al-Shaykh's exile to Portugal and Spain, see Alonso Acero (2006, 91–109); and Oliver Asín (2008, 55–61).

23 For an analysis of Bernardo Asturiano's painting, see Enrique Gómez Martínez et al. (1997); specifically, pages 69–112 relate how the visual content of the canvas coincides with Manuel de Salcedo Olid's description of the pilgrimage in his *Panegírico* (1677).

24 For more on Cervantes's description of the Virgin of la Cabeza, see Carlos Romero Múñoz's note in his edition of the *Persiles* (1997, 487–8n21); see also de Torres (2006).

25 Oliver Asín identifies this friar from the monastery of Nuestra Señora de la Victoria as the historical Fray Juan Macías, the prince's catechist from the outskirts of Andújar (2008, 111).

26 The friar mentions the following images of the Virgin in his instruction of Marian iconography: the Virgin of la Cabeza, Virgin of Montserrat, Virgin del Pilar, Virgin of Guadalupe, Virgin of la Peña de Francia, Virgin del Sagrario, Virgin of San Clemente, Virgin of Atocha, and the Virgin of los Reyes (vv. 1882–1939). As Pontón notes in his edition to Lope's play, the Fenix mistakenly places the Virgin of San Clemente in Valladolid instead of the Virgin of San Lorenzo, patroness of the city (2012, 907n1915–40).

27 For more on the Prophet Muhammad's destruction of the idols in Mecca, see Chapter 2.

28 For a similar case in Granada, see Pereda (2007, 347).

29 See miracles 16, 123, 144, 234 (Burgos 1605, 60r; 113v–114r;127v–129r; 188r–189v). For more on the different editions of Burgos's book, see Altés i Aguiló (2003); Foster (2015, 20–1n5).

30 Francisco de Pereda recounts the same miracle in his *Historia de la santa y devotíssima imagen de Nuestra Señora de Atocha* published in 1604 (170r–171v). This author also attributes another Muslim's conversion to the power of the Virgin (241r–245v).

31 Talavera includes a variety of miracles related to Muslims' conversion to Christianity because of the Virgin of Guadalupe's influence (1597, 234v–235r; 247v–248v; 273v–274r; 289r–289v; 315v–316v). See the discussion on this topic and footnotes in Remensnyder (2014a, 189–90, 410–11).

32 "Pues si tanta eficacia tienen las palabras que se oyen o leen, para mudar nuestros afectos, con mucha mayor violencia penetrarán dentro de nosotros aquellas figuras que respiran piedad, devoción, modestia y santidad"

33 "Mas hablando de las imágines Christianas, digo que el fin principal será persuadir los ombres a la piedad, y llevarlos a Dios"

34 "Dios nos enseña las cosas invisibles por las visibles"

35 "La facilidad está en que por los colores, i faiciones esteriores, en una vista de ojos ponen dentro del alma el conocimiento de mil cosas, que por el oído no hallaran camino en gran pieça de tiempo. Son tan capazes los ojos, i tienen tanta semejança al entendimiento, que con admirable presteza de una vista comprehenden innumerables cosas, que los demás sentidos reciben parte por parte, con gran tardança."

36 For more on the significance of images in "The Captive's Tale" in Cervantes's *Don Quixote*, see Chapter 6, where I analyse this episode in detail.

37 "Porque muchas dellas son / del tiempo que destruisteis / nuestra cristiana nación / en España, cuando hicisteis / a Muza español Nerón. / Enterraban los cristianos / estos bultos soberanos / por los montes; que temían / que en sus reliquias pondrían / aquellas bárbaras manos"

38 I thank Javier Irigoyen-García for generously sharing his digital images of the documents referring to Muley al-Shaykh from the Archive of Carmona.

39 Oliver Asín believes that Lope de Vega is referencing a historical figure from Muley al-Shaykh's time in Andújar, but he does not offer any proposition as to who this may be (2008, 114–15).

40 "También escrivió su Magestad a Don Francisco Sarmiento, Obispo entonces de Jaen, ordenándole que viniesse a instruir en nuestra Santa Ley al Príncipe, como lo hizo desde quince de Junio que entró en Andújar, donde estuvo dos meses y medio enseñándole la Doctrina, visitándole en su posada cada día dos vezes, hasta fin de Agosto de aquel año, que el Príncipe de Marruecos partió de esta Ciudad a Madrid, donde recibió el Sagrado Bautismo"

41 "Con justa causa la llamas / sol, luna, rosa y estrella. / A burlarme aquí venía, / y hele cobrado afición"

42 "Dio una al Príncipe de Marruecos, que se hallava en las Platicas, y recibiéndola, con grande reverencia de rodillas dixo: Padre Roxas, confiesso a vuesa Paternidad que no merezco esta merced, y favor de la Madre de Dios, y besándola, y poniéndola sobre su cabeça, y prosiguió: Pondréla en oro para traerla siempre conmigo."

43 "el príncipe era, indudable un hombre de sincera devoción mariana"

44 Gianolio di Cherasco includes Muley al-Shaykh's will at the end of his biography. The three churches where he sent his money were in Vigevano and two in Madrid (1795, 82–3). See also Oliver Asín (2008, 212–13). On Muley al-Shaykh's possession and donation of the tapestries, see Forti Grazzini (1992, 157).

45 Oliver Asín identifies this character in Lope's play with Muley al-Shaykh's historical servant. The character also appears in Manuel de Salcedo Olid's *Panegírico* in which he also converts and is renamed José (2008, 110).

46 "¿No has oído desta ermita / de la que llaman bendita / los cristianos, y aun los moros, / tan rica de mil tesoros / que le ofrecen?"

47 "Turchi, e Mori, ed altri, che profittando della opportunità facean vendita di varie merci"

48 For scenes in Lope's plays that portray Moriscos with an inclination to reject images, see the discussion of Lope's plays in Chapter 5.

49 On the Moriscos' representation in this scene, see especially Usandizaga (2014, 245–8); Belloni (2017); Pontón (2012, 809); see also Oliver Asín (2008, 105–6).

50 For other examples of Mary as intercessor for Muslims who do not convert, see Cuffel (2003, 43–6).

51 "carta de presentación"

52 "… parece que es temprano para que V.M. aya de proveer en ello ni procurar se dispense con él en tantas cosas aviendo tan poco que el susodicho reçivió el agua del Bautismo y tiene conocimiento de las cosas de nuestra Religión christiana y que sería conviniente [*sic*] esperar a que tomase estado y ver con quién se casa"

53 The play was published in 1618 in the *Décima parte*. See Valdés (2001, 166n2).

54 See Montesinos (1923, 191) and Valdés (2001, 183), who cite this passage and reference to the Morisco expulsion in their effort to accurately date Lope's play.

55 "BALTASAR. ¿Pues de dónde eres tú? / TOMAR. Soy de muy lejos, / y aunque no soy de África, soy moro. / ¿Eres tú noble? / BALTASAR. Noble y caballero / de un linaje que tiene su principio / en quien a España libertó del moro. / TOMAR. ¿Luego libre de moros está España? / BALTASAR. Sí, por las armas de un Fernando Santo / y de otro que llamaron el Católico. / TOMAR. Pues dijéronme a mí que entre vosotros / vivían moros. / BALTASAR. Esos son esclavos, / y algún día también saldrán de España. / TOMAR. Pésame de ser moro en este tiempo"

5 Images of Mary on the Battlefield

1 "no hay autor que no escriba comedias ni representante que no haga su farsa de moros y cristianos; que me acuerdo yo antes, que si no eran comedias del buen Lope de Vega, y Ramón, no había otra cosa"

2 Due to the ideological implications of the notion of "Reconquista," I use this term sparingly. On the historical and contemporary contentions

surrounding this word, see García Sanjuán (2012). For more on the festivals and *comedias* of Moors and Christians in early modern Spain, see especially Carrasco Urgoiti (1996, 2003); Childers (2009); González Alcantud (2003); and Harris (2000, 206–15). See Irigoyen-García (2017, 9–11) for a definition of the festivals of *moros y cristianos* in juxtaposition to the game of canes.

3 In creating this list, I draw on Carrasco Urgoiti (1996, 60–1) for many of the titles.

4 For a summary of Lope de Vega's plays that deal with Christian-Muslim encounters, see Case (1993). For all of these authors, see Carraso Urgoiti (1996).

5 "locura y desatino"

6 Spanish Erasmians also expressed doubt about some miracles; see Christian (1981b, 103–5).

7 Cardiloro evokes his noble blood from the line of the Abencerrajes in act 1 (800). On the inclusion of the noble Moor in the play, see Case (1993, 90). Pascual Barea (2010) has also suggested an influence from Alfonso X's *Cantigas de Santa María*, as well as the *Primera Crónica General*, throughout other parts of Lope's play.

8 "¡Virgen del Fuerte, Señora, / que rescaté de Granada / cautiva entre gente mora! / ¡Alzad vos también la espada, / pelead, valedme ahora! / ¿Yo no os saqué de cautiva?, ¡pues libradme de cautivo! / Vuestra imagen, ¿no está viva? / ¡Ayudadme mientras vivo!"

9 Míkel de Epalza, among other scholars, highlights how Jesus is referred to as "Son of Mary" (*Ibnu Maryam*) in the Qur'an, and specifically not as "Son of God." Likewise, the ex-Morisco Ibrāhīm Ṭaybilī also describes Jesus as "Son of Mary" in this work (Epalza Ferrer 1999, 166–8).

10 "Una Señora. / ¡Por Mahoma, lindo encuentro! / ¡Todo temblar en miralda! / … / Parece en estar merando / me la he cobrado afición"

11 On the legends of these hidden images of Mary, see Christian (1981b, 75–91); Pereda (2004; 2007, 145–58); Rodríguez Becerra (2014); Velasco (2000, 2003). Surprisingly, this motif has barely been examined in early modern Spanish literature. See, however, Carrasco Urgoiti (1996, 60–1, 85–7; 2003, 34–5).

12 José María Asencio makes a case for attributing this work to Cervantes, although scholars have generally doubted his authorship. On the question of authorship, the different publications of this play, and its comparison to other dramas on the Virgin of Guadalupe in early modern Spain, see Crémoux (2000).

13 "Yo soy, Señora, quien fui / y quien por vos vuelvo a ser"

14 On the Castle of Enesa and legend of the Virgin of El Puig, Tirso de Molina dedicates seventeen folios to this in his *Historia general de la Orden de Nuestra Señora de las Mercedes* (1639). See Devesa's edition of these folios in his *El*

monasterio de El Puig y su Virgen (Tirso de Molina 1968). See also Jerónimo Jacinto de Espinosa's visual rendering of this same miracle, "Hallazgo de la Virgen del Puig," located at the Museum of Fine Arts in Valencia (Pérez Sánchez 2000, 184–5).

15 See also Christian (1981a, 88–93); Velasco (2000, 92–3; 2003, 405); Rodríguez Becerra (2014, 117–18). While shepherds were most frequently associated with these miracles of discovery, the "inventor" in these legends varied, especially in urban spaces and coastal towns (Velasco 2000, 91).

16 Aside from the examples already mentioned, in this chapter I examine a number of early modern plays employing this motif, among them Rojas Zorrilla's *Nuestra Señora de Atocha* ([1645] 2014). See also Carrasco Urgoiti (1996, 84–6). For a notable exception, see Irigoyen-García (2014, 88–9).

17 Valbuena Briones considers this *comedia* Calderón's first extant three-act play (1980, 753–6).

18 This tripartite structure of Calderón's *comedia* has been the subject of a number of studies. See especially Aparicio Maydeu (2000); Calvo (2002); Sáez (2014, 488–9).

19 On the iconography of the crescent moon in relation to Muslim characters in early modern Spanish texts, see the section of Chapter 1 titled "Of Crescent Moons and Other Images."

20 On Queen Constanza's appropriation of this space in the name of the Virgin, see de Armas, who reads these verses of the play as a masked statement supporting the expulsion of the Moriscos from Spain (2014, 138).

21 These legends of buried treasures were to some extent fueled by cases of historical Moriscos. As Barrios Aguilera makes clear, it is important to consider that these tales flourished at a time when Moriscos were being expelled from Spain and that these exiles were not necessarily concealing "treasures" but were more likely protecting their belongings (Barrios Aguilera (1996).

22 "encantado tesoro"

23 "moros hechiceros"

24 On François Delpech's theories of the Moor's buried treasures in other interpretations of the literature of early modern Spain, see Irigoyen-García who looks at the "cultural nostalgia" in Jacinto de Espinel Adorno's *El premio de la constancia* (2014, 200–1, 275n35).

25 The poetry composed for the *certamen* is included as roughly the last two hundred pages in Pedro de Herrera's *Descripción de la Capilla de Nuestra Señora del Sagrario* (1617).

26 On the Virgin of Atocha's prominence in Madrid and her connection to the monarchy, see Schrader (2006); Civil (1998).

27 See Suárez Miramón (2009), who studies Rojas's play as a reflection on early modern theories of art and representation.

28 "In protectione Mariæ vinces"

29 "erografías." Alcalá Galán (2009) studies the multiplicity of portraits of Auristela and the desire they incite in Cervantes's *Persiles*.

30 See Covarrubias's entries for "barragán" and "amancebado" in his *Tesoro* ([1611] 2006, 294–5, 147).

31 "perdida reliquia"

32 For a comparison of other literary sources, especially theater, on the Virgin of Atocha, see González Cañal (2011). See also Marcello's prologue to Rojas's *Nuestra Señora de Atocha* (2014, 13–35).

33 Lope de Vega's *El Isidro* ([1599] 2010) is the first work to include the legend of the Virgin of Atocha, which he later revisits in *El alcaide de Madrid* ([1599] 1993) and *La niñez de San Isidro* (1965). See also Salas Barbadillo's poem *Patrona de Madrid restituida* (González Cañal 2011, 281–2).

34 Very little has been written about this playwright. Diego Símini has edited a complete collection of his *comedias* with a critical introduction (Fajardo y Acevedo 2000), and discusses *Origen de Nuestra Señora de las Angustias* in relation to others that also stage the War of the Alpujarras in a separate article (Simini 2007). See also Irigoyen-García, who has dedicated a few pages to this play, examining how Fajardo y Acevedo constructs the characters' identities through sartorial difference (2017, 177–9).

35 "lobos carniceros"

36 "por cuyos divinos filos / de siete espadas, a todos / passaremos a cuchillo"

37 "le acataban, reverenciaban y adoraban como cosa divina"

38 "María de las A[n]gustias / es deste efecto la causa, / porque al ver el estandarte / con su efigie soberana, / al braço faltó el aliento, / y al brío faltó la espada"

39 The little-known play composed by Miguel González de Cunedo, *A un traidor dos alevosos y a los dos el más leal* (1653) also stages Fernando de Válor's conversion to Christianity at the end of the play, but here without the intervention of the Virgin of las Angustias (102v–103r). For more on this play in relation to Fajardo y Acevedo's *comedia*, see Símini (2007, 227).

40 See Francisco José Cano Hila for the most comprehensive information about the historical Aben Humeya, including his conversion to Christianity at the end of his life (2009, 20). On the chroniclers' mention of his conversion, see Mármol Carvajal ([1600] 1991, 7:11, 199–200); Hurtado de Mendoza (1852, 118); Pérez de Hita (1998, 219).

6 Captive Images and Forged Identities

1 "sacrílegos atrevimientos"

2 At least six early modern historians and writers give an account of this image's capture and ransom, including González Dávila (1623, 252);

Granados de los Ríos (1648, 23–4); Quintana (1629, 418v); León Pinelo ([1701] 1971, 220); Arcos (1670, 412–13); and Silvestre (1690, 280). For more on this ransomed Marian icon, venerated as *Nuestra Señora del Rescate*, see Rumeu de Armas (1974). The Prado Museum in Madrid holds an anonymous eighteenth-century watercolour of the image (catalogue number D001946). Years before this image was taken captive, an image of the Virgin of Guadalupe was also taken off the coast of the Canary Islands during a corsair raid, although this time it was brought to Morocco. For the seventeenth-century account of this image's trajectory, see *Breve relación* (1664). Fraga Gonçalez (1980), who first discovered this document, and Clar Fernández (1995) also include a transcription and commentary on this case in their cited studies.

3 Garcés (2002), Hershenzon (2018), Ohanna (2011), and Rodríguez-Rodríguez (2013), among other scholars, offer illuminating analyses of early modern Spanish captivity narratives. See also Camamis (1970), Mas (1967), and Teijeiro Fuentes (1987) for bibliographies on primary sources. On other early modern captivity narratives from Britain, see Vitkus (2001) and Matar (2014); from France, see Weiss (2011); and on the Atlantic, see Voigt (2009). Yet, aside from Carlos Varona's important article (2011), the question of captive religious images has been touched on only minimally. Apart from the particular context of religious images described in captivity narratives, other studies that focus on the material exchanges in the early modern Mediterranean provide a useful starting point to delve into this topic. On this, see especially Jardine (1996); Jardine and Brotton (2000); Fusaro Omri, and Heywood (2010).

4 The *Topografía e historia general de Argel*, published under the name of Diego de Haedo, has been attributed for some time now to Antonio de Sosa. For a summary of the authorship of this text, see María Antonia Garcés (2002, 32–4; 70–2; 2011, 51–4) and George Camamis (1977, 124–50). Antonio de Sosa offers a summary of what happened to these images taken captive on the Mediterranean Sea by 'Ulūj 'Alī and how they later ended up in Algiers: "one of them was the image of St John the Baptist, which 'Ulūj 'Alī had taken from one of the galleys of Malta in 1570, next to Licata, a city in Sicily also called by the name of St John. Another image was of the Apostle St Paul that they took from the galley *San Pablo* of Malta in 1577 on the first day of April, next to Sardinia. And the third was of the saintly angel, which they took from the galley *Santángel*, on 27 April 1578, next to the Isle of Capri, when the Duke of Terranova was sailing from Sicily to Naples and Spain ("una dellas era la imagen de San Juan Baptista, que el Ochali tomó en una de las galeras de Malta el año 1570, junto a la Licata, ciudad de Sicilia, y que se llamaba del nombre del mismo santo San Juan, y otra era del apóstol San Pablo, que tomaron en la galera *San Pablo*, de Malta, el año 1577, el primer

    día de abril junto a Cerdeña, y la tercera era del Angel santo, que tomaron en la galera *Santángel*, a los veintisiete de abril 1578, junto a la isla de Capri, pasando el duque de Terranova de Sicilia para Nápoles y España") (Haedo [1612] 1927–9, 1:159).

5 "llevasen a la puerta de su casa las tres imágenes que diximos, y en una plaçuela que allí delante está, por orden de los morabutos, las hicieron pedazos y quemaron en un gran fuego"

6 On these images that renegades damaged or destroyed, see Andrew Hess (1978). He suggests that the renegade Hasan Veneciano publicly broke and burned three Christian images in Algiers in 1579, thus demonstrating the Islamic identity of the city (177–8). However, as suggested in Antonio de Sosa's *Topografía*, it seems more likely that Hasan's real motivation could have been the drought that the city was suffering and the belief that the images were to blame for the dry spell (Haedo [1612] 1927–9, 1:158–9).

7 "tomaron los corsarios moros de Argel un vajel de cristianos, y aportando con él a su muelle al desbalijar la ropa, toparon con un grande y formado Crucifijo"

8 For more on the *Cristo del rescate* image in Valencia, see Lazcano (2010), Rodrigo Zarzosa (2010), and Arciniega García (2009). On Jerónimo Jacinto de Espinosa's painting, see the exhibition catalog edited by Alfonso E. Pérez Sánchez (2000, 32–3, 70–3).

9 "redimieron diez y siete Imágenes Sagradas, con todos los Ornamentos, Cruzes, y Vasos Sagrados, que los Moros avían cogido en el Presidio de la Mamora"

10 María Cruz de Carlos Varona (2011) studies the trajectory of the Christ of Medinaceli image between North Africa and Spain within the context of other rescued images of the same time period. For more on this fascinating statue, see Fernández Villa (1982) and Witko (2004).

11 "Del mejor cautivo rescatado"

12 "una en el Duan, donde se vende lo que apresan los Turcos; otra del Turco que la vendió al Judío, y la tercera vez, quando se la compré"

13 "Papaz, detente, y cómprame este Christo tuyo, por lo que quisieres, que yo te le daré barato"

14 "el que dexa al arbitrio del comprador lo que vende, es señal, o que no sabe su valor, o que lo estima en poco"

15 As María Cruz de Carlos Varona has noted while analysing the rescued Christ of Medinaceli image, the amount of money that is agreed upon for the sale of the statue is not arbitrary, since in this case and in others of the same nature, thirty coins were used as a way to link the history of the image with the Passion of Christ (2011, 335).

16 On the increasing value that captive images acquired after circulating around North Africa and the wider Mediterranean world, it is worth

mentioning a similar case observed and narrated by the Belgian ex-captive
Emanuel d'Aranda in *Les captifs d'Alger* ([1656] 1997). In his thirteenth
account, he recalls his experience in Tetouan, where he witnessed how a
Muslim privateer tried to sell a wooden image of the Virgin that was stolen
from a Christian ship to a group of Spanish captives. Seeing the fervour
with which these Christians wanted to own the statue, the corsair decided
to increase the price to four times as much and also threatened to burn
it if no agreement was met, to which the captives responded: "We do not
buy the image for its value, but rather so that it does not receive any harm"
("Nous n'achetons pas l'image par sa valeur, mais afin qu'elle ne reçoive
aucune injure") (141). But finally, after d'Aranda intervened, the image
was purchased at a lower price. Either way, it is interesting to note that this
case also portrays the Spanish with an irresistible desire to possess sacred
representations and willing to pay any amount in exchange for a captive
image. On the other hand, the Muslim privateer is only interested in the
materiality of the image as he tries to exploit the situation for financial gain,
rather than treating the effigy in a certain way based on what it represents.

17 "Hízose la Processión en esta Corte tan solemne, y del concurso, qual no
se veió jamás, con los Cautivos, y el Santíssimo Christo, como el principal
rescatado." Gómez de Losada does not specify exactly where in Madrid that
this effigy of Christ ended up once it was rescued. In the index of his work,
however, he reveals that "The [image] of the Holy Christ is rescued from
Algiers, and it is venerated in the Royal Convent of Our Lady of Mercy in
Madrid ("Rescatase en Argel, la del Santissimo Christo, que se venera en el
Real Convento de Nuestra Señora de la Merced de Madrid").

18 Miguel Ángel de Bunes Ibarra and Beatriz Alonso Acero point out in their
introduction to *Tratado de la redención de cautivos* (2004) how Jerónimo
Gracián describes his experience in captivity in Tunis while clearly
connecting it to the Passion of Christ (Bunes Ibarra and Alonso Acero 2006,
12). In the same way, José María Parreño notices this same parallel in the
work of Antonio de Sosa (1990, 16).

19 "Y para el assumpto del capítulo hemos de entrar en una meditación de
la sacrosanta Passión de Jesu Christo, y es que en qualquier passo della, le
hallaremos, no solamente con dolores intensíssimos, y acervos, sino también
sumamente injuriado, lleno de afrentas, oprobios, y valdones"

20 This episode refers to how the Valencian friar Miguel de Aranda was
martyred in retaliation for the death of the Morisco Alicax, as Antonio
de Sosa describes in his work (Haedo [1612] 1927–9, 3:137–55). Steven
Hutchinson (2012a, 67–8), as well as Emilio Sola and José F. de la Peña
(1995, 130–1, 196–203), among others, have studied this act of martyrdom
in the work of Sosa and Cervantes. See also Ohanna (2016) for Lope de
Vega's treatment of this martyrdom in his play *Los cautivos de Argel*.

21 "Prendieron éste a gran priesa / para ejecutar su hecho, / porque vieron
que en el pecho / traía la cruz de Montesa, / y esta señal de victoria / que
le cupo en buena suerte, / si le dio en el suelo muerte, / en el cielo le
dio gloria; / porque estos ciegos sin luz, / que en él tal señal han visto, /
pensando matar a Cristo, / matan al que trae su cruz"

22 On this comparison, see especially Hutchinson (2012a, 68–9).

23 "Miró, en efeto, la cruz, / y queriendo el enemigo / hacer la misma en el
pecho / que adoraba en el vestido, / otra le hizo (¡ay de mí, / piedra soy,
pues esto os digo!) / con un cuchillo afilado, / que fue pincel el cuchillo. /
La sangre dio la color, / la tabla el pecho bendito, / y así, en cruz, quedó en
él / de esmalte rojo encendido. / Si le queréis ver, miralde, / al sacerdote
divino, / ofreciendo a Cristo el alma / que es hostia del sacrificio"

24 "saca una cruz de palo"

25 Diálogo de los mártires de Argel is the third book of Antonio de Sosa's
Topografía e historia general de Argel (Haedo [1612] 1927–9).

26 "con los dedos de la mano derecha hacía de continuo la señal de la cruz"

27 On the cultural hybridity in this scene, see Irigoyen-García (2010). For more
on Christian captives' practice of religion in North Africa, see Friedman
(1975; 1983, 77–90).

28 "Atado está a una columna, / hecho retrato de Cristo, / de la cabeza a los
pies / en su misma sangre tinto"

29 In his edition to Los baños de Argel, Jean Canavaggio, among other scholars,
notes the connection between this scene and the Passion of Christ,
underscoring that "Francisquito becomes a figure of Christ, whom he will
imitate with his martyrdom, while the person of the cadi, his executioner,
brings to mind Pontius Pilate" ("Francisquito viene a ser figura de Cristo,
a quien imitará en el martirio, en tanto que en el ser del cadí, su verdugo,
revive Poncio Pilatos") ([1615] 1983, 180; emphasis in original).

30 On the imagery of the Christ child with symbols of the Passion in Baroque
culture, see Juan Antonio Sánchez López (1994) and Ana García Sanz
(2010). The latter also highlights how some early modern Spanish writers,
such as Lope de Vega and Calderón de la Barca, included this subject in
some of their works (302–3).

31 "para avivar en su devoción la de los Fieles, que ha de ser muy grande,
sabiendo el origen de su libertad, los portentos, y maravillas, que ha obrado
después que está entre Católicos"

32 "semejança con su original"

33 In their study on Spaniards in North Africa in early modern times,
Mercedes García Arenal and Miguel Ángel de Bunes Ibarra calculate that,
during periods of increased corsair activity, anywhere between a quarter and
a third of Christian captives held against their will in North Africa reneged
on their faith (1992, 244).

34 "[los renegados] son más que todos los otros vecinos moros y turcos y judíos de Argel, porque no hay nación de cristianos en el mundo de la cual no haya renegado y renegados en Argel"

35 On renegades and the rise in the conversions to Islam in the early modern Mediterranean, see Bennassar (1983, 1999); Bennassar and Bennassar (1989); Braga (1998); Bunes Ibarra (1990); Gonzalez-Raymond (1992); Greene (2003); Hutchinson (2015); Rodríguez-Rodríguez (2013, 89–104); Rostagno (1983); and Scaraffia (1993). For the particular case of renegade women, see Dursteler (2011) and Hutchinson (2015). On the coexistence of images and frontier figures, see Infante (2013, 2018). See also Garcés (2009, 2013) and Ohanna (2009) for illuminating analyses of renegades in Cervantes's work.

36 "el renegado entendió que no acaso se había hallado aquel papel, sino que realmente a alguno de nosotros se había escrito; y así nos rogó que si era verdad lo que sospechaba, que nos fiásemos dél y se lo dijésemos, que él aventuraría su vida por nuestra libertad. Y diciendo esto, sacó del pecho un crucifijo de metal, y con muchas lágrimas juró por el Dios que aquella imagen representaba, en quien él, aunque pecador y malo, bien y fielmente creía, de guardarnos lealtad y secreto en todo cuanto quisiésemos descubrirle, porque le parecía, y casi adevinaba, que por medio de aquella que aquel papel había escrito había él y todos nosotros de tener libertad, y verse él en lo que tanto deseaba, que era reducirse al gremio de la santa Iglesia, su madre, de quien como miembro podrido estaba dividido y apartado, por su ignorancia y pecado" (Cervantes 1978, 1:40, 490).

37 "be careful who you ask to read it: do not trust any Moor" (1:40, 347) ["mira a quién lo das a leer: no te fíes de ningún moro" (1:40, 490).

38 "antes que del todo me declarase con él, le dije que me leyese aquel papel, que acaso me había hallado en un agujero de mi rancho" (1:40, 489).

39 "Con tantas lágrimas y con muestras de tanto arrepentimiento dijo esto el renegado, que todos de un mesmo parecer consentimos, y venimos en declararle la verdad del caso; y así, le dimos cuenta de todo, sin encubrirle nada" (1:40, 490).

40 "sacaron por la mesma ventana una pequeña cruz hecha de cañas, y luego la volvieron a entrar. Esta señal nos confirmó en que alguna cristiana debía de estar cautiva en aquella casa, y era la que el bien nos hacía; pero la blancura de la mano, y las ajorcas que en ella vimos, nos deshizo este pensamiento, puesto que imaginamos que debía de ser cristiana renegada, a quien de ordinario suelen tomar por legítimas mujeres sus mesmos amos, y aun lo tienen a ventura, porque las estiman en más que las de su nación. En todos nuestros discursos dimos muy lejos de la verdad del caso" (1:40, 487).

41 "al *renegar* … Zoraida se coloca en la misma zona tornadiza que el renegado murciano, quien da encarecidas muestras de querer salir del exilio y volver a su tierra y religión natales"

42 For the dating and questions about Guillén de Castro's authorship of this play, see Bruerton (1944).

43 "Por mi testigo os elijo: / bien sabéis vos, Virgen pía, / lo que conmigo podía / la imagen del Crucifijo. / Nunca os vi crucificado, / que no llorase y llorando / me hallaron, vos sabéis cuándo, / besando vuestro costado. / Y para mayor abono, / *Saca un Crucifijo pequeño del seno, y prosigue:* / Vos, mi dulce compañía, / si me descuidé algún día, / decildo aquí, yo os perdono. / Bien sabéis que renegué, / y que me acordé de Vos, / para teneros por Dios, / pues del reniego os saqué"

44 "hacía burla de que adorasen los cristianos las imágenes, diciendo que era un pecado"

45 "niega también la adoración de las imágenes, diciendo que no se deben adorar, ni a Cristo, ni a los santos, ni ninguna reliquia"

46 "L'inquisiteur intervient si l'on peut établir que le blasphémateur nie Dieu en parole et en action. Et que dire de celui qui effacerait l'image de Dieu, ou de la Sainte Vierge, ou d'un saint, ou qui les détruirait, ou qui les jetterait par terre, ou qui peindrait des images ou écrirait le nom de Dieu dans des lieux où leur présence serait un affront à la divinité ? Que dire ? Que contre celui qui agirait de la sorte la vengeance serait dure, sévère la peine, quelle que fût la condition, la dignité, le grade du délinquant"

47 As the Bennassars explain, repentant renegades returning to Christian lands who presented themselves voluntarily before a tribunal of the Holy Office oftentimes faced more favorable circumstances (1989, 22–3).

48 "fazia reverencia as imagens com mostras de christam"

49 "Y por dar a entender a los Turcos, lo era como ellos, hizo aquel sacrilegio tan grande, como arrojar al fuego la Santíssima Imagen de Nuestra Señora"

50 "Lo primero que haçían en Casa del Rey era una cruz en tierra y escupirla y pisarla y a grandes bozes decir que heran moros negando al verdadero Jesucristo por Dios." The anonymous letter is located at the Archivo General de Simancas (Estado, leg. 475, año 1550), and is included as an appendix in Martínez Torres's *Prisioneros de los infieles* (2004, 171–5).

51 "una cruz, escupir tres veces encima y arrojarla al mar"

52 "porque suelen algunos renegados, cuando tienen intención de volverse a tierra de cristianos, traer consigo algunas firmas de cautivos principales, en que dan fe, en la forma que pueden, como el tal renegado es hombre de bien, y siempre ha hecho bien a cristianos, y que lleva deseo de huirse en la primera ocasión que se le ofrezca. Algunos hay que procuran estas fees con buena intención; otros se sirven dellas a caso y de industria; que viniendo a robar a tierra de cristianos si a dicha se pierden o los cautivan, sacan sus firmas y dicen que por aquellos papeles se verá el propósito con que venían, el cual era de quedarse en tierra de cristianos, y que por eso

venían en corso con los demás turcos. Con esto se escapan de aquel primer ímpetu, y se reconcilian con la Iglesia, sin que se les haga daño; y cuando veen la suya, se vuelven a Berbería a ser lo que antes eran. Otros hay que usan destos papeles, y los procuran con buen intento, y se quedan en tierra de cristianos" (Cervantes 1978, 1:40, 488–9). In line with what the Murcian renegade does here, the Bennassars offer a variety of examples of real renegades that also collected signatures while in captivity to serve as letters of safe-conduct in case they returned to Christian lands (Bennassar and Bennassar 1989, 511–14). Márquez Villanueva also highlights a passage from *Los baños de Argel* in which the renegade Hazén collects some signatures from Christian captives with the hope of returning to his homeland (2010, 84).

53 For more on the scene in which Zoraida and the renegade enter the church in Vélez Málaga, where he instructs her in Marian iconography, see Gerli (1995, 51); Hutchinson (2011, 158); Infante (2013, 200); and Márquez Villanueva (1975, 131–2; 2010, 108–9).

54 Even though Zoraida is Algerian and not a Morisca, scholars have noted the similarities between this character and the Morisca community in Spain, since upon her arrival to the Iberian Peninsula she could be considered as one of them, especially since this takes place in the years leading up to the expulsion of the Moriscos. For more on this, see Avilés (2002, 184–5); Childers (2006, 178–80); and Hutchinson (2011, 159–60).

55 For more on Cipriano de Valera's Protestant perspective of human captivity, see Ohanna (2012). See also Bunes Ibarra and Alonso Acero's (2004) introduction to Cipriano de Valera's work for a succinct summary of treatise and his main arguments.

56 "nuestros adversarios"

57 "verdaderos cristianos"

58 "De estos diez mandamientos nuestros adversarios, como traidores y alevosos que son contra el Dios que los crió, han totalmente quitado el Segundo, que es contra las imágenes"

59 "No se contentan con invocar los santos, sino que invocan sus imágenes, sus estatuas, o por mejor decir, sus ídolos"

60 "Esto de la cruz he dicho como de pasada, para que ninguno tome de este lugar pretexto de adorar la cruz de palo o de plata; porque hacer así es superstición y [*sic*] idolatría"

61 "Unas mezquitas bien hechas, salvo que ni tienen sanctos ni altar. Aborresçen mucho las figuras, teniéndolas por gran pecado"

62 "Sí, y que no hay más de uno, y sólo aquél tiene de ser adorado, y de aquí viene que aborresçen tanto las imágines, que en la iglesia, ni en casa, ni en parte ninguna no las pueden tener, ni retratos, ni en paramentos"

63 When Mátalascallando asks Pedro what to do with the reliquary, Pedro
    recommends tossing the relics into the river, to which Mátalascallando
    responds: "¿Las reliquias se han de echar en el río? Grandemente me habéis
    turbado. Mirad no traiáis alguna punta de luterano desas tierras extrañas"
    ["The relics should be thrown into the river? You have greatly troubled me.
    See that you don't bring any Lutheran trace back from those foreign lands"]
    (125). As Agustin Redondo notes, Pedro later has to soften his critique,
    since the Inquisition processed those who questioned the cult of relics
    (1988, 412).
64 "¿Para qué pensáis vos que da el otro a entender que una imagen de
    madera va a sacar cautivos y que quando buelve toda sudando, sino para
    atraer el simple vulgo a que offrescan a aquella imagen cosas de que él
    después se puede aprovechar? Y no tiene temor de Dios de engañar assí la
    gente. ¡Como si Nuestra Señora, para sacar un cativo, hobiesse menester
    llevar consigo una imagen de madera! Y seyendo una cosa ridícula, créelo el
    vulgo por la auctoridad de los que lo dizen"
65 "algunas Turcas y Moras les dieron algunas vezes velas de cera, para que
    ardiesen delante del Santíssimo, y otras cosas tan particulares, de que se
    podría hazer un largo tratado"
66 In one case he explains how, after he was captured, a Turk marked the soles
    of his feet with a hot iron rod, leaving behind the symbol of the cross. When
    Gracián inquires about this practice, some Christian captives clarify that "in
    disgrace of the cross of Jesus Christ they do it on the sole of the foot of the
    priest whom they find" ("en oprobio de la cruz de Jesucristo la hacen en
    la planta del pie del sacerdote que hallan") (92). The French Trinitarian
    father Pierre Dan describes a similar practice in his *Histoire de Barbarie et de
    ses corsaires* (1637), where he recounts how in Algiers the form of a cross
    was marked on the soles of Christians' feet to repudiate Christianity and its
    followers (328).
67 In 1619, Andrés del Mármol published a biography on the life and works
    of Jerónimo Gracián titled *Excelencias, vida y trabajos del padre fray Gerónimo
    Gracián de la Madre de Dios Carmelita*. In this text, his biographer includes
    an amplified version of Gracián's *Peregrinación de Anastacio* ([c.1613] 2006),
    with additional details about his time as a captive in Tunis. The fact that
    only ten years had gone by between Gracián's death and the publication of
    his biography and the understanding that these two knew each other have
    led Miguel Ángel de Bunes Ibarra and Beatriz Alonso Acero to believe that
    the additions included in Mármol's version could be from a lost draft of the
    work or from what the biographer heard first-hand from Gracián (2006, 23).
68 "turcazo borracho"
69 "daba un áspero o dos para aceite de la lámpara y se enojaba mucho si la
    hallaba muerta"

CONCLUSION

1 Stories of this effigy of Christ ransomed by Gabriel Gómez de Losada continued to be used in liturgical settings throughout the seventeenth and eighteenth centuries. In 1708 a novena dedicated to this particular *Cristo del rescate* effigy was printed in Puebla, Mexico (*Novena del primero Redemptor y mexor cautivo Christo*) and at least one other was published in Mexico in 1725 by Fray Miguel de Torres (*Novena del primer redemptor y mejor cautivo, Christo*).

Works Cited

Abd-El-Jalil, Juan Mohamed. 1951. "El islam ante la Virgen María." *Arbor* 19
(65): 1–27.

"Acusación y sentencia del proceso inquisitorial contra Francisco de Espinosa,
morisco de El Provencio (Cuenca), 1561–62." 1975. In *Los moriscos*, ed.
Mercedes García Arenal, 97–106. Madrid: Editora Nacional.

Alcalá Galán, Mercedes. 2009. *Escritura desatada: poéticas de la representación en
Cervantes*. Alcalá de Henares: Centro de Estudios Cervantinos.

– 2017. "La noción de museo en el *Persiles*: las colecciones de arte en la
imaginación literaria." *Revista de Occidente* 439: 61–76.

– 2020. "From Literary Painting to Marian Iconography: The Cult of Auristela
in Cervantes's *Persiles y Sigismunda*. In *Millennial Cervantes: New Currents in
Cervantes Studies*, ed. Bruce R. Burningham, 3–24. Lincoln: University of
Nebraska Press.

Alcázar, Luis de. 1614. *Vestigatio arcani sensus Apocalypsi*. Antwerp: Joannem
Keebergium.

Alfonso X. 1986. *Cantigas de Santa María*, ed. Walter Mettmann. 3 vols.
Madrid: Castalia.

Alonso Acero, Beatriz. 2006. *Sultanes de Berbería en tierras de la cristiandad: exilio
musulmán, conversión y asimilación en la Monarquía hispánica (siglos XVI–XVII)*.
Barcelona: Edicions Bellaterra.

Alpert, Michael. 1997. "Did Spanish Crypto-Jews Desecrate Christian Sacred
Images and Why? The Case of the Cristo de la Paciencia (1629–32),
the Romance of 1717 and the Events of November 1714 in the Calle del
Lobo." In *Faith and Fanaticism: Religious Fervour in Early Modern Spain*, ed.
Lesley K Twomey, Robert Hooworth-Smith, and Michael Truman, 95–104.
Aldershot, UK: Ashgate.

Altés i Aguiló, Francesc Xavier. 2003 "La santa imatge de Montserrat i la seva
'morenor' a través de la documentació i de la història." In *La imatge de la*

Mare de Déu de Montserrat, ed. Francesc Xavier Altés i Aguiló et al., 93–179. Barcelona: Publicaciones de l'Abadia de Montserrat.

Álvarez, Lourdes María. 2007. "Prophecies of Apocalypse in 16th-Century Morisco Writings and the Wondrous Tale of Tamīm al-Dārī." *Medieval Encounters: Jewish, Christian and Muslim Culture in Confluence and Dialogue* 13 (3): 566–601.

Andreu de San Joseph, Antonio Juan. 1625. *Relación del milagroso rescate del Crucifixo de las monjas de S. Joseph de Valencia, que está en Santa Tecla, y de otros.* Valencia: Juan Chrysostomo Garriz.

Ángeles, Tomás de los. 1610. *Verdadera relación en la qual se declara el gran número de moriscos que renegaron de la fe católica, en la ciudad de Alarache, que confina con Berbería. Y del martyrio de cinco que no quisieron renegar, naturales de la ciudad de Córdoba.* Zaragoza: Lorenço de Robles.

Antolínez de Burgos, Justino. [c. 1611] 1996. *Historia eclesiástica de Granada*, ed. Manuel Sotomayor. Granada: Universidad de Granada.

Aparicio Maydeu, Javier. 2000. "Del parateatro litúrgico al teatro religioso: sobre la práctica escénica de *Origen, pérdida y restauración de la Virgen del Sagrario* de Calderón." In *Estudios sobre Calderón*, vol. 2, ed. Javier Aparicio Maydeu, 744–59. Madrid: Istmo.

Appadurai, Arjun. 1986. "Introduction: Commodities and the Politics of Value." In *The Social Life of Things: Commodoties in Cultural Perspective*, ed. Arjun Appadurai, 3–63. Cambridge: Cambridge University Press.

Arciniega García, Luis. 2009. "Procesión, a su paso por el palacio del Real, por la llegada a Valencia del Cristo del Rescate." In *La gloria del Barroco. Valencia 2009–10. Catálogo*, ed. Felipe V. Garín Llombart and Vicente Pons Alós, 268–73. Valencia: Generalitat Valenciana/La Llum de les Imatges.

Aranda, Emanuel d'. 1997. *Les captifs d'Alger*, ed. Latifa Z'Rari. Paris: J.-P. Rocher.

Arcos, Francisco de. 1670. *Primera parte de la vida del venerable y reverendísimo padre maestro fray Simón de Roxas.* Madrid: por Julián de Paredes.

Arnaldi, Ivan. 1990. *Nostra Signora di Lampedusa: storia civile e materiale di un miracolo mediterraneo.* Milan: Leonardo Editore.

Avilés, Luis F. 2002. "El lenguaje oculto de Zoraida: tensión histórica y revelación narrativa en Cervantes." In *Morada de la palabra: homenaje a Luce y Mercedes López-Baralt*, vol. 1, ed. William Mejías López, 180–9. San Juan: Editorial de la Universidad de Puerto Rico.

Aznar Cardona, Pedro. 1612. *Expulsión justificada de los moriscos españoles.* Huesca: Pedro Cabarte.

al-Azraqī, Abu al-Walīd Muhammad. 1969. *Akhbār Makka*, 2 v., ed. Rushdī al-Ṣāliḥ Malḥas. Beirut: Dār al-Andalus.

Baer, Eva. 2004. *The Human Figure in Islamic Art.* Costa Mesa, CA: Mazda.

"Bando de expulsión de los moriscos de Valencia." 1975. In *Los moriscos*, ed. Mercedes García Arenal, 251–5. Madrid: Editora Nacional, 1975.

Barceló, Carmen, and Ana Labarta. 2009. *Archivos moriscos: textos árabes de la minoría islámica valenciana, 1401–1608*. Valencia: Universitat de València.

Barkaï, Ron. 1983. "Une invocation musulmane au nom de Jésus et de Marie." *Revue de l'histoire des religions* 200 (3): 257–68.

Barletta, Vincent. 2005. *Covert Gestures: Crypto-Islamic Literature as Cultural Practice in Early Modern Spain*. Minneapolis: University of Minnesota Press.

Barrios Aguilera, Manuel. 1996. "Tesoros moriscos y picaresca." *Espacio, Tiempo y Forma, Serie IV, Historia Moderna* 9: 11–24.

– 2006. "Pedro de Castro y los plomos del Sacromonte: invención y paradoja: una aproximación crítica." In *Los plomos del Sacromonte: invención y tesoro,* ed. Manuel Barrios Aguilera and Mercedes García Arenal, 17–50. Valencia: Universitat de València.

Barrios Aguilera, Manuel, and Mercedes García Arenal, eds. 2006. *Los plomos del Sacromonte: invención y tesoro*. Valencia: Universitat de València.

– 2008. *¿La historia inventada? Los libros plúmbeos y el legado sacromontano*. Granada: Universidad de Granada.

Barrios Aguilera, Manuel, and Valeriano Sánchez Ramos. 2001. *Martirios y mentalidad martirial en las Alpujarras (de la rebelión morisca a las Actas de Ugíjar)*. Granada: Universidad de Granada.

Bas, Cristóbal. 1670. *Dispertador espiritual y oración evangélica del Redentor redimido o santo Cristo del Rescate, del Real Convento de Nuestra Señora de la Merced Calçada, redempción de cautivos de la villa de Madrid*. Valencia: Gerónimo Vilagrasa.

Bass, Laura R. 2008. *The Drama of the Portrait: Theater and Visual Culture in Early Modern Spain*. University Park: Penn State University Press.

Baticle, Jeannine. 1987. *Zurbarán*. New York: Metropolitan Museum of Art.

Beaugé, Gilbert, and J.-F. Clément, eds. 1995. *L'image dans le monde arabe*. Paris: CNRS éditions.

Bellino, Francesca. 2018. "Idols and Idolatry in the Legendary Maġāzī Literature." *Annali, Sezione Orientale* 78: 104–34.

Belloni, Benedetta. 2014. "Lope de Vega y el encargo aprovechado: algunas reflexiones sobre *El bautismo del Príncipe de Marruecos*, pieza de corte histórico-político." In *Páginas que no callan: historia, memoria e identidad en la literatura hispánica*, ed. A. García-Reidy, L.M. Romeu, E. Soler, and L.C. Souto, 89–100. Valencia: Universitat de València, 2014.

– 2017. "La presencia morisca en la romería de la Virgen de la Cabeza en la obra *El bautismo del príncipe de Marruecos* de Lope de Vega." In *Serenísima palabra: Actas del X Congreso de la Asociación Internacional Siglo de Oro (Venecia, 14–18 de julio de 2014)*, ed. Anna Bognolo et al. 395–403. Venice: Veni Edizioni Ca'Foscari.

Bennassar, Bartolomé. 1983. "Renégats et inquisiteurs (XVIᵉ–XVIIᵉ siècles)." In *Les problèmes de l'exclusion en Espagne (XVIᵉ–XVIIᵉ siècles): idéologie et discours*, ed. Augustin Redondo, 105–11. Paris: Publications de la Sorbonne.

– 1992. "Le procès de Guillaume Bedos devant l'inquisition de Palerme (1619–1625)." In *Ketzerverfolgung im 16. und frühen 17. Jahrhundert*, ed. Hans Rudolf Guggisberg, Bernd Moeller, and Silvana Seidel Menchi, 119–23. Wiesbaden: Harrassowitz.

– 1999. "El Mediterráneo de los renegados en la época de Felipe II." In *Felipe II y el Mediterráneo*, ed Ernest Belenguer Cebriá, 313–17. Madrid: Sociedad Estatal para la Conmemoración de los Centenarios de Felipe II y Carlos V.

Bennassar, Bartolomé, and Lucile Bennassar. 1989. *Los cristianos de Alá: la fascinante aventura de los renegados*, trans. José Luis Gil Aristu. Madrid: NEREA.

Bergmann, Emilie L. 1979. *Art Inscribed: Essays on Ekphrasis in Spanish Golden Age Poetry*. Cambridge, MA: Harvard University Press.

Bermúdez de Pedraza, Francisco. 1608. *Antigüedad y excelencias de Granada*. Madrid: Luis Sánchez.

Bernabé Pons, Luis F. 1996. "Una nota sobre Aḥmad Ibn Qāsim al-Ḥaŷarī Bejarano." *Sharq al-Andalus* 13 (1996): 123–8.

– 1997. "La asimilación cultural de los musulmans de España: lengua y literatura de mudéjares y moriscos." In *Chrétiens et musulmanes á la Renaissance*, ed. Bartolomé Bennassar and Robert Sauzet, 317–35. Paris: Honoré Campion Éditeur.

– 1997–8. "Una crónica de la expulsión de los moriscos valencianos: los cuadros de la Fundación Bancaja." *Sharq al-Andalus* 14–15: 535–8.

– 2001. "Estudio preliminar." In Miguel de Luna, *Historia verdadera del Rey Don Rodrigo*, ed. Luis F. Bernabé Pons, vii–lxx. Granada: Universidad de Granada.

– 2007. "Desheredados de al-Andalus: la cultura de mudéjares y moriscos." In *La herencia de al-Andalus*, ed. Fátima Roldán Castro, 49–72. Sevilla: Fundación El Monte.

– 2008. "Los libros plúmbeos de Granada desde el pensamiento islámico." In *¿La historia inventada? Los libros plúmbeos y el legado sacromontano*, ed. Manuel Barrios Aguilera and Mercedes García Arenal, 57–81. Granada: Universidad de Granada.

– 2009. *Los moriscos: conflicto, expulsión y diáspora*. Madrid: Catarata.

– 2010. "Los manuscritos aljamiados como textos islámicos." In *Memoria de los moriscos: escritos y relatos de una diáspora cultural: Biblioteca Nacional de España, del 17 de junio al 26 de septiembre de 2010*, ed. Alfredo Mateos Paramio and Juan Carlos Villaverde Amieva, 27–44. Madrid: Sociedad Estatal de Conmemoraciones Culturales.

– 2013a. "De los moriscos a Cervantes." *eHumanista/Cervantes* 2: 156–82.

– 2013b. "*Taqiyya, niyya* y el islam de los moriscos." *Al-Qanṭara* 34 (2): 491–527.

– 2014a. "The Lead Books of Sacromonte." In *Christian-Muslim Relations 1500–1900*, vol. 6, ed. David Thomas and John Chesworth, 273–81. Leiden, Brill.

– 2014b. "The Mufti of Oran." In *Christian-Muslim Relations 1500–1900*, vol. 6, ed. David Thomas and John Chesworth, 67–72. Leiden: Brill.

– 2016. "La paradoja de Epiménides, Cervantes, y de nuevo sus moriscos." *eHumanista/Cervantes* 5: 85–102.

Bleda, Jaime. 1600a. *Libro de la Cofradía de la Minerva*. Valencia: Pedro Patricio Mey.

– 1600b. *Quatrocientos milagros y muchas alabanças de la Santa Cruz: con unos tratados de las cosas más notables desta divina señal*. Valencia: Pedro Patricio Mey.

– 1610. *Breve relación de la expulsión de los moriscos del reyno de Valencia. Defensio fidei in causa neophytorum siue Morischorum Regni Valentiae totiusque Hispaniae*. Valencia: Ioannem Chrysostomum Garriz, 581–618.

– 1618. *Corónica de los moros de España*. Valencia: Felipe Mey.

Bonilla, Alonso de. [1614] 2004. *Peregrinos pensamientos de misterios divinos*, ed. Juan Cruz Cruz. Pamplona: Universidad de Navarra.

Bouzineb, Hossain. 1987. "Culture et identité morisques." *Revue de l'Occident Musulman et de la Méditerranée* 43: 118–29.

Braga, Isabel M.R. Mendes Drumond. 1998. *Entre a cristandade e o islão (séculos XV–XVII): cativos e renegados nas franjas de duas sociedades em confronto*. Ceuta: Instituto de Estudios Ceutíes.

Braudel, Fernand. 1972. *The Mediterranean and the Mediterranean World in the Age of Philip II*, 2v., trans. Siân Reynolds. New York: Harper.

Breve relación de la invasión de Lanzarote llevada a cabo por los turcos. Real Sociedad Económica de Amigos del País de Tenerife, Rodríguez Moure Collection, 31-1-1664, RM 129 (20/39).

Bruerton, Courtney. 1944. "The Chronology of the Comedias of Guillén de Castro." *Hispanic Review* 12 (2): 89–151.

Bunes Ibarra, Miguel Ángel. 1990. "Reflexiones sobre la conversión al Islam de los renegados en los siglos XVI y XVII." *Hispania Sacra* 42 (85): 181–98.

Bunes Ibarra, Miguel Ángel de, and Beatriz Alonso Acero. 2004. "Introducción." In Cipriano de Valera, *Tratado para confirmar los pobres cautivos de Berbería en la católica y antigua fe y religión cristiana, y para los consolar, con la palabra de Dios, en las aflicciones que padecen por el Evangelio de Jesucristo*, ed. Miguel Ángel de Bunes Ibarra and Beatriz Alonso Acero, 9–41. Valencina de la Concepción, Sevilla: Ediciones Espuela de Plata.

– 2006. "Crónica de cautiverio y misión." In Jerónimo Gracián, *Tratado de la redención de cautivos* [includes *Tratado de la redención de cautivos*, "Del cautiverio del Padre Gracián," and *Peregrinación de Anastasio*], ed. Miguel

Angel de Bunes Ibarra and Beatriz Alonso Acero, 9–24. Sevilla: Espuela de Plata, 2006.

– 2008. "Estudio preliminar." In *Vida de don Felipe de África: Príncipe de Fez y Marruecos, 1566–1621*, ed. Miguel Ángel de Bunes Ibarra and Beatriz Alonso Acero, vii–lxvii. Madrid: CSIC.

Burgos, Pedro de. 1605. *Libro de la historia y milagros hechos a inuocacion de Nuestra Señora de Montserrate*. Barcelona: en casa Sebastián de Cormellas.

Cabrera de Córdoba, Luis. 1998. *Historia de Felipe II, Rey de España*, 4 v., ed. José Martínez Millán and Carlos Javier de Carlos Morales. Valladolid: Junta de Castilla y León.

Calatrava, Juan. 2000. "Arquitectura e *imago urbis*: Granada en la época de Felipe II." *Felipe II y las Artes. Actas del Congreso Internacional (9–12 de diciembre de 1998)*. Madrid: Universidad Complutense, 199–207.

– 2006. "Contrarreforma e imagen de la ciudad: la Granada de Francisco Bermúdez de Pedraza." In *Los plomos del Sacromonte: invención y tesoro*, ed. Manuel Barrios Aguilera and Mercedes García Arenal, 419–58. Valencia: Universitat de València.

Calderón de la Barca, Pedro. 1960a. *El gran príncipe de Fez: obras completas, Comedias*, vol. 2, ed. Ángel Valbuena Briones, 1365–1409. Madrid: Aguilar.

– 1960b. *Origen, pérdida y restauración de la Virgen del Sagrario: obras completas, Comedias*, vol. 2, ed. Ángel Valbuena Briones, 573–601. Madrid: Aguilar.

– 2008. *Amar después de la muerte*, ed. Erik Coenen. Madrid: Cátedra.

Calvo, Florencia. 2002. "*Origen, pérdida y restauración de la Virgen del Sagrario*: un modelo dramático abandonado." In *El gran teatro de la historia: Calderón y el drama barroco*, ed. Melchora Romanos y Florencia Calvo, 119–33. Buenos Aires: Universidad de Buenos Aires.

Camamis, George. 1977. *Estudios sobre el cautiverio en el Siglo de Oro*. Madrid: Editorial Gredos.

Cano Hila, Francisco José. 2009. "Apuntes históricos sobre el linaje morisco de los Córdova y Válor." *FARUA* 12: 1–48.

Cantineau, J. 1927. "Lettre du Moufti d'Oran aux Musulmans d'Andalousie." *Journal Asiatique* 210: 1–17.

Cardaillac, Louis. 2004. *Moriscos y cristianos: un enfrentamiento polémico (1492–1640)*, trans. Mercedes García Arenal. México: Fondo de cultura económica.

Carlos Varona, María Cruz de, et al., eds. 2008. *La imagen religiosa en la monarquía hispánica: usos y espacios*. Madrid: Casa de Velázquez.

Carlos Varona, María Cruz de. 2011. "'Imágenes rescatadas' en la Europa Moderna: el caso de Jesús de Medinaceli." *Journal of Spanish Cultural Studies* 12 (3): 327–54.

Caro Baroja, Julio. 1957. *Los moriscos del reino de Granada*. Madrid: Instituto de estudios políticos.

Carrasco Urgoiti, María Soledad. 1996. *El moro retador y el moro amigo: (estudios sobre fiestas y comedias de moros y cristianos)*. Granada: Universidad de Granada.

– 1997. "Musulmanes y moriscos en la obra de Cervantes: beligerancia y empatía." *Fundamentos de Antropología* 6–7: 66–79.

– 2003. "La escenificación del triunfo del cristiano en la comedia." In *Moros y cristianos: representaciones del otro en las fiestas del Mediterráneo occidental*, ed. Marlène Albert-Llorca and José Antonio González Alcantud, 25–44. Toulouse: Presses Universitaires du Mirail.

"Carta de don Pedro Vaca de Castro, Arzobispo de Sevilla, al rey Felipe III, con motivo de la cédula de expulsión de los Moriscos." 2003. In *Historia de los moriscos: vida y tragedia de una minoría*, ed. Antonio Domínguez Ortiz and Bernard Vincent, 281–2. Madrid: Alianza.

Case, Thomas E. 1993. *Lope and Islam: Islamic Personages in his* Comedias. Newark, NJ: Juan de la Cuesta.

"Casida morisca enviada al Sultán otomano en petición de ayuda." 1975. In *Los moriscos*, ed. Mercedes García Arenal, 33–41. Madrid: Editora Nacional.

Castries, Henry de. 1928. "Trois princes marocains convertis au christianisme." In *Memorial Henri Basset. Nouvelles études nord-africaines et orientales publiées par l'institut des hautes études marocaines*, vol. 1, 141–58. Paris: Librairie orientaliste Paul Geuthner.

Castillo, Alonso del. 1852. *Cartulario de la sublevación de los moriscos granadinos. Memorial histórico español*, vol. 3, ed. José Rodriguez, 1–164. Madrid: Real Academia de la Historia.

Castro y Bellvís, Guillén. [c. 1592–1600] 1925. *El renegado arrepentido: obras de Don Guillén de Castro y Bellvís*, vol. 1, ed. Eduardo Juliá Martínez, 206–45. Madrid: Imprenta de la Revista de Archivos, Bibliotecas y Museos.

Cavero de Carondelet, Cloe. 2019. "The Virgin Embracing the Virgin: Eugenio Cajés' Short-Lived Iconography of Our Lady del Sagrario in Counter-Reformation Toledo." *Bulletin of Spanish Studies*: 1–30.

Ceballos Viro, Ignacio. 2009. "El romance *El zancarrón de* Mahoma y la pervivencia de una leyenda medieval." In *Medievalismo en Extremadura: estudios sobre literatura y cultura hispánicas de la Edad Media*, ed. Jesús Cañas Murillo, Fco. Javier Grande Quejigo, and José Roso Díaz, 305–17. Caceres: Universidad de Extremadura.

Centurión y Córdoba, Adán. 1632. *Información para la historia del sacro monte llamado de Valparaíso y antiguamente illipulitano, junto a Granada*. Granada: Bartolomé de Lorenzana.

Cervantes Saavedra, Miguel de. [c. 1582] 1996. *El trato de Argel*, ed. Florencio Sevilla Arroyo and Antonio Rey Hazas. Madrid: Alianza.

– [1613] 1980. *El amante liberal: novelas ejemplares*, vol. 1, ed. Harry Sieber, 137–88. Madrid: Cátedra.

– [1615] 2010. *"The Bagnios of Algiers" and "The Great Sultana": Two Plays of Captivity*, ed. and trans. Barbara Fuchs and Aaron J. Ilika. Philadelphia: University of Pennsylvania Press.

– [1615] 1983. *Los baños de Argel*, ed. Jean Canavaggio. Madrid: Taurus.

– [1615] 1999. *La gran sultana: obras completas*, ed. Florencio Sevilla Arroyo, 1001–30. Madrid: Editorial Castalia.

– [1617] 2004. *Los trabajos de Persiles y Sigismunda*, ed. Carlos Romero Muñoz. Madrid: Cátedra.

– 1978. *Don Quijote de la Mancha*, 2 v. 5th ed., ed. Luis Andrés Murillo. Madrid: Castalia.

– 2003. *Don Quixote*, trans. Edith Grossman. New York: Harper Collins.

Céspedes y Meneses, Gonzalo. [1626] 1975. *Varia fortuna del soldado Píndaro*, ed. Arsenio Pacheco. Madrid: Espasa-Calpe.

Chejne, Anwar G. 1983. *Islam and the West: The Moriscos*. Albany: State University of New York.

Chicharro Chamorro, Dámaso. 1988. *Alonso de Bonilla en el conceptismo: estudio y antología*. Jaen: Instituto de Estudios Giennenses.

Childers, William. 2006. *Transnational Cervantes*. Toronto: University of Toronto Press.

– 2009. "Manzanares, 1600: Moriscos from Granada Organize a Festival of Moors and Christians." In *The Conversos and Moriscos in Late Medieval Spain and Beyond*, vol. 1, *Departures and Change*, ed. Kevin Ingram, 287–310. Leiden: Brill.

Christian Jr., William A. 1981a. *Apparitions in Late Medieval and Renaissance Spain*. Princeton, NJ: Princeton University Press.

– 1981b. *Local Religion in Sixteenth-Century Spain*. Princeton, NJ: Princeton University Press.

– 2009. "Images as Beings in Early Modern Spain." In *Sacred Spain. Art and Belief in the Spanish World*, ed. Ronda Kasl et al., 75–99. Indianapolis: Indianapolis Museum of Art.

Civil, Pierre. 1998. "Devoción y literatura en el Madrid de los Austrias: el caso de Nuestra Señora de Atocha." *Edad de Oro* 17: 31–47.

Clar Fernández, José Manuel. 1995. "La Virgen de Guadalupe en la historia de Lanzarote." In *VI Jornadas de Estudios sobre Lanzarote y Fuerteventura: 26–30 de septiembre de 1994*. Arrecife: Cabildo Insular de Lanzarote, 316–47.

Coleman, David. 2003. *Creating Christian Granada: Society and Religious Culture in an Old-World Frontier City, 1492–1600*. Ithaca, NY: Cornell University Press.

Colombo, Emanuele. 2013. "A Muslim Turned Jesuit: Baldassarre Loyola Mandes (1631–1667)." *Journal of Early Modern History* 17 (5–6): 479–504.

Colón, Fernando. [1517] 1988. *Descripción y cosmografía de España: manuscrito de la Biblioteca Colombina*. 3 v. Sevilla: Padilla Libros.

Contreras, Alonso de. [c. 1630–41] 1982. *Vida del capitán Contreras*, ed. Joan Estruch. Barcelona: Editorial Fontamara.

– 1996. *Derrotero universal del Mediterráneo. Manuscrito del siglo XVII*, ed. Ignacio Fernández Vial. Málaga: Algazara.

Coronas Tejada, Luis. 1991. *La inquisición en Jaén*. Jaén: Diputación Provincial de Jaén.

Corriente Córdoba, Federico, ed. 1990. *Relatos píos y profanos del manuscrito aljamiado de Urrea de Jalón*. Zaragoza: Institución Fernando el Católico.

Cosgrove, Denis E. 1998. *Social Formation and Symbolic Landscape*. Madison: University of Wisconsin Press.

Covarrubias Horozco, Sebastián de. [1611] 2006. *Tesoro de la lengua castellana o española*, ed. Ignacio Arellano and Rafael Zafra. Madrid/ Frankfort: Universidad de Navarra/ Iberoamericana/ Vervuert.

Cowan, J.M. 1994. *Arabic-English Dictionary. The Hans Wehr Dictionary of Modern Written Arabic*. 4th ed. Urbana, IL: Spoken Language Services.

Crémoux, Françoise. 2000. "Escenificación de un culto popular: la fortuna literaria de la Virgen de Guadalupe." In *Actas del XIII Congreso de la Asociación Internacional de Hispanistas: Madrid 6–11 de julio de 1998*, vol. 1, ed. Florencio Sevilla Arroyo and Carlos Alvar Ezquerra, 476–84. Madrid: Castalia.

Cuffel, Alexandra. 2003. "'Henceforward All Generations Will Call Me Blessed': Medieval Christian Tales of Non-Christian Marian Veneration." *Mediterranean Studies* 12: 37–60.

Dadson, Trevor J. 2007. *Los moriscos de Villarrubia de los Ojos (siglos XV–XVIII). Historia de una minoría asimilada, expulsada y reintegrada*. Madrid: Iberoamericana.

Dan, Pierre. 1646. *Histoire de Barbarie, et de ses corsaires*. 2nd ed. Paris: Pierre Rocolet.

de Armas, Frederick A. 2004. *Writing for the Eyes in the Spanish Golden Age*. Lewisburg, PA: Bucknell University Press.

– 2006. *Ekphrasis in the Age of Cervantes*. Lewisburg, PA: Bucknell University Press.

– 2014. "La geografía y mito de Europa en el teatro de Calderón (*El origen, pérdida y restauración de la Virgen del Sagrario* y *Los tres mayores prodigios*)." In *Violencia en el teatro de Calderón: XVI Coloquio Anglogermano sobre Calderón, Utrecht y Ámsterdam, 16–22 de julio de 2011*, ed. Robert Folger, Yolanda Rodríguez Pérez, and Antonio Sánchez Jiménez, 129–50. Vigo: Editorial Academia del Hispanismo.

Delgado-Gómez, Ángel. 1987. "Una visión comparada de España y Turquía: *El viaje de Turquía*." *Cuadernos Hispanoamericanos* 444: 35–64.

Delpech, François. 2002. "Un mito andaluz: el reino oculto de Boabdil y los moros encantados." In *Las tomas: antropología de la ocupación territorial del reino de Granada*, ed. José Antonio González Alcantud and Manuel Barrios Aguilera, 565–616. Granada: Diputación de Granada.

de Poorter, Nora. 1978. *The Eucharist Series*, vol 1. London: Harvey Miller.

de Torres, José Carlos. 2006. "'La fiesta de Nuestra Señora de la Cabeza' según Miguel de Cervantes (*Persiles*, III, VI)." *Boletín del Instituto de Estudios Giennenses* 193: 157–70.

Devaney, Thomas C. 2019. "Everyday Miracles in Seventeenth-Century Spain." In *Lived Religion and Everyday Life in Early Modern Hagiographic Material*, ed. Jenni Kuuliala, Rose-Marie Peake, and Päivi Räisänen-Schröder, 189–213. Cham, Switzerland: Palgrave Macmillan.

Le dictionnaire des inquisiteurs [*Repertorium inquisitorum*, Valencia, 1494]. 1981. Trans. Louis Sala-Molins. Paris: Éditions Galilée.

Domínguez Ortiz, Antonio, and Bernard Vincent. 1978. *Historia de los moriscos: vida y tragedia de una minoría*. Madrid: Revista de Occidente.

Dopico Black, Georgina. 2003. "Ghostly Remains: Valencia, 1609." *Arizona Journal of Hispanic Cultural Studies* 7: 91–100.

Drayson, Elizabeth. 2016. *The Lead Books of Granada*. Basingstoke, UK: Palgrave.

Dursteler, Eric. 2011. *Renegade Women: Gender, Identity, and Boundaries in the Early Modern Mediterranean*. Baltimore: Johns Hopkins University Press.

Epalza Ferrer, Míkel de. 1985. "Arabismos en el manuscrito castellano del morisco tunecino Ahmad Al-Hánafi." In *Homenaje a Alvaro Galmés de Fuentes*, vol. 2, 515–27. Oviedo: Universidad de Oviedo.

– 1999. *Jesús entre judíos, cristianos y musulmanes hispanos (siglos VI–XVII)*. Granada: Universidad de Granada.

Escolano, Gaspar. 1879–80. *Décadas de la historia de la insigne y coronada ciudad y reino de Valencia*, 3v., ed. Juan B Perales. Valencia: Terraza, Aliena y Compañía.

Escovar, Antonio de. 1909. "Lettre de Antonio de Escovar a D. Diego de Ibarra." In *Les Sources Inédites l'Histoire du Maroc*, vol. 2, ed. Henry de Castries, 204. Paris: Ernest Leroux.

Espinosa, Pedro, ed. 1605. *Flores de poetas ilustres de España*. Valladolid: Luys Sánchez.

Ettinghausen, R. 2014. "Hilāl." *Encyclopaedia of Islam*. 2nd ed., ed. P Bearman et al. *Brill Online*, 5 February. Online at http://referenceworks.brillonline.com.ezproxy.library.wisc.edu/entries/encyclopaedia-of-islam-2/hilal-COM_0286.

Fajardo y Acevedo, Antonio. [1675] 2000. *Origen de Nuestra Señora de las Angustias y rebelión de los moriscos: comedias*, ed. Diego Símini, 147–90. Lecce: Adriatica Editrice.

Fernández Dougnac, José Ignacio. 2007. "Sobre la recepción poética de los Plomos del Sacromonte (siglos XVI–XVII)." *Academia de Buenas Letras de Granada*: 8–34.

– 2008. "Los plomos del Sacromonte en la poesía barroca." In *¿La historia inventada? Los libros plúmbeos y el legado sacromontano*, ed. Manuel Barrios Aguilera and Mercedes García Arenal, 311–46. Granada: Universidad de Granada.

– 2011. "La presencia de los libros plúmbeos en el poema *Granada* de Agustín Collado del Hierro." *AnMal* 34 (2): 397–433.

Fernández García, Francisco, et. al. 2003. *La Santa Vera Cruz de Caravaca: textos y documentos para su historia (1517–2001)*. Caravaca: Centro Internacional de Estudios de la Vera Cruz de Caravaca.

Fernández Medina, Esther. 2012. "The Seal of Solomon: From Magic to Messianic Device." In *Seals and Sealing Practices in the Near East. Developments in Administration and Magic from Prehistory to the Islamic Period. Proceedings of an International Workshop at the Netherlands-Flemish Institute in Cairo on December 2–3, 2009*, ed. Ilona Regulski, Kim Duistermaat, and Peter Verkinderen, 175–88. Leuven: Peeters.

Fernández de Ribera, Rodrigo. n.d. *La asinaria*. Biblioteca Nacional de España. Ms. 1473.

– [1473] 1947. *La asinaria*, ed. Carlos Petit Caro. Sevilla: Editorial Hispalense.

– 1617. *Canción al Monte Santo de Granada*. Granada: Bartolomé de Lorençana.

Fernández Villa, Domingo. 1982. *Historia del Cristo de Medinaceli*. León: Editorial Everest.

Flores Arroyuelo, Francisco J. 1989. *Los últimos moriscos (Valle de Ricote, 1614)*. Murcia: Academia Alfonso X el Sabio.

Fonseca, Damián. 1612. *Justa expulsión de los moriscos de España: con la instrvcción, apostasía, y trayción dellos: y respuesta a las dudas que se ofrecieron acerca desta materia*. Rome: Iacomo Mascardo.

Forti Grazzini, Nello. 1992. "La serie 'gialla' di Audenarde." In *Mirabilia Ducalia: Gli arazzi dell'ultimo degli Sforza e dell'Infante d'Africa*, 88–101. Vigevano: Diakronia.

Foster, Elisa A. 2015. "The Black Madonna of Montserrat: An Exception to Concepts of Dark Skin in Medieval and Early Modern Iberia?" In *Envisioning Others: Race, Color, and the Visual in Iberia and Latin America*, ed. Pamela A. Patton, 18–50. Leiden: Brill.

Fournel-Guérin, Jaqueline. 1979. "Le livre et la civilisation écrite dans la communauté morisque aragonaise (1540–1620)." *Melanges de la Casa de Velázquez* 15: 241–60.

Fraga González, María del Carmen. 1980. "Esculturas de la Virgen de Guadalupe en Canarias: tallas sevillanas y americanas." *Anuario de estudios americanos* 37: 697–707.

Franco Llopis, Borja. 2008a. "Evangelización, arte y conflictividad social: la conversión morisca en la vertiente mediterránea." *Pedralbes. Revista de Historia Moderna* 28 (1): 377–92.

– 2008b. *La pintura valenciana entre 1550 y 1609: cristología y adoctrinamiento morisco*. Lleida: Universitat de Lleida.

– 2010a. "Los moriscos y la Inquisición. Cuestiones artísticas." *Manuscrits* 28: 87–101.

– 2010b. "Redescubriendo a Jaime Prades, el gran tratadista olvidado de la Reforma católica." *Ars Longa* 19: 83–93.

– 2010c. "San Francisco de Borja y las artes." In *San Francisco de Borja, Grande de España: arte y espiritualidad en la cultura hispánica de los siglos XVI y XVII*, ed. Ximo Company and Joan Aliaga Morell, 99-113. Catarroja: Afers.

– 2011a. "Arte y misión. San Francisco de Borja y la difusión de la doctrina católica en las Indias interiores." In *Francisco de Borja y su tiempo: Política, religión y cultura en la Edad Moderna*, ed. Enrique García Hernán and María del Pilar Ryan, 698–741. Valencia; Rome: Albatros Ediciones and Institutum Historicum Societatis Iesu.

– 2011b. "En defensa de una identidad perdida: los procesos de destrucción de imágenes en Valencia durante la Edad Moderna." *Goya: Revista de arte* 335: 116–25.

– 2011–13. "Consideraciones sobre el uso y abuso de la imagen en la Península Ibérica en el siglo XVI a través de los procesos inquisitoriales: una visión multicultural del arte: moriscos, protestantes y cristianos viejos." *Sharq al-Andalus: Estudios Mudéjares y Moriscos* 20: 129–52.

– 2014. "Aproximación al carácter polisémico e intercultural de las representaciones marianas en el imaginario valenciano del siglo XVI." In *Imatge, devoció i identitat a l'època moderna (segles XVI–XVIII)*, ed. Sílvia Canalda and Cristina Fontcuberta, 101–15. Barcelona: Edicions Universitat Barcelona.

– 2017. "Mercédaires, musulmans et Morisques: usages artistiques de l'ordre de la Merci et création d'une iconographie anti-islamique au XVIe siècle." In *Morisques (1501–1614): une histoire si familière*, ed. Youssef El Alaoui, 143–60. Mont-Saint-Aignan: Presses Universitaires de Rouen et du Havre.

– 2019. "Art of Conversion? The Visual Policies of the Jesuits, Dominicans, and Mercedarians in Valencia." In *Polemical Encounters: Christians, Jews, and Muslims in Iberia and Beyond*, ed. Mercedes García-Arenal and Gerard Wiegers, 179–202. University Park: Pennsylvania State University Press.

Franco Llopis, Borja, and Francisco Javier Moreno Díaz del Campo. 2018. "The Moriscos' Artistic Domestic Devotions Viewed through Christian Eyes in Early Modern Iberia." In *Domestic Devotions in the Early Modern World*, ed. Marco Faini and Alessia Meneghin, 107–25. Leiden: Brill.

– 2019. *Pintando al converso. La imagen del morisco en la península ibérica (1492–1614)*. Madrid: Cátedra.

Freedberg, David. 1989. *The Power of Images: Studies in the History and Theory of Response*. Chicago: University of Chicago Press.

Friedman, Ellen G. 1975. "The Exercise of Religion by Spanish Captives in North Africa." *Sixteenth Century Journal* 6 (1): 19–34.

– 1983. *Spanish Captives in North Africa in the Early Modern Age*. Madison: University of Wisconsin Press.

Fuchs, Barbara. 2003. *Passing for Spain: Cervantes and the Fictions of Identity*. Urbana: University of Illinois Press.

Fusaro, Maria, Mohammed-Salah Omri, and Colin Heywood, eds. 2010. *Trade and Cultural Exchange in the Early Modern Mediterranean: Braudel's Maritime Legacy*. London: Tauris Academic Studies.

Gallego y Burín, Antonio. 1996. *Granada: guía artística e histórica de la ciudad*, ed. Francisco Javier Gallego Roca. Granada: Editorial Comares.

Galmés de Fuentes, Álvaro. 1957. "Lle-yeísmo y otras cuestiones lingüísticas en un relato morisco del siglo XVI." In *Estudios dedicados a Menéndez Pidal*, vol. 7, 273–307. Madrid: CSIC.

– 1975a. Introducción. *Libro de las batallas: narraciones épico-caballerescas*, vol. 1, ed. Álvaro Galmés de Fuentes, 9–97. Madrid: Gredos.

–, ed. 1975b. *Libro de las batallas. Narraciones épico-caballerescas*, vol. 1. Madrid: Gredos.

Garcés, María Antonia. 2002. *Cervantes in Algiers: A Captive's Tale*. Nashville: Vanderbilt University Press.

– 2009. "'Grande amigo mío': Cervantes y los renegados." In *USA Cervantes: 39 cervantistas en Estados Unidos*, ed. Georgina Dopico Black and Francisco Layna Ranz, 545–82. Madrid: CSIC/Ediciones Polifemo.

– 2011. Introduction. *An Early Modern Dialogue with Islam. Antonio de Sosa's Topography of Algiers (1612)*, ed. María Antonia Garcés, trans. Diana de Armas Wilson, 1–78. Notre Dame, IN: University of Notre Dame Press.

– 2013. "'Alabado por sus acciones:' Maḥmud Siciliano en *El amante liberal*." *Cervantes y el Mediterráneo. eHumanista/Cervantes: Journal of Iberian Studies* 2: 427–61.

García Arenal, Mercedes. 1975. *Los moriscos*. Madrid: Editora Nacional.

– 1985. "Los moros en las *Cantigas* de Alfonso X el Sabio." *Al-Qantara: Revista de Estudios Árabes* 6: 133–52.

– 1992. "El problema morisco: propuestas de discusión." *Al-Qantara* 13 (2): 491–503.

– 2006. "El entorno de los plomos: historiografía y linaje." In *Los plomos del Sacromonte: invención y tesoro*, eds. Manuel Barrios Aguilera and Mercedes García Arenal, 51–78. Valencia: Universitat de València.

– 2009. *Ahmad Al-Mansur: The Beginnings of Modern Morocco*. Oxford: OneWorld.

– 2010. "Miguel de Luna y los moriscos de Toledo: 'No hay en España mejor moro.'" *Chronica Nova* 36: 253–62.

– 2015. "Granada as a New Jerusalem: The Conversion of a City." In *Space and Conversion in Global Perspective*, ed. Giuseppe Marcocci, 15–43. Leiden: Brill.

García Arenal, Mercedes, and Miguel Ángel de Bunes Ibarra. 1992. *Los españoles y el Norte de África. Siglos XV-XVII.* Madrid: Editorial MAPFRE.

García Arenal, Mercedes, and Fernando Rodríguez Mediano. 2008. "Miguel de Luna, cristiano árabigo de Granada." In *¿La historia inventada? Los libros plúmbeos y el legado sacromontano*, ed. Manuel Barrios Aguilera and Mercedes García Arenal, 83–136. Granada: Universidad de Granada.

– 2010. *Un oriente español: los moriscos y el Sacromonte en tiempos de Contrarreforma.* Madrid: Marcial Pons.

– 2013. *The Orient in Spain: Converted Muslims, the Forged Lead Books of Granada, and the Rise of Orientalism*, trans. Consuelo López-Morillas. Leiden: Brill.

García Arenal, Mercedes, and Gerard Wiegers. 2013. *Los moriscos: expulsión y diáspora. Una perspectiva internacional.* Valencia: Universidad de Valencia.

– 2014. *The Expulsion of the Moriscos from Spain: A Mediterranean Diaspora.* Leiden: Brill.

García Fuentes, José María. 1981. *La Inquisición en Granada en el siglo XVI: fuentes para su estudio.* Granada: Departamento de Historia Moderna de la Universidad de Granada.

García Sanjuán, Alejandro. 2012. "Al-Andalus en la historiografía del nacionalismo españolista (siglos XIX–XXI): entre la Reconquista y la España musulmana." In *A 1300 años de la conquista de al-Andalus (711–2011): Historia, cultura y legado del Islam en la Península Ibérica*, ed. Diego Melo Carrasco and Francisco Vidal Castro, 65–104. Coquimbo: Centro Cultural Mohamed V.

García Sanz, Ana. 2010. "Los Niños de pasión: la infancia y la muerte." *El Niño Jesús en el Monasterio de las Descalzas Reales de Madrid*, 299–387. Madrid: Patrimonio Nacional.

Gerli, E. Michael. 1995. *Refiguring Authority: Reading, Writing, and Rewriting in Cervantes.* Lexington: University Press of Kentucky.

–, ed. 2003. *Medieval Iberia: An Encyclopedia.* New York: Routledge.

– 2016a. "The Expulsion of the Moriscos: Seven Monumental Paintings from the Kingdom of Valencia." In *The Routledge Companion to Iberian Studies*, ed. Javier Muñoz-Basols, Laura Lonsdale, and Manuel Delgado, 184–200. New York: Routledge.

– 2016b. "Xadraque Xarife's Prophecy, *Persiles* III, 11: The Larger Setting and the Lasting Irony." *eHumanista/Cervantes* 5: 265–83.

al-Ghassānī, Muhammad ibn 'Abd al-Wahhāb. 2005. *Riḥlat al-Wazīr fī Iftikāk al-Asīr (The Journey of the Ambassador for the Redemption of Captives)*, ed.

Abderrahim Benhadda. Tokyo: Research Institute for Languages and Cultures of Asia and Africa.

Gianolio di Cherasco, Matteo. 1795. *Memorie storiche intorno la vita del Real Principe di Marocco Muley Xeque chiamato nel suo battesimo Don Filippo d'Austria Infante d'Africa, religiosamente morto in Vigevano.* Torino: Dalla Stamp. di Giacomo Fea.

Gila Medina, Lázaro. 1992. "La Cruz de Guadix en el Sacromonte granadino." *Boletín del Instituto de Estudios "Pedro Suárez"* 5: 51–55.

Giner, Francisco. 1962. "Cervantes y los moriscos valencianos." *Anales del centro de cultura valenciana* 47: 131–49.

Glazer-Eytan, Yonatan. 2019. "Jews Imagined and Real: Representing and Prosecuting Host Profanation in Late Medieval Aragon." In *Jews and Muslims Made Visible in Christian Iberia and Beyond, 14th to 18th Centuries*, ed. Borja Franco Llopis and Antonio Urquízar-Herrera, 40–69. Leiden: Brill.

Gómez de Losada, fray Gabriel. 1670. *Escuela de trabajos.* Madrid: Julián de Paredes.

Gómez Martínez, Enrique, et al. 1997. *La romería de la Virgen de la Cabeza en una pintura del siglo XVII.* Córdoba: Publicaciones Obra Social y Cultural Cajasur.

Góngora y Argote, Luis de. 1982. *Sonetos completos.* 5th ed., ed. Biruté Ciplijauskaité. Madrid: Clásicos Castalia.

González Alcantud, José Antonio. 2003. "Para sobrevivir a los estereotipos culturales: estructuras paródicas de las fiestas de moros y cristianos. El caso andaluz oriental." In *Moros y cristianos: representaciones del otro en las fiestas del Mediterráneo occidental*, ed. Marlène Albert-Llorca and José Antonio González Alcantud, 45–60. Toulouse: Presses Universitaires du Mirail.

González Cañal, Rafael. 2011. "La Virgen de Atocha en el teatro español del Siglo de Oro." In *Actas del I Congreso Ibero-Asiático de Hispanistas Siglo de Oro e Hispanistas general*, ed. Vibha Maurya and Mariela Insúa Cereceda, 279–93. Pamplona: Universidad de Navarra/Biblioteca Áurea Digital del GRISO.

González Dávila, Gil. 1623. *Teatro de las grandezas de la Villa de Madrid.* Madrid: Tomás Iunti.

González de Cunedo, Miguel. 1653. *A un traidor dos alevosos y a los dos el más leal. Parte tercera de comedias de los mejores ingenios de España*, 84r-106v. Madrid: por Melchor Sánchez.

Gonzalez-Raymond, Anita. 1992. *La croix et le croissant: les inquisiteurs des îles face à l'Islam, 1550–1700.* Éditions du Centre Nationale de la Recherche Scientifique.

Grabar, Oleg. 1987. *The Formation of Islamic Art.* New Haven, CT: Yale University Press.

Gracián, Jerónimo. [1613] 2006. *Tratado de la redención de cautivos.* [Includes *Tratado de la redención de cautivos*, "Del cautiverio del Padre Gracián," and

Peregrinación de Anastasio], ed. Miguel Angel de Bunes Ibarra and Beatriz Alonso. Sevilla: Espuela de Plata.

Granados de los Ríos, Cristóbal. 1648. *Historia de Nuestra Señora de los Remedios de la Fuensanta*. Madrid: Por Diego Díaz de la Carrera.

Granja, Fernando de la. 1968. "Milagros españoles en una obra polémica musulmana (El "Kitāb maqāmiʿ al-Ṣulbān" del Jazraŷī")." *Al-Andalus* 33 (2): 311–65.

Green-Mercado, Marya T. 2013. "The Mahdī in Valencia: Messianism, Apocalypticism and Morisco Rebellions in Late Sixteenth-Century Spain." *Medieval Encounters* 19: 193–220.

– 2018. "Morisco Prophecies at the French Court (1602–1607)." *Journal of the Economic and Social History of the Orient* 61: 91–123.

– 2019. *Visions of Deliverance: Moriscos and the Politics of Prophecy in the Early Modern Mediterranean*. Ithaca, NY: Cornell University Press.

Greene, Molly. 2003. "Resurgent Islam." In *The Mediterranean in History*, ed David Abulafia, 219–49. Los Angeles: J. Paul Getty Museum.

Gruber, Christiane J., ed. 2019. *The Image Debate: Figural Representation in Islam and across the World*. London: Gingko.

Guadalajara y Xavier, Marcos. 1613. *Memorable expulsión y justísimo destierro de los moriscos de España*. Pamplona: Nicolás de Assiayn.

– 1614. *Prodición y destierro de los moriscos de Castilla, hasta el Valle de Ricote*. Pamplona.

Guillén Robles, Francisco. 1885–6. *Leyendas moriscas sacadas de varios manuscritos existentes en las Bibliotecas Nacional, Real y de D. P. de Gayangos*. 3 v. Madrid.

Haedo, fray Diego de [Antonio de Sosa]. [1612] 1927–9. *Topografía e historia general de Argel*. 3 v., ed. Ignacio Bauer y Landauer. Sociedad de Bibliófilos Españoles.

Hagerty, Miguel José. 1980. *Los libros plúmbeos del Sacromonte*. Madrid: Editora Nacional.

Harris, A. Katie. 2002. "The Sacromonte and the Geography of the Sacred in Early Modern Granada." *Al-Qanṭara* 23 (2): 517–43.

– 2006. "El Sacromonte y la geografía sacra de la Granada moderna." In *Los plomos del Sacromonte: invención y tesoro*, ed. Manuel Barrios Aguilera and Mercedes García Arenal, 459–80. Valencia: Universitat de València.

– 2007. *From Muslim to Christian Granada: Inventing a City's Past in Early Modern Spain*. Baltimore: Johns Hopkins University Press.

– 2017. "Sacred Landscape in Early Modern Granada: Muslim Past and Christian Present." In *Layered Landscapes: Early Modern Religious Space across Faiths and Cultures*, ed. Eric Nelson and Jonathan Wright, 30–42. London: Routledge.

Harris, Dianne Suzette, and D. Fairchild Ruggles. 2007. "Landscape and Vision." In *Sites Unseen: Landscape and Vision*, 5–29. Pittsburgh: University of Pittsburgh Press.

Harris, Max. 2000. *Aztecs, Moors, and Christians: Festivals of Reconquest in Mexico and Spain*. Austin: University of Texas Press.

Harvey, L.P. 1959. "The Morisco who was Muley Zaidan's Spanish Interpreter." *Miscelánea de estudios árabes y hebraicos* 8 (1): 67–97.

– 1964. "Crypto-Islam in Sixteenth-Century Spain." In *Actas del primer congreso de estudios árabes e islámicos (Córdoba 1962)*, 163–78. Madrid: Comité Permanente del Congreso de Estudios Árabes e Islámicos.

– 2005. *Muslims in Spain, 1500 to 1614*. Chicago: University of Chicago Press.

Hasleton, Richard. 2001. *Strange and Wonderful Things Happened to Richard Hasleton...in His Ten Years' Travails in Many Foreign Countries. Piracy, Slavery, and Redemption: Barbary Captivity Narratives from Early Modern England*, ed. Daniel J. Vitkus, 71–95. New York: Columbia University Press.

Hawkins, John P. 1988. "A Morisco Philosophy of Suffering: An Anthropological Analysis of an Aljamiado Text." *Maghreb Review* 13 (3–4): 199–217.

Hawting, G.R. 1999. *The Idea of Idolatry and the Emergence of Islam: From Polemic to History*. New York: Cambridge University Press.

Hegyi, Ottmar. 1972. "El uso del alfabeto árabe por minorías musulmanas y otros aspectos de la literatura aljamiada, resultantes de circunstancias históricas y sociales análogas." In *Actas del coloquio internacional sobre literatura aljamiada y morisca. 10–16 July 1972, Universidad de Oviedo*, ed. Álvaro Galmés de Fuentes, 147–64. Madrid: Editorial Gredos.

–, ed. 1981. *Cinco leyendas y otros relatos moriscos. (MS. 4953, BN)*. Madrid: Editorial Gredos.

Herrera, Pedro de. 1617. *Descripción de la Capilla de Nuestra Señora del Sagrario*. [Includes *Certamen*]. Madrid: Luis Sánchez.

Hershenzon, Daniel. 2018. *The Captive Sea: Slavery, Communication, and Commerce in Early Modern Spain and the Mediterranean*. Philadelphia: University of Pennsylvania Press.

Hess, Andrew. 1978. *The Forgotten Frontier: A History of the Sixteenth Century Ibero-African Frontier*. Chicago: University of Chicago Press.

Hesse, Everett W. 1955. "Calderón's Popularity in the Spanish Indies." *Hispanic Review* 23 (1): 12–27.

Hildburgh, W.L. 1942. "Lunar Crescents as Amulets in Spain." *Royal Anthropological Institute of Great Britain and Ireland* 42: 73–84.

Hitos, Francisco A. 1993. *Mártires de la Alpujarra en la rebelión de los moriscos (1568)*, ed. Manuel Barrios Aguilera. Granada: Universidad de Granada.

Horden, Peregrine, and Nicholas Purcell. 2006. "The Mediterranean and 'the New Thalassology.'" *American Historical Review* 111: 722–40.

Hurtado de Mendoza, Diego. 1852. *Guerra de Granada*, ed. Cayetano Rosell, 65–122. Madrid: M. Rivadeneyra.

Hutchinson, Steven. 2011. "Fronteras cervantinas: Zoraida en el exilio." In *Variantes de la modernidad: estudios en honor de Ricardo Gullón*, ed. Carlos Javier García and Cristina Martínez-Carazo, 147–67. Newark, NJ: Juan de la Cuesta.

– 2012a. "Martirios en Cervantes: contextos históricos y literarios." *eHumanista/Cervantes* 1: 57–80.

– 2012b. "The Morisco Problem in its Mediterranean Dimension: Exile in Cervantes' *Persiles*." In *The Conversos and Moriscos in Late Medieval Spain and Beyond* ed. Kevin Ingram, 187–202. Leiden: Brill.

– 2012c. "Renegades as Crossover Figures: Forgers of the Early Modern Mediterranean." *Journal of Levantine Studies* 2 (1): 41–69.

– 2015. "Renegadas in Early Modern Spanish Literature." In *Perspectives on Early Modern Women in Iberia and the Americas: Studies in Law, Society, Art and Literature in Honor of Anne J. Cruz*, ed. Adrienne L. Martín y María Cristina Quintero, 528–48. New York: Escribana Books.

– 2020. *Frontier Narratives: Liminal Lives in the Early Modern Mediterranean.* Manchester: Manchester University Press.

Ibn ʿAbd al-Rafīʿ al-Andalusī, Muhammad. 2009. In *Al-Anwār al-Nabawīyya fī Ābāʾ Khayr al-Barīyya. Europe Through Arab Eyes, 1578–1727*, ed. Nabil Matar, 194–200. New York: Columbia University Press.

Ibn Ḥazm. 1984. *Kitāb al-fiṣal. Abenházam de Córdoba y su historia crítica de las ideas religiosas.* 5 v., ed. Miguel Asín Palacios. Madrid: Ediciones Turner.

Ibn Qāsim al-Ḥajarī, Aḥmad. [c. 1637] 1997. *Kitāb Nāṣir al-Dīn ʿalā al-Qawm al-Kāfirīn (The Supporter of Religion against the Infidels)*, ed. P.S. Van Koningsveld, Q. Al-Samarrai, and G.A. Wiegers. Madrid: CSIC.

Infante, Catherine. 2012. Los moriscos y la imagen religiosa: la cruz de Rafala en el *Persiles* rebatiendo a los apologistas de la expulsión." *eHumanista/Cervantes* 1: 285–99.

– 2013. "Imágenes cautivas y la convivencia con las imágenes en el Mediterráneo de Cervantes." *Cervantes y el Mediterráneo. eHumanista/Cervantes: Journal of Iberian Studies* 2: 183–204.

– 2018. "El renegado cervantino y el poder de las imágenes." *Hispanic Review* 86 (3): 307–27.

Informaciones de don Pedro de Castro: Los mártires de las Alpujarras, Volumen I, Informaciones (1569–1621). 2014. Ed. J. Carlos Vizuete Mendoza, 81–222. Granada: Editorial Nuevo Inicio.

Irigoyen-García, Javier. 2010. "'La música ha sido hereje:' Pastoral Performance, Moorishness, and Cultural Hybridity in *Los baños de Argel*." *Bulletin of the Comediantes* 62 (2): 45–62.

– 2014. *The Spanish Arcadia: Sheep Herding, Pastoral Discourse, and Ethnicity in Early Modern Spain.* Toronto: University of Toronto Press.

– 2017. *Moors Dressed as Moors: Clothing, Social Distinction, and Ethnicity in Early Modern Iberia.* Toronto: University of Toronto Press.

Jardine, Lisa. 1996. *Worldly Goods: A New History of the Renaissance.* New York: W.W. Norton.

Jardine, Lisa, and Jerry Brotton. 2000. *Global Interests: Renaissance Art between East and West.* London: Reaktion Books.

Jiménez de Rada, Rodrigo. [c. 1243] 1989. *Historia de los hechos de España.* Ed. Juan Fernández Valverde. Madrid: Alianza Editorial.

Johnson, Paul Michael. 2020. *Affective Geographies: Cervantes, Emotion, and the Literary Mediterranean.* Toronto: University of Toronto Press.

Kagan, Richard L. 1998. "*Urbs* and *Civitas* in Sixteenth- and Seventeenth-Century Spain." In *Envisioning the City: Six Studies in Urban Cartography*, ed. David Buisseret, 75–108. Chigago: University of Chicago Press.

Kasl, Ronda, et al., eds. 2009. *Sacred Spain: Art and Belief in the Spanish World.* Indianapolis: Indianapolis Museum of Art.

Kimmel, Seth. 2015. *Parables of Coercion: Conversion and Knowledge at the End of Islamic Spain.* Chicago: University of Chicago Press.

Labarta, Ana. 1980. "Inventario de los documentos árabes contenidos en procesos inquisitoriales contra moriscos valencianos conservados en el Archivo Histórico Nacional de Madrid (legajos 548–556)." *Al-Qantara: Revista de estudios árabes* 1: 115–64.

–, ed. 1993. *Libro de dichos maravillosos. (Misceláneo morisco de magia y adivinación).* Madrid: CSIC.

– 2011–13. "La cultura de los moriscos valencianos." *Sharq al-Andalus* 20: 223–47.

Laguna, Ana María G. 2009. *Cervantes and the Pictorial Imagination: A Study on the Power of Images and Images of Power in Works by Cervantes.* Lewisburg, PA: Bucknell University Press.

Lane, Edward William. 1984. *Arabic-English Lexicon.* 2 v. Cambridge: Islamic Texts Society.

Las Casas, Ignacio de. 2006. "Al supremo consejo de la sancta Inquisición de España: carta para el señor inquisidor general." In *Jésuites, Morisques et Indiens. Étude comparative des méthodes d'évangélisation de la Compagnie de Jésus d'après les traités de José de Acosta (1588) et d'Ignacio de las Casas (1605–1607)*, ed. Youssef El Alaoui, 536–65. Paris: Honoré Champion Éditeur.

Lapiedra Gutiérrez, Eva. 1997. *Cómo los musulmanes llamaban a los cristianos hispánicos.* Alicante: Instituto Juan Gil-Albert.

Lazcano, Rafael. 2010. "Avatares de la imagen del Cristo del Rescate de Valencia." In *Los crucificados: religiosidad, cofradías y arte. Actas del Simposium, 3 al 6 de septiembre de 2010*, ed. Francisco Javier Campos y Fernández de

Sevilla, 355–72. San Lorenzo del Escorial: Real Centro Universitario Escorial-María Cristina.

Leahy, Chad. 2016. "'Dineros en cruzados': The *Morisco* Expulsion, Numismatic Propaganda, and the Materiality of Ricote's Coins." *Hispanic Review* 84 (3): 273–98.

Lee, Christina H. 2015. *The Anxiety of Sameness in Early Modern Spain*. Manchester: Manchester University Press.

León Pinelo, Antonio de. [1701] 1971. *Anales de Madrid (desde el año 447 al de 1658)*, ed. Pedro Fernández Martín. Madrid: Instituto de Estudios Madrileños.

La leyenda de la doncella Carcayona. 2000. Ed. Pino Valero Cuadra. Alicante: Universidad de Alicante.

Libro de Cuentas. n.d. Archivo Municipal de Carmona, caja 1068.

Libro de redención de cautivos hecha en Argel en 1667 por los Padres mercedarios Pedro de la Concepción, Gabriel Gómez de Losada y Juan de Luque. n.d. Biblioteca Nacional de España. Ms. 3613.

Long, Rebecca. 2009. "Saint Pedro Nolasco Recovering the Image of the Virgin of El Puig, 1630." In *Sacred Spain. Art and Belief in the Spanish World*, ed. Ronda Kasl et al., 274–5. Indianapolis: Indianapolis Museum of Art.

López Baralt, Luce. 1992. *Islam in Spanish Literature: From the Middle Ages to the Present*. Leiden: Brill.

– 2009. *La literatura secreta de los últimos musulmanes de España*. Madrid: Editorial Trotta.

López Madera, Gregorio. 1601. *Discursos de la certidumbre de las reliquias descubiertas en Granada desde el año de 1588 hasta el de 1598*. Granada: Sebastián de Mena.

Lugo Acevedo, María Luis, ed. 2008. *Libro de las luces*. Madrid: SIAL Ediciones.

Luna, Miguel de. [1592] 2001. *Historia verdadera del Rey Don Rodrigo*, ed. Luis F. Bernabé Pons. Granada: Editorial Universidad de Granada.

Lybarger, Loren D. 2000. "Gender and Prophetic Authority in the Qur'anic Story of Maryam: A Literary Approach." *Journal of Religion* 80 (2): 240–70.

Magnier, Grace. 2006. Introduction. *Sobre el pergamino y láminas de Granada*. By Pedro de Valencia. Oxford: Peter Lang.

– 2010. *Pedro de Valencia and the Catholic Apologists of the Expulsion of the Moriscos: Visions of Christianity and Kingship*. Leiden: Brill.

Mancebo de Arévalo. 2003. *Tratado [tafsira]*, ed. María Teresa Narváez Córdova. Madrid: Trotta.

Marcello, Elena E. 2004. "De Valdivielso a Calderón: *Origen, pérdida y restauración de la Virgen del Sagrario*." *Criticón* 91: 79–91.

– 2014. "Prólogo." *Nuestra Señora de Atocha: obras completas.*, vol. 5, by Francisco de Rojas Zorrilla, ed. Elena E. Marcello, 13–35. Cuenca: Universidad de Castilla-La Mancha.

Marchant Rivera, Alicia. 2010. "Aspectos sociales, prácticas y funciones de los escribanos públicos castellanos del Siglo de Oro." In *El nervio de la República: El oficio de escribano en el Siglo de Oro*, ed. Enrique Villalba y Emilio Torné, 201–21. Madrid: Calambur.

Mariscal, George. 1990. "Symbolic Capital in the Spanish Comedia." *Renaissance Drama* 21: 143–69.

Mármol, Andrés del. 1619. *Excelencias, vida y trabajos del Padre Fray Jerónimo Gracián de la Madre de Dios*. Valladolid.

Mármol Carvajal, Luis. [1600] 1991. *Historia del [sic] rebelión y castigo de los moriscos del reino de Granada*, ed. Ángel Galán. Málaga: Editorial Arguval.

Márquez Villanueva, Francisco. 1975. *Personajes y temas del Quijote*. Madrid: Taurus.

– 1981. "La voluntad de leyenda de Miguel de Luna." *Nueva Revista de Filología Hispánica* 30 (2): 359–95.

– 1998. *El problema morisco: (desde otras laderas)*. Madrid: Ediciones Libertarias.

– 2010. *Moros, moriscos y turcos de Cervantes: ensayos críticos*. Barcelona: Bellaterra.

Martín Morán, José Manuel. 2004. "Identidad y alteridad en *Persiles y Sigismunda*." *Peregrinamente peregrinos*. In *Actas del V Congreso Internacional de la Asociación de Cervantistas*, vol. 1, ed. Alicia Villar Lecumberri, 561–91. Alcalá de Henares: Asociación de Cervantistas.

Martínez-Burgos García, Palma. 1990. *Ídolos e imágenes: la controversia del arte religioso en el siglo XVI español*. Valladolid: Universidad de Valladolid.

Martínez Medina, Francisco Javier. 2006. "Los hallazgos del Sacromonte a la luz de la Historia de la Iglesia y de la Teología católica." In *Los Plomos del Sacromonte: invención y tesoro*, ed. Manuel Barrios Aguilera and Mercedes García Arenal, 79–111. Valencia: Universitat de València.

Martínez Rojas, Francisco Juan. 2004. *El episcopado de D. Francisco Sarmiento de Mendoza (1580–1595): la reforma eclesiástica en el Jaén del XVI*. Jaén: Instituto de Estudios Giennenses.

Martínez Torres, José Antonio. 2004. *Prisioneros de los infieles: vida y rescate de los cautivos cristianos en el Mediterráneo musulmán (siglos XVI–XVII)*. Barcelona: Ediciones Bellaterra.

Mas, Albert. 1967. *Les Turcs dans la littérature espagnole du siècle d'or*. 2 v. Paris: Centre de Recherches Hispaniques.

Matar, Nabil. 2009. *Europe Through Arab Eyes, 1578–1727*. New York: Columbia University Press.

– 2014. *British Captives from the Mediterranean to the Atlantic, 1563–1760*. Leiden: Brill.

Matar, Nabil, and Tina P. Christodouleas. 2005. "The Mary of the Sacromonte." *Muslim World*. 95: 199–215.

Mitchell, W.J.T. 1994. *Picture Theory*. Chicago: University of Chicago Press.

–, ed. 2002a. *Landscape and Power.* 2nd ed. Chicago: University of Chicago Press.

– 2002b. "Showing Seeing: A Critique of Visual Culture." *Journal of Visual Culture* 1 (2): 165–81.

– 2003. "Word and Image." In *Critical Terms for Art History.* 2nd ed., ed. Robert S. Nelson and Richard Shiff, 51–61. Chicago: University of Chicago Press.

– 2005. *What Do Pictures Want? The Lives and Loves of Images.* Chicago: University of Chicago Press.

Monnot, Guy. 2019. "Wathaniyya." In *Encyclopaedia of Islam.* 2nd ed., ed. P. Bearman et al. Brill Online. http://dx.doi.org/10.1163/1573-3912_islam _SIM_7893, accessed 10 October 2019.

Monroe, James T. 1966. "A Curious Morisco Appeal to the Ottoman Empire." *Al-Andalus* 31 (1): 281–303.

Montaigne, Michel de. 1962. *Journal de voyage en Italie, par la Suisse et l'Allemagne, en 1580 et 1581. Oeuvres complètes,* ed. Maurice Rat, 1099–342. Paris: Éditions Gallimard.

Montaner Frutos, Alberto. 2010. "La literatura aljamiada." In *Memoria de los moriscos: escritos y relatos de una diáspora cultural: Biblioteca Nacional de España, del 17 de junio al 26 de septiembre de 2010,* ed. Alfredo Mateos Paramio and Juan Carlos Villaverde Amieva, 45–55. Madrid: Sociedad Estatal de Conmemoraciones Culturales.

Montesinos, José F. 1923. "The Chronology of Lope de Vega's Plays." *Revista de Filología Española* 10: 190–2.

Morales, Cristóbal de. 1658. *La estrella de Monserrate: comedias nuevas escogidas de los mejores ingenios de España, duodécima parte.* Madrid: por Andrés García de la Iglesia.

Moreno Nieto, Luis. 1995. *La Reina de Toledo: historia de la Virgen del Sagrario.* Toledo: Luis Moreno Nieto.

Morgan, David. 2005. *The Sacred Gaze: Religious Visual Culture in Theory and Practice.* Berkeley: University of California Press.

Mufti of Oran. 1975. "Respuesta que hizo el Muftí de Orán a ciertas preguntas que le hicieron desde la Andalucía." In *Los moriscos,* ed. Mercedes García Arenal, 43–5. Madrid: Editora Nacional.

Narraciones y leyendas. Consejo Superior de Investigaciones Científicas (CSIC), Biblioteca Tomás Navarro Tomás, ms. RESC/57.

Narváez Córdova, María Teresa. 1976. "El Mancebo de Arévalo frente a Jesús y María: tradición y novedad." In *La littérature aljamiado-morisque: hybridisme linguistique et univers discursif,* ed. Abdeljelil Temimi, 109–15. Tunis: Centre de Recherche en Bibliothéconomie et Sciences de l'Information.

– 1995. "Conocimientos místicos de los moriscos: puesta al día de una confusión." In *Actes du VI Symposium International d'Études Morisques,* ed.

Abdeljelil Temimi, 227–38. Zaghouan: Publications du Centre d'Études et de Recherches Ottomanes, Morisques, de Documentation et d'Information.

– 2003. Estudio preliminar. *Tratado [tafsira]*. By Mancebo de Arévalo, ed. María Teresa Narváez Córdova, 13–96. Madrid: Trotta.

Natif, Mika. 2011. "The Painter's Breath and Concepts of Idol Anxiety in Islamic Art." In *Idol Anxiety*, ed. Josh Ellenbogen and Aaron Tugendhaft, 41–55. Stanford, CA: Stanford University Press.

Neuwirth, Angelika. 2014. *Scripture, Poetry and the Making of a Community: Reading the Qur'an as a Literary Text*. Oxford: Oxford University Press.

Nietzsche, Fredrich. 2006. *Human, All-Too-Human: Parts One and Two*, trans. Helen Zimmern and Paul V. Cohn. Mineola, NY: Dover Publications.

Nora, Pierre. 1989. "Between Memory and History: *Les Lieux de Mémoire*." *Representations* 26: 7–24.

Novena del primero Redemptor y mexor cautivo Christo, rescatado en su sagrada y milagrosa imagen del poder de un judío que estaba en Argel prisionero de los moros por el M. R. P. M. Fr. Gabriel Gómez de Lozada. 1708. Puebla: en la Imprenta Nueva de D. Joseph Pérez. Biblioteca Nacional de Chile. E.G. 1–12–3(40).

Ohanna, Natalio. 2009. "Cervantes, los musulmanes nuevos y la *Información* de Argel." *Anales Cervantinos* 41: 267–84.

– 2011. *Cautiverio y convivencia en la edad de Cervantes*. Alcalá de Henares: Centro de Estudios Cervantinos.

– 2012. "Heterodoxos en cautiverio: de Cipriano de Valera a los protestantes del norte de África." *Hispanic Review* 80 (1): 21–40.

– 2016. "*Los cautivos de Argel* y la expulsión de los moriscos." *Hispanic Review* 84 (4): 361–79.

Oliver Asín, Jaime. 2008. *Vida de don Felipe de África: Príncipe de Fez y Marruecos, 1566–1621*, ed. Miguel Ángel de Bunes Ibarra and Beatriz Alonso Acero. Madrid: CSIC.

Orozco Díaz, Emilio. 1965. *El poema* Granada *de Collado de Hierro*. Granada: Patronato de la Alhambra.

– 1983. "Sobre la teatralización y comunicación de masas en el Barroco. La visualización espacial de la poesía." In *Homenaje a José Manuel Blecua*, 497–512. Madrid: Gredos.

– 2000. *Granada en la poesía barroca*, ed. José Lara Garrido. Granada: Universidad de Granada.

– 2002. *Los sonetos de Góngora (Antología comentada)*, ed. José Lara Garrido. Cordoba: Diputación de Córdoba.

Orozco Pardo, José Luís. 1985. *Christianópolis: urbanismo y Contrarreforma en la Granada del Seiscientos*. Granada: Diputación Provincial de Granada.

Ostrow, Steven F. 1996. "Cigoli's Immacolata and Galileo's Moon: Astronomy and the Virgin in Early Seicento Rome." *Art Bulletin* 78 (2): 218–35.

Osuna, Inmaculada, ed. 2000. *Poética silva: un manuscrito granadino del Siglo de Oro*. 2 v. Cordoba: Universidad de Córdoba.

– 2003. *Poesía y academia en Granada en torno a 1600: la* Poética Silva. Sevilla: Universidad de Sevilla.

Pacheco, Francisco. 1649. *Arte de la pintura, su antigüedad y grandeza*. Sevilla: por Simon Faxardo.

Pallares Garzón, María Berta. 2012. "A la sombra de un redentor: el Padre Fray Gabriel Gómez de Losada, mercedario y su *Escuela de trabajos*." In *Relazioni religiose nel Mediterraneo: Schiavi, redentori, mediatori (secc. XVI–XIX)*, ed. Sara Cabibbo and Maria Lupi, 101–33. Roma: Viella.

Pareja, Félix M. 1960. "Un relato morisco sobre la vida de Jesús y María." *Estudios ecclesiasticos* 34: 859–71.

Parreño, José María. 1990. "Experiencia y literatura en la obra de Antonio de Sosa." In *Diálogo de los mártires de Argel*, ed. Emilio Sola and José María Parreño, 9–23. Madrid: Hiperión.

Pascual Barea, Joaquín. 2010. "La divina vencedora de Lope de Vega: Caracterización del protagonista como Hércules y como otros personajes míticos de la Antigüedad y la Biblia." *Anagnórisis* 2: 105–30.

Pedraza Jiménez, Felipe B. 1997. "Ecos de Alcazarquivir en Lope de Vega: *la tragedia del rey don Sebastián* y la figura de Muley Xeque." In *El siglo XVII hispanomarroquí*, ed. Mohamed Salhi, 133–46. Rabat: Facultad de Letras de Rabat.

– 2012. "Episodios de la historia contemporánea en Lope de Vega." *Anuario Lope de Vega* 18: 1–39.

Pelikan, Jaroslav. 1996. "The Heroine of the Qur'ān and the Black Madonna." In *Mary Through the Centuries. Her Place in the History of Culture*, 67–79. New Haven, CT: Yale University Press.

Perceval, José María. 1987. "En busca del 'tesoro de los moros.'" *Boletín del Instituto de Estudios Almerienses. Letras* 7: 175–82.

– 1997. *Todos son uno: Arquetipos, xenofobia y racismo: la imagen del morisco en la monarquía española durante los siglos XVI y XVII*. Almería: Instituto de Estudios Almerienses.

Pereda, Felipe. 2004. "Palladia: antiguas y nuevas imágenes de la cruzada andaluza." In *Los Reyes Católicos y Granada: Hospital Real (Granada) 27 de noviembre de 2004–20 de enero de 2005*, 201–12. Madrid: Sociedad Estatal de Conmemoraciones Culturales.

– 2007. *Las imágenes de la discordia: política y poética de la imagen sagrada en la España del cuatrocientos*. Madrid: Marcial Pons.

– 2019. *Images of Discord: Poetics and Politics of the Sacred Image in Fifteenth-Century Spain*, trans. Consuelo López Morillas. London: Harvey Miller.

Pereda, Francisco de. 1604. *Historia de la santa y devotíssima imagen de Nuestra Señora de Atocha*. Valladolid: por Sebastián de Cañas.

Pérez de Chinchón, Bernardo. [1532] 2000. *Antialcorano. Diálogos christianos. Conversión y evangelización de moriscos*, ed. Francisco Pons Fuster. Alicante: Universidad de Alicante.

Pérez Galdeano, Ana María. 2016. *La historia de la Abadía del Sacromonte a través de sus grabados*. Granada: Ideal-Fundación Abadía del Sacromonte.

Pérez de Hita, Ginés. 1998. *La guerra de los moriscos (segunda parte de las guerras civiles de Granada)*, ed. Paula Blanchard-Demouge. Granada: Universidad de Granada.

Pérez Sánchez, Alfonso E., ed. 2000. *Jerónimo Jacinto de Espinosa: Museo de Bellas Artes de Valencia, del 28 de septiembre al 12 de noviembre de 2000*. Valencia: Consorci de Museus de la Comunitat Valenciana.

Perry, Mary E. 2003. "Patience and Pluck: Job's Wife, Conflict and Resistance in Morisco Manuscripts Hidden in Sixteenth-Century Spain." In *Women, Texts and Authority in Early Modern Spain*, ed. Marta Vicente and Luis Corteguera, 91–106. New York: Ashgate.

– 2005. *The Handless Maiden: Moriscos and the Politics of Religion in Early Modern Spain*. Princeton, NJ: Princeton University Press.

– 2012. "Morisco Stories and the Complexities of Resistance and Assimilation." In *The Conversos and Moriscos in Late Medieval Spain and Beyond*, ed. Kevin Ingram, 161–85. Leiden: Brill.

Pons Fuster, Francisco. 2014. "Bernardo Pérez de Chinchón." In *Christian-Muslim Relations: A Bibliographical History*, vol. 6, ed. David Thomas and John A. Chesworth, 119–24. Leiden: Brill.

Pontón, Gonzalo. 2012. Prólogo. *Comedias, Parte XI*, vol. 2, ed. Laura Fernández and Gonzalo Pontón, 793–821. Madrid: Gredos.

Portús Pérez, Javier. 1999. *Pintura y pensamiento en la España de Lope de Vega*. Guipúzcoa: Nerea.

– 2000. *El culto a la Virgen en Madrid durante la Edad Moderna*. Madrid: Comunidad de Madrid.

Pozo Martínez, Indalecio. 2017. "Bibliografía histórica sobre la Santa Cruz de Caravaca (1541–1900)." *Carth* 33 (63): 151–80.

Proceso de fe contra Guillaume Bedos, alias "Xavan de Raez," cristiano renegado (1619–1624). Archivo Histórico Nacional, sección Inquisición, legajo 1748, expediente 11.

Quevedo, Francisco de. [1626] 2012. *La vida del buscón*, ed. Fernando Cabo Aseguinolaza. Barcelona: Galaxia Gutenberg.

Quinn, Mary B. 2013. *The Moor and the Novel: Narrating Absence in Early Modern Spain*. New York: Palgrave.

Quintana, Jerónimo de. 1629. *A la muy antigua, noble y coronada villa de Madrid: historia de su antigüedad, nobleza y grandeza*. Madrid: en la Imprenta del Reyno.

– 1637. *Historia del origen y antigüedad de la imagen de Nuestra Señora de Atocha*. Madrid: Imprenta del Reino.

The Qur'an. Trans. M. A. Abel Haleem. New York: Oxford University Press, 2005.

Redondo, Agustin. 1983. "El primer plan sistemático de asimilación de los moriscos granadinos: El del doctor Carvajal (1526)." In *Les morisques et leur temps,* 113–23. Paris: Centre National de la Recherche Scientifique.

– 1988. "Devoción tradicional y devoción erasmista en la España de Carlos V: De la *Verdadera información de la Tierra Santa* de Fray Antonio de Aranda al *Viaje de Turquía.*" In *Homenaje a Eugenio Asensio,* ed. Luisa López Griguera and Augustin Redondo, 391–416. Madrid: Gredos.

Reeves, Eileen. 1997. *Painting the Heavens: Art and Science in the Age of Galileo.* Princeton, NJ: Princeton University Press.

Remensnyder, Amy G. 2011. "Beyond Muslim and Christian: The Moriscos' Marian Scriptures." *Journal of Medieval and Early Modern Studies* 41 (3): 545–76.

– 2014a. *La Conquistadora: The Virgin Mary at War and Peace in the Old and New Worlds.* Oxford: Oxford University Press.

– 2014b. "Warrior and Diplomat: Mary between Islam and Christianity." In *Picturing Mary: Woman, Mother, Idea,* ed. Timothy Verdon et al., 39–50 Washington, DC: National Museum of Women in the Arts.

Roa, Martín de. 1623. *Antigüedad, veneración i fruto de las sagradas imágenes, i reliquias.* Sevilla: Gabriel Ramos Vejarano.

Robinson, Cynthia. 2013. *Imagining the Passion in a Multiconfessional Castile: The Virgin, Christ, Devotions, and Images in the Fourteenth and Fifteenth Centuries.* University Park: Pennsylvania State University Press.

Robles Corbalán, Juan de. 1615. *Historia del misterioso aparecimiento de la Santíssima Cruz de Carabaca, e innumerables milagros que Dios N. S. ha obrado y obra por su devoción.* Madrid: en casa de la viuda de Alonso Martín.

Rodrigo Zarzosa, Carmen. 2010. "El Santísimo Cristo del Rescate de Valencia." In *Los crucificados: religiosidad, cofradías y arte. Actas del Simposium, 3 al 6 de septiembre de 2010,* ed. Francisco Javier Campos y Fernández de Sevilla, 341–54. San Lorenzo del Escorial: Real Centro Universitario Escorial-María Cristina.

Rodríguez Becerra, Salvador. 2014. "Las leyendas de apariciones marianas y el imaginario colectivo." *Etnicex: revista de estudios etnográficos* 6: 101–21.

Rodríguez G. de Ceballos, Alfonso. 2009. "Image and Counter-Reformation in Spain and Spanish America." In *Sacred Spain. Art and Belief in the Spanish World,* ed. Ronda Kasl et al., 15–35. Indianapolis: Indianapolis Museum of Art.

Rodríguez-Rodríguez, Ana M. 2013. *Letras liberadas: cautiverio, escritura y subjetividad en el Mediterráneo de la época imperial española.* Visor Libros.

Roisse, Philippe. 2006. "'La Historia del Sello de Salomón': estudio, edición crítica y traducción comparada." In *Los plomos del Sacromonte: invención y tesoro*, ed. Manuel Barrios Aguilera and Mercedes García Arenal, 141–72. Valencia: Universitat de València.

Rojas Zorrilla, Francisco de. [1645] 2014. *Nuestra Señora de Atocha: obras completas*, vol. 5, ed. Elena E. Marcello, 37–164. Cuenca: Universidad de Castilla-La Mancha.

Romanos, Melchora. 1999. "Felipe II en la *Tragedia del rey don Sebastián y el bautismo del Príncipe de Marruecos* de Lope de Vega." *Edad de Oro* 18: 177–91.

Romero Múñoz, Carlos. 1997. "Ecos de la *Topografía e historia general de Argel* en el *Persiles*." In *Un lume nella notte: studi di iberistica che allievi ed amici dedicano a Giuseppe Bellini*, ed. Silvana Serafin, 265–74. Rome: Bulzoni Editore.

Rosa-Rodríguez, María del Mar. 2010. "Simulation and Dissimulation: Religious Hybridity in a Morisco Fatwa." *Medieval Encounters* 16: 143–80.

Rostagno, Lucia. 1983. *Mi faccio turco: esperienze ed immagini dell'islam nell'Italia moderna*. Istituto per l'Oriente C.A. Nallino.

Rubiera Mata, María Jesús. 1972. "De nuevo sobre las tres morillas." *Al-Andalus: Revista de las Escuelas de Estudios Árabes de Madrid y Granada* 37 (1): 133–43.

Ruiz Lagos, Manuel. 1999. Introducción. *Expulsión de los moriscos de España*, by Gaspar Aguilar, ed. Manuel Ruiz Lagos, 11–114. Sevilla: Guadalmena.

Rumeu de Armas, Antonio. 1974. "La Virgen del Rescate, símbolo espiritual del Lanzarote heróico." *Anuario de estudios atlánticos* 20: 711–23.

Saborit Badenes, Pere. 1996. "El obispo Figueroa y la evangelización de los moriscos." *Anales Valentinos* 44: 429–45.

Sáez, Adrián. 2014. "Paradigmas y estructuras en las comedias triples del Siglo de Oro." *Revista de Literatura* 76: 479–93.

Said, Edward W. 1978. *Orientalism*. New York: Vintage Books.

Salas Barbadillo, Alonso Jerónimo. 1979. *Patrona de Madrid restituida*. Madrid: Albatros.

Salcedo Olid, Manuel de. 1677. *Panegírico historial de N.S. de la Cabeza de Sierra Morena*. Madrid: por Julián de Paredes.

San Juan, fray Raphael de. 1686. *De la redención de cautivos. Sagrado instituto del Orden de la SS^{ma} Trinidad. De su antigüedad, calidad, y privilegios que tiene, y de las contradiciones que ha tenido*. Madrid: Por Antonio Gonçalez de Reyes.

Sánchez Álvarez, Mercedes, ed. 1982. *El manuscrito misceláneo 774 de la Biblioteca Nacional de París. (Leyendas, itinerarios de viajes, profecías sobre la destrucción de España y otros relatos moriscos)*. Madrid: Editorial Gredos.

Sánchez Jiménez, Antonio. 2011. *El pincel y el Fénix: pintura y literatura en la obra de Lope de Vega Carpio*. Madrid/Frankfurt: Iberoamericana/Vervuert.

– 2019. "El zancarrón de Mahoma: un chiste antiislámico en Lope de Vega." *Revista de Filología Española* 99: 191–209.

Sánchez López, Juan Antonio. 1994. "Contenidos emblemáticos de la iconografía del Niño de Pasión en la cultura del Barroco." In *Actas del*

I Simposio Internacional de Emblemática, Teruel, 1 y 2 de octubre de 1991,
  ed. Santiago Sebastián López, 685–718. Teruel: Instituto de Estudios
  Turolenses.

Scaraffia, Lucetta. 1993. *Rinnegati: per una storia della identità occidentale.*
  Laterza.

Schimmel, Annemarie. 1970. *Islamic Calligraphy.* Leiden: Brill.

– 1984. *Calligraphy and Islamic Culture.* New York: New York University
  Press.

Schleifer, Aliah. 1993. "Maryam in Morisco Literature: A Factor in the
  Preservation of Their Muslim Identity." In *Actes du Ve Symposium international
  d'études morisques sur le Ve centenaire de la chute de Grenade, 1492–1992,* ed.
  Abdeljelil Temimi, 2:679–94. Zaghouan: Centre d'Études et de Recherches
  Ottomanes, Morisques, de Documentation et d'Information.

– 1997. *Mary the Blessed Virgin of Islam.* Louisville, KY: Fons Vitae.

Schrader, Jeffrey. 2006. *La Virgen de Atocha: los Austrias y las imágenes milagrosas.*
  Madrid: Ayuntamiento de Madrid.

– 2011. "*In hoc signo vinces*: The Virgin of Atocha, St Luke and Spanish
  Habsburg Power." In *La imagen Sagrada y sacralizada,* ed. Peter Krieger,
  2:497–512. Mexico: Universidad Nacional Autónoma de México.

Schroeder, H.J., ed. 1978. *Canons and Decrees of the Council of Trent.* Rockford,
  IL: Tan Books.

Sepúlveda, Jerónimo de. 1924. *Historia de varios sucesos y de las cosas notables
  que han acaecido en España y otras naciones desde el año 1584 hasta el de 1603.
  Documentos para la Historia del Monasterio de San Lorenzo el Real de El Escorial,*
  vol. 4, ed. Julián Zarco Cuevas. Madrid: Imprenta Helénica.

Serato, Gaspar. 1612. *Relación verdadera que se sacó del libro donde están escritos los
  milagros de Nuestra Señora de la Caridad de Sanlúcar de Barrameda.* Málaga: por
  Juan Rene.

Sigüenza, José de. 2000. *Historia de la Orden de San Jerónimo.* 2 v., ed. Francisco
  J. Campos y Fernández de Sevilla. Valladolid: Junty de Castilla y León.

Silvestre, Francisco Antonio. 1690. *Fundación histórica de los hospitales que la
  religión de la Santíssima Trinidad, redempción de cautivos, de calçados, tiene en la
  ciudad de Argel.* Madrid: Julián de Paredes.

Símini, Diego. 2007. "La rebelión de las Alpujarras en tres comedias del Siglo
  de Oro (Calderón, Fajardo, Cunedo)." In *Jornadas de Teatro del Siglo de Oro
  XXI–XXIII,* ed. Antonio Serrano, 221–31. Almeria: Instituto de Estudios
  Almerienses.

Smith, Jane I., and Yvonne Y. Haddad. 1989. "The Virgin Mary in Islamic
  Tradition and Commentary." *Muslim World* 79 (3–4): 161–87.

*La soberana Virgen de Guadalupe y sus milagros y grandezas de España: obras
  completas.* [1605] 1970. Ed. Ángel Valbuena Prat, 2:1994–2005. Madrid:
  Aguilar.

Sola, Emilio, and José F. de la Peña. 1995. *Cervantes y la Berbería: Cervantes, mundo turco-berberisco y servicios secretos en la época de Felipe II.* México: Fondo de Cultura Económica.

Stewart, Devin. 2006. "The identity of the 'muftī of Oran,' Abū-l-ʿAbbās Aḥmad b. Abī Jumʿah al-Maghrāwī al-Wahrānī (d. 917/1511)." *Al-Qanṭara* 27: 265–301.

Suárez Miramón, Ana. 2009. "Iconografía y pintura en *Nuestra Señora de Atocha*, de Rojas Zorrilla." In *En buena compañía: estudios en honor de Luciano García Lorenzo*, ed. Joaquín Álvarez Barrientos et al., 709–16. Madrid: CSIC.

Surtz, Ronald E. 2001. "Morisco Women, Written Texts, and the Valencia Inquisition." *Sixteenth-Century Journal* 32 (2): 421–33.

Szpiech, Ryan. 2012. "Preaching Paul to the Moriscos: The Confusión o confutación de la secta mahomética y del Alcorán (1515) of 'Juan Andrés.'" *La corónica: A Journal of Medieval Hispanic Languages, Literatures, and Cultures* 41 (1): 317–43.

Talavera, Gabriel de. 1597. *Historia de nuestra señora de Guadalupe.* Toledo: en casa de Thomás de Guzmán.

al-Tamaghrūtī, ʿAlī ibn Muhammad. [c. 1591] 2007. *Al-Nafḥat al-Miskiyya fī al-Sifārat al-Turkiyya*, ed. Muhammad Salihi. Beirut: Al-Muʾassasa al-ʿArabiyya li-l-Dirāsāt wa-l-Nashr.

Taybili, Ybrahim. 1988. *El cantico islámico del morisco hispanotunecino Taybili*, ed. Luis F. Bernabé Pons. Zaragoza: Institución Fernando el Católico.

Teijeiro Fuentes, Miguel Ángel. 1987. *Moros y turcos en la narrativa áurea (el tema del cautiverio).* Cáceres: Universidad de Extremadura.

Temimi, Abdeljelil. 1989. "Une lettre des morisques de Grenade au Sultan Suleiman al-Kanuni en 1541." In *Le gouvernement ottoman et le problème morisque*, 23–32 (French); 27–38 (Arabic). Zaghouan: Publications du Centre d'Études et de Recherches Ottomanes, Morisques, de Documentation et d'Information.

Terry, Elizabeth Ashcroft. 2015. "The Granada Venegas Family, 1431–1643: Nobility, Renaissance and Morisco Identity." PhD diss., University of California-Berkeley.

Tirso de Molina. 1968. *El Monasterio de El Puig y su Virgen*, ed. P. Juan Devesa. Valencia: Ayuntamiento de Valencia.

Torres, fray Miguel de. 1725. *Novena del primer redemptor y mejor cautivo, Christo, rescatado en su sagrada y milagrosa imagen del poder de un judío, que estaba en Argel prisionero de los moros.* Mexico: por Joseph Bernardo de Hogal. Texas A & M Cushing Memorial Library. BX2170.H5 P38 1775.

Torres Sánchez, Rafael. 1986. "La esclavitud en Cartagena en los siglos XVII y XVIII." *Contrastes. Revista de Historia Moderna* 2: 81–101.

al-Turkī, Abdelmajid. 1967. "Wathāʾiq ʿan al-Hijra al-Andalusiyya al-Akhīra ilā Tūnis." *Hawliyyāt al-Jāmiʿa al-Tūnisiyya* 4: 23–82.

Urquízar-Herrera, Antonio. 2017. *Admiration and Awe: Morisco Buildings and Identity Negotiations in Early Modern Spanish Historiography*. Oxford: Oxford University Press.

Usandizaga, Guillem. 2014. *La representación de la historia contemporánea en el teatro de Lope de Vega*. Madrid/Frankfurt: Iberoamericana/Vervuert.

Valbuena Briones, Ángel. 1980. "La primera 'comedia' de Calderón." In *Actas del Sexto Congreso Internacional de Hispanistas*, ed. Alan M. Gordon and Evelyn Rugg, 753–6. Toronto: University of Toronto.

Valdés, Alfonso de. [1527] 1956. *Diálogo de las cosas ocurridas en Roma*, ed. José F. Montesinos. Madrid: Espasa-Calpe.

Valdés, Ramón. 2001. "Claves e hipótesis para la interpretación de *La octava maravilla*: fuentes, motivos simbólicos y trasfondo histórico." *Anuario de Lope de Vega* 7 (2001): 165–89.

Valdivielso, José de. [1616a] 1983. *Auto de la descensión de Nuestra Señora en la santa Iglesia de Toledo, quando trujo la casulla al gloriossíssimo San Ildefonso su santo arçobispo y patrón nuestro*, ed. Joseph T. Snow. Exeter: University of Exeter.

– 1616b. *Sagrario de Toledo*. Madrid: Luis Sánchez.

Valera, Cipriano de. [1594] 2004. *Tratado para confirmar los pobres cautivos de Berbería en la católica y antigua fe y religión cristiana, y para los consolar, con la palabra de Dios, en las aflicciones que padecen por el Evangelio de Jesucristo*, ed. Miguel Ángel de Bunes Ibarra and Beatriz Alonso Acero. Valencina de la Concepción, Sevilla: Ediciones Espuela de Plata.

Valero Cuadra, Pino. 2000. Introducción. *La leyenda de la doncella Carcayona*, ed. Pino Valero Cuadra, 15–229. Alicante: Universidad de Alicante.

Van Koningsveld, P.S., Q. Al-Samarrai, and G.A. Wiegers. 1997. Introduction. *Kitāb Nāṣir al-Dīn ʿalā al-Qawm al-Kāfirīn (The Supporter of Religion against the Infidels)*, by Aḥmad Ibn Qāsim al-Ḥajarī, ed. P.S. Van Koningsveld, Q. Al-Samarrai, and G.A. Wiegers, 11–59. Madrid: CSIC.

Vega, Lope de. [c. 1593–1603] 2012. *El bautismo del Príncipe de Marruecos*. Comedias, Parte XI, ed. Laura Fernández and Gonzalo Pontón, 2:823–954. Madrid: Gredos.

– [1599] 1993. *El alcaide de Madrid*. Comedias, VI, ed. Jesús Gómez and Paloma Cuenca, 3–103. Madrid: Turner/Biblioteca Castro.

– [1599] 2010. *El Isidro*, ed. Antonio Sánchez Jiménez. Madrid: Cátedra.

– [c. 1599] 2017. *Los cautivos de Argel*, ed. Natalio Ohanna. Barcelona: Clásicos Castalia.

– [1599–1603] 1993. *La divina vencedora*. Comedias, X, ed. Jesús Gómez and Paloma Cuenca, 767–871. Madrid: Turner/Biblioteca Castro.

– [c. 1609] 1917. *La octava maravilla: obras de Lope de Vega publicadas por la Real Academia Española*, 8:246–85. Madrid: Tipografía de la Revista de Archivos, Bibliotecas y Museos.

– 1965. *La niñez de San Isidro: obras de Lope de Vega, X*, ed. Marcelino Menéndez Pelayo, 325–60. Madrid: Atlas.

Velasco, Honorio M. 2000. "Las leyendas de hallazgo y de singularización de imágenes marianas en España." In *Religiosidad y costumbres populares en Iberoamérica: actas del Primer Encuentro Internacional celebrado en Almonte-El Rocío (España) del 19 al 21 de febrero de 1999*, ed. David González Cruz, 89–102. Huelva: Universidad de Huelva.

– 2003. "Las leyendas de hallazgos y de apariciones de imágenes. Un replanteamiento de la religiosidad popular como religiosidad local." In *La religiosidad popular. II Vida y muerte: la imaginación religiosa*, ed. Carlos Álvarez, María Jesús Buxó, and Salvador Rodríguez, 401–10. Barcelona: Anthropos.

Vespertino Rodríguez, Antonio. 1978. "Las figuras de Jesús y María en la literatura aljamiada-morisca." In *Actas del coloquio internacional sobre literatura aljamiada y morisca*, 259–94. Madrid: Gredos.

– 1983. *Leyendas aljamiadas y moriscas sobre personajes bíblicos*. Madrid: Gredos.

Viaje de Turquía. [c. 1557] 1980. Ed. Fernando García Salinero. Madrid: Cátedra.

Villalmanzo Cameno, Jesús. 1997. "La colección pictórica sobre la expulsión de los moriscos. Autoría y cronología." In *La expulsión de los moriscos del reino de Valencia*, 34–68. Valencia: Fundación Bancaja.

Villanueva Fernández, Juan Manuel. 1992. *Historia de la literatura de Caravaca de la Cruz*. Caravaca: UNED.

– 1999. *Historia de Caravaca de la Cruz*. Cartagena: Centro Asociado de Cartagena.

Vincent, Bernard. 2001. "Musulmans et conversion en Espagne aux XVIIe siècle." In *Conversions islamiques: identités religieuses en islam méditerranéen*, ed. Mercedes García Arenal, 193–205. Paris: Maisonneuve et Larose.

Vitkus, Daniel J. 2001. *Piracy, Slavery, and Redemption: Barbary Captivity Narratives from Early Modern England*. New York: Columbia University Press.

Vizuete Mendoza, J. Carlos. 2012. "Nuestra Señora del Martirio de Ugíjar (Granada): Origen, voto y fiesta." In *Advocaciones Marianas de Gloria: Actas del Simposium*, 121–38. San Lorenzo de El Escorial: Ediciones Escurialenses.

Voigt, Lisa. 2009. *Writing Captivity in the Early Modern Atlantic: Circulations of Knowledge and Authority in the Iberian and English Imperial Worlds*. Chapel Hill: University of North Carolina Press.

Wasyliw, Patricia Healy. 2008. *Martyrdom, Murder, and Magic: Child Saints and Their Cults in Medieval Europe*. New York: Peter Lang.

Weiss, Gillian. 2011. *Captives and Corsairs: France and Slavery in the Early Modern Mediterranean*. Stanford, CA: Stanford University Press.

Wiegers, Gerard. 1992. "A Life between Europe and the Maghrib. The Writings and Travels of Aḥmad b. Qâsim ibn Aḥmad ibn al-Faqîh Qâsim ibn al-Shaykh al-Ḥajarî al-Andalusî (born c. 977/1569–70)." In *The Middle East and Europe: Encounters and Exchanges,* ed. G.J. Van Gelder and E. de Moor, 87–115. Amsterdam: Rodopi.

– 2017. "Aḥmad ibn Qāsim al-Ḥajarī." In *Christian-Muslim Relations: A Bibliographical History,* vol. 10, ed. David Thomas et al., 200–20. Leiden, Brill.

Witko, Andrzej. 2004. *Jesús Nazareno Rescatado.* Rome: Curia Generalizia dei Trinitari.

Wood, Donald W. 2019. "Yā Maryam/Ave Maria: Textual Appropriations and Diglossia in Aljamiado-Morisco Marian Texts." *eHumanista* 41: 155–70.

Wunder, Amanda. 2017. *Baroque Seville: Sacred Art in a Century of Crisis.* University Park: Pennsylvania State University Press.

Ximénez, Francisco. 1934. *Colonia trinitaria de Túnez,* ed. Ignacio Bauer y Landauer. Tetuan: Tipografía de Gomariz.

Index

Toronto Iberic